The *Satyricon* of Petronius

THE SATYRICON
OF PETRONIUS

A Literary Study

J. P. SULLIVAN

Professor of Classics
at the University of Texas

INDIANA UNIVERSITY PRESS
Bloomington and London

Printed in Great Britain

COLLEGIIS
DIVI IOANNIS EVANGELISTAE
APUD CANTABRIGIENSES
ET
APUD OXONIENSES REGINENSI
ET LINCOLNIENSI
ALUMNUS OLIMVE SOCIUS
HUNC LIBELLUM

Contents

9

List of Abbreviations

Abbreviations for standard classical periodicals, where not obvious, usually conform to the conventions of *L'Année Philologique*; for ancient authors cited in the notes, to the lists in Lewis and Short and Liddell-Scott-Jones. *RE* is one of the standard abbreviations for *Pauly-Wissowa-Kroll-Mittelhaus, Real-Encyklopädie der classischen Altertumswissenschaft*. The following list of abbreviations is peculiar to this book:

BC   *Carmen de bello civili*, chapters 119–124.1 of the *Satyricon*.

Bücheler   *Petronii Saturae recensuit Franciscus Buecheler*. Berlin, 1862.

Burman   *Titi Petronii Arbitri Satyricôn quae supersunt*. Curante Petro Burmanno. Editio altera. Amsterdam, 1743.

Ciaffi   Ciaffi, V., *La Struttura del Satyricon*. Turin, 1955.

Collignon Collignon, A., *Étude sur Pétrone*. Paris, 1892.

Gaselee   Gaselee, S., *Materials for an Edition of Petronius* (1907–1908). Unpublished Thesis. Cambridge University Library.

Müller   *Petronii Arbitri Satyricon cum Apparatu Critico* edidit Konrad Müller. Munich, 1961.

Müller[2]   *Petronius Satyrica*. Lateinisch-Deutsch von Konrad Müller und Wilhelm Ehlers. Munich, 1965.

Maiuri   Maiuri, A. *La Cena di Trimalchione di Petronio Arbitro*. Naples, 1945.

Paratore   Paratore, E., *Il Satyricon di Petronio*. Vols. I and II. Florence, 1933.

Rose   Rose, K. F. C., *The Date and Author of the Satyricon* (1962). Unpubld. Thesis. Bodleian Library, Oxford.

*L'artiste doit s'arranger de façon à faire croire
à la postérité qu'il n'a pas vécu.*

G. Flaubert

Introduction

It is nineteen hundred years since Petronius committed suicide and this seems an appropriate time for a full-length study of an author who, for various reasons, has been largely neglected in England from all but the historical and textual sides. The reason for this neglect may by seen in the words of R. Y. Tyrrell: 'The "Satyricon" is not in the hands of many, and indeed ought by no means to be recommended for general perusal . . .' (*Latin Poetry*, 1895, p. 275), or, as a Frenchman put it, *on lit Pétrone, on ne le cite pas.* Petronius, however, should appeal to modern sensibilities in other ways than that alluded to by Tyrrell and I do not think that a straightforward study will excite much distaste, provided certain characteristics of the work are not allowed to colour our view of the whole. D. H. Lawrence's comment in a letter to Lady Ottoline Morrell (1st February 1916) is worth recalling:

> I send you also Petronius. He startled me at first, but I liked him. He is a gentleman when all is said and done . . . Petronius is straight and above board. Whatever he does, he doesn't try to degrade and dirty the pure mind in him.

I have not of course burked certain problems presented by Petronius, but I do not think the Common Reader will be unduly shocked in these days, although some scholars may be disturbed in a different way by my psychoanalytical explanations of some parts of the work.

This book is, in the main, intended as a literary study. Originally it was planned as something larger and more definitive, something which would include all the more or less settled results of Petronian scholarship. But it seemed better to reserve many of the minor points on which disagreement would be non-existent, or

limited, for the much needed commentary which I hope to produce in the near future with the collaboration of Kenneth Rose.
This book simply states at length my critical views of the *Satyricon*
as a whole. I have therefore tried to keep the footnotes down to a
decent minimum and avoid clogging the text with attributions
and the many trivial, inconclusive, or worthless items that would
figure in a full Petronian bibliography. Of course, with an author
like Petronius, many large and small scholarly debts are accumu-
lated, and the more important are, I hope, fully acknowledged, but
the bibliography is meant to be as selective as the notes are meant
to be relevant. But despite such good intentions, some chapters
have suffered more than others, and I am aware that perhaps a
fondness for certain by-ways into which one is led in Petronian
studies may have increased the number of the notes beyond the
strictly necessary. Here I must ask the reader's indulgence, and
hope that some of the otiose remarks may prove of interest. I have
also felt it my duty, since this is the only general study of Petronius
in English, to give some guidance to the student beginning work
on this author. Hence also the reconstruction of the missing parts
of the work, which, it may be felt, is a mere exercise in speculation
or, at best, a work of detection that has no place in a literary study.
I am aware that I can only offer a plausible story, a sort of εἰκὼς
μῦθος, in the conviction that, if not this, then something like this,
must have been the case. Nevertheless, if we do not bear in mind
the nature of the parts we have lost, our analysis may become
subtly distorted and our evaluation prejudiced by the merits of
the *Cena Trimalchionis*, where, it may be argued, Petronius surpassed himself. Those who are familiar with the problems and the
evidence would be well advised to pass over these preliminary
chapters and content themselves with their own dreams.

In the hope that a critical study of Petronius may be of interest
to students of literature in general, I have adopted the growing
practice of translating many of the Latin quotations: most of the
translations are taken from my version of the *Satyricon* in the
Penguin Classics (1965). For the same reason some of the notes
are rather fuller and sometimes more explicit than the average
classical scholar might expect.

I have assumed that my task was to explain why the work is what it is and not any other thing, and then to attempt to evaluate it. In neither of these activities did I feel confident of success, but the book is meant to stimulate discussion rather than stifle it. I may have been presumptuous even in this aim. Certainly the general reader will find no specific principles of criticism which he can deduce from the following pages. But my aims are perhaps justified in that most of the scholars who have worked on Petronius have limited themselves to the many historical, philological, and textual problems that the *Satyricon* presents. The only specifically literary problem that has tempted some away from this *embarras de richesse* has been the question of Petronius' literary models and predecessors. It was generally felt that on this prior question depended the classification of this apparently unique work. There have been therefore few attempts to assess the *Satyricon* as a work of art. The strained exclamations, prefacing a bare recital of the plot, such as we find in our literary histories and introductions, are as much a hindrance to any evaluation of the work as were the harsh judgments passed by earlier scholars on the sexual immorality portrayed in some of the fragments.

I am aware that to some my concluding chapter will seem rather hard on the author on whom I have obviously spent a considerable amount of time. But the second-rate author's value frequently consists in refining our concept of the first-rate and I have learnt much from my study of Petronius. It is surely a mistake to think that the judgment of more mature reason on a favourite author of our youth, even if it abates considerably our initially high estimate of him, is not a gain to us. I am also aware that the judgment of much of Latin literature must be for a time tentative, until the status and position of the Augustans are properly established in our critical studies, for that will entail a radical re-assessment, if not re-orientation, of our present views of the whole character and direction of Latin literature. Until that long-distant day, most books on Latin authors must be offered as stop-gaps and I hope that this book will be so considered.

My task has been greatly aided by the appearance in 1961 of the new edition of Petronius produced by Konrad Müller and the text quoted in these pages is based upon this and his revision in *Petronius Satyrica* (Munich, 1965), pp. 425 ff. One assumption of this book is that Petronius is a very careful and precise writer and this is an assumption more easily granted now that Müller's labours have cleared the work of much that was conjectured, corrupt or otiose.

Parts of this book have appeared in different form in *Critical Essays in Roman Literature: Satire* (London, 1963); in the introduction to my translation of Petronius in the Penguin Classics; and in such journals as *The American Imago* and *Arion*. Other parts of it may be familiar to my lecture and seminar audiences in Oxford and Austin, but the book was conceived as a whole, and is intended to bring together, and qualify, my earlier views on the subject.

Acknowledgements are due to Lincoln College, who helped me to buy photostats and gave me hospitality; to the Craven Fund of the University of Oxford for their help towards certain topographical researches in Italy; to the American Council of Learned Societies for a travel grant in 1963; to the Research Institute of the University of Texas for its generous financial support for study leave and typing expenses; and to the Widener Library at Harvard for its facilities. More personal acknowledgements for general or scholarly help are due to D. S. Carne-Ross, Wendell Clausen, J. G. Griffith, C. I. Levene, L. D. Reynolds, W. W. Robson, Niall Rudd, Mrs. Stephanie West, and Edward Whittle. The careful and severe castigation of Robin Seager removed a number of infelicities from the manuscript; Sylvia Chilver's proof reading compensated for my inadequacies in the art; and Philippa Coetzee's typing produced order from chaos. Particular thanks are due to my friend and colleague, Kenneth Rose, who read over the whole of this book several times in manuscript and proof, helped generously with discussion and criticism, and saved me from a number of errors. The mistakes that remain are due to my obstinacy or obtuseness. Various slips of a different kind were removed by Graham Speake, who kindly checked most of the classical references. For permission to quote from D. H. Lawrence's *Lady Chatterley's Lover* I am indebted to Wm. Heinemann Ltd., Laurence Pollinger Ltd., and the Estate of the late Mrs. Frieda Lawrence.

I would like to thank also those gracious English and American ladies whose hospitality and kindness in other ways considerably furthered or lightened my labours: Mrs. Lizbeth Atkinson, Mrs. Molly Barger, Miss Kirsten Barger, Mrs. Rosemary Bowie, Miss Linda Dew, Mme Janine Scarcella, Miss Linda Reese Vaughn, and last, but by no means least, my mother and sister.

28th October 1966

CHAPTER I

The Date and Authorship
of the *Satyricon*

The fragmentary work, known as the *Satyricon* of Petronius Arbiter, although only the size of a shortish modern novel, presents more puzzles and has aroused more controversy than perhaps any other ancient text. It has been described as the work of a moralist and a work of the most profound immorality; it has been regarded as satire, as a picaresque novel, as a parody of a romance or an epic, and as a mixture of several such genres. Even estimates of its original length vary enormously. And the puzzles begin immediately with the most basic facts about it. When was the work written and who wrote it?

Although it is not my intention to discuss the history of the so-called 'Petronian question' or the many arguments discovered and exploded in the course of it,[1] every critic of Petronius is bound to have a view on the inter-related problems of its date and authorship. The issues are these: is the work Neronian or not? If so, may we plausibly identify the author whom the manuscripts and the *testimonia* call Petronius, Arbiter, or Petronius Arbiter[2] with Nero's

---

[1] The literature on the date and authorship of the work is immense. Articles offering particular arguments are cited in the appropriate note. The general surveys, which come out for and against the Neronian date, vary in quality and importance, but mention should be made of Iannelli, Studer, Beck, Haley, Bagnani, Marmorale, and Rose, and also of earlier opinions recorded in Burman (1709 and 1743). A discussion of many of these by K. F. C. Rose may be found in *Arion* 5 (1966), 275 ff.

[2] See Müller, p. 1.

courtier, the Petronius referred to by Pliny the Elder, Tacitus and Plutarch?[1]

The evidence for the date of the work is all internal. None of the writers who cite the work or the author is earlier than A.D. 200 and their testimony, despite scholarly efforts to manipulate it, establishes nothing except that A.D. 200, the generally accepted date for Terentianus Maurus, is the approximate *terminus ante quem*. The earliest possible date, because of the obvious imperial allusions in the work, is of course the reign of Augustus.

If we dismiss such subjective grounds as the unlikelihood of a work of such merit being written later than the first century A.D., or the lack of unanimity among those who argue for any date other than the Neronian period, the arguments which carry conviction fall into three types: historical, linguistic and literary.

i. *Historical Arguments*

There are a number of allusions in the *Satyricon* to personages, events, social customs and economic facts, which scholars have used to establish the Neronian date. Many of these however cannot be shown as demonstrably Neronian, or even first century, and it would be unprofitable to hash over such things as the supposed reference to *manumissio per mensam* at 70.11. Indeed there is a general argument which must first be considered against using any of these allusions to prove a definite date. Perhaps Petronius, writing at a much later date than the Neronian age, deliberately set the time of his story in the near or remote past and carefully inserted appropriate allusions to his selected period. The difficulty with this idea is that such a literary plan, although found in Plato for very special reasons, is more modern than ancient. There is a good deal of realism in Petronius, but the concept of the historical novel, the period piece which shuns anachronisms and adds historical flavour by carefully documented detail, is alien to the canons of ancient

---

[1] I accept the almost certainly independent evidence of Pliny and Plutarch as against that of Tacitus (or his MS, which may be easily emended) that the courtier's *praenomen* was Titus. The best discussion of this vexed question, which takes into account the previous work on the subject, is by Rose, *Latomus* 20 (1961), 821–5.

writing, which made a distinction between poetry or fiction and what we might call 'scientific' writing. If anything, ancient writers were readier to dilute 'scientific' work such as history with material more suitable to poetry than the other way round. In fact, one of the characters in the *Satyricon*, who is expressing, as I shall show later, Petronius' own views on poetry, chides writers of historical epic for incorporating into their work too much history and not enough myth. Since the *Satyricon*, for all its realism in certain sections, is clearly a fictitious narration with large elements of poetry and sheer invention, Petronius would be directly contravening his own principles. So far from being a realistic and accurate *historical* novel, the *Satyricon*, for Petronius' literary purposes, permits the introduction of such undatable fantasies as the Croton episode. The low-life, though not the sexual, realism is almost entirely confined to one episode – the *Cena Trimalchionis* – and the historical allusions are found there simply as a means of reproducing with some verisimilitude the small-time gossip of Trimalchio's circle. But the purpose is contemporary or literary satire, not the resuscitation of a bygone age. If this is granted, we may turn with more confidence to the very few, but more or less convincing, allusions to persons and conditions of the first century in general, and to Neronian times in particular.

Now it has to be admitted that there are no references to people of contemporary importance. Petronius, despite the realism of the *Cena*, avoids mentioning Lucan in 118, although his criticism is clearly directed at him, and he contents himself with such vague imperial titles as *Caesar* or *Augustus*, when referring to an emperor. We know, for instance, that the story of the unbreakable glass (51) is associated by the elder Pliny with Tiberius. Petronius keeps his literary and critical references non-topical. No poet later than Vergil or Horace is mentioned by name. The decision, I believe, was artistic – to avoid too close a test of verisimilitude – and it may be likened to modern habits of setting fictional scenes in certain but unspecified Eastern or Iron Curtain countries. Unimportant or long-dead figures however did not come under this ban and there is one set of allusions which have to be taken together. The allusions seem to point to three important entertainers of Neronian and pre-Neronian times and to each in his proper chronological setting. At 64.3 Plocamus tells the company that he now has gout, but that when he was quite young (*adulescentulus*) his only equal at singing was Apelles, clearly a famous *artiste*. Now there was a notable singer in the reign of Caligula (A.D. 37–41),[1] who would fit the implied chronology. Again, at 73.3 Trimalchio butchers some songs of Menecrates, who flourished under Nero.[2] Finally, we discover that Trimalchio is a great fan of a gladiator named Petraites (52.3, 71.6); archaeological evidence has recently been adduced for the existence of a famous gladiator of that name under Nero.[3]

Separately, each of these allusions might be taken as a co-incidence, but together they make a convincing case. The other supposed allusions to people or things of Neronian or pre-Neronian times, while they are not incompatible with a Neronian date, are not, by themselves, truly convincing, because they are open to alternative explanations.

One would class among these some of the allusions collected by Iannelli, such as the anointing of the guests' feet, a custom introduced by the future Emperor Otho, the use of *lapis specularis*, and the reference to *horti Pompeiani*.[4]

To the historical arguments proper may be added the various elements of the social and economic background which fit a first-century dating. *Latifundia*, slave labour as opposed to *coloni* on Trimalchio's estates, the significance of gold rings, competition in municipal elections, and the prosperity of Puteoli, all fit a first-century rather than a second-century dating.[5] The other socio-

---

[1] Suet. *Calig.* 33.2; Dio 59.5.2; Philo, *Leg. ad Gaium* §203 (Smallwood).

[2] Suet. *Ner.* 30.5.

[3] H. T. Rowell, *TAPA* 89 (1958), 14–24. The three allusions were further developed into an argument by Rose, *CQ* 12 (1962), 166–8.

[4] The argument developed by P. Veyne, in *Hommages à Albert Grenier* (Brussels 1962), pp. 1617–24, that Trimalchio has an *agnomen* (*Maecenatianus*), a custom which died out among freedmen after the first century A.D., is of no value, for Trimalchio puts it only on his tomb (71.12, cp. 30.2); it is not on the inscription at 30.2. See Rose, *TAPA* 93 (1962), 407.

[5] On the position of freedmen, see A. M. Duff, *Freedmen in the Early Roman Empire* (Cambridge, 1958), *passim*. On the wine trade and Trimalchio's estates,

economic arguments, while they will not disprove a first-century dating, do not stand up to detailed scrutiny.

ii. *Linguistic Arguments*

Although the narrative prose of the *Satyricon* must be discussed in the light of its own stylistic canons, we can say with certainty of the *Cena Trimalchionis* that it offers in the dialogue and monologue a realistic picture of Trimalchio's uneducated circle of friends. The rest of the work is written in a literary approximation to the *sermo urbanus*, which constitutes the style of Encolpius' basic narrative and is chosen as usual in accordance with the methods of Menippean satire; this is broken intermittently by a more elevated—or parodic—style used by various speakers when discussing larger issues of literature and culture. All of the language can be paralleled from the first-century sources. In particular, the language of Trimalchio's circle finds a number of significant parallels in the Pompeian wall inscriptions,[1] which of course all date from before the eruption of Mount Vesuvius in A.D. 79.

Equally interesting are the parallels in language between Seneca's *Apocolocyntosis* and the *Cena Trimalchionis*. The former work can be dated with certainty to A.D. 54, shortly after the death of the emperor Claudius, whom it satirizes. The parallels have been collected by Bagnani and others.[2] Now the language and style, common to the two works, were probably dictated by the choice of Menippean satire as the literary form. But so close are some of the linguistic resemblances that, although it may be going too far to suggest, as Bagnani does, that they have a common author, it is

see H. C. Schnur, *Latomus* 18 (1959), 790–9 and the references there given. On competition for offices, which declined after the first century A.D., see L. Debray, *NRD* 43 (1919), 5 ff., 127 ff. On gold rings, *latifundia*, and *coloni* see R. Browning, *CR* 63 (1949), 12–14. On Puteoli's first-century prosperity, see R. Meiggs, *Roman Ostia* (Oxford, 1960), pp. 60 ff. For the identity of the *colonia* with Puteoli, see below, p. 47.

[1] For these resemblances see A. von Guericke, *De linguae vulgaris reliquiis apud Petronium et in inscriptionibus parietariis Pompeianis* (Gumbinnen, 1875) and Maiuri, pp. 227–35.

[2] See *Arbiter of Elegance* (Toronto, 1954), pp. 80–2, and other references there cited.

hard to believe that the two works are widely separated in time. In particular, if parts of the *Satyricon* are radically unclassical or late in their language, as has been argued by such opponents of the Neronian dating as Marmorale, then the *Apocolocyntosis* is so too. But this is manifestly absurd.

iii. *Literary Arguments*

There are a great many dubious literary arguments which can be offered for the Neronian date or something close to it. But one argument which is of decisive value is the imitation or parody found in the *Satyricon*, the *Bellum Civile*, which bears a close and deliberate relation to Lucan's *Pharsalia*.[1] The action of the *Bellum Civile* covers, roughly, the action of the first book of the *Pharsalia*. The diction echoes the first three books and there are some signs that indicate that Petronius was acquainted with the ending of Lucan's poem.[2] All this may be used to argue that the author of the *Satyricon* wrote the *Bellum Civile* while the *Pharsalia* was in process of publication. But what is surely clear is that the *Bellum Civile* has more point if it is roughly contemporary with Lucan's late poetic career (he died in A.D. 65). Particularly significant is the general criticism of Lucan's poetic principles in Eumolpus' remarks prefacing the poem and the omission of Lucan's name, which would make no sense if our author was writing much later than Lucan. Whatever the explanation of the *Bellum Civile*, whatever the situation of Lucan at the time, whether out of favour, still acceptable in Neronian circles, or even recently dead, we are forced to the conclusion that the *Bellum Civile* and the introductory criticism are pointless unless they are contemporary productions of late Neronian times.

This is the main literary argument, but there are others of a less obvious sort. Moving from the stronger to the weaker, one may point out that the literary criticism in general, which, as we shall

---

[1] The fullest collection of resemblances and imitations may be found in Rose, pp. 167 ff. and 276 ff., which incorporates all of the earlier work by Collignon, Baldwin and others on the subject. Some of the evidence is cited in his article mentioned above, p. 24, n. 3.

[2] Cp. *BC* 290–4 with *Phars.* 10.545–6, as Rose suggests (*art. cit.*).

see, has much in common with that of Persius' first satire, and some of the subjects of satire legacy hunting (*captatio*) and freedmen, are typically early Empire and may be paralleled, for example, in the elder Seneca (*passim*), Horace (*Sat.* 2.5), and Persius (5.73 ff.). It has to be added, however, that such views and themes continue to be found in Tacitus, Martial and Juvenal, and the highly literary nature of the *Satyricon* makes this argument less convincing.

There seems to be also a number of glances, often for parodic purposes, at Seneca's *Epistulae Morales*.[1] Many of these might be attributed to some common source of Stoic platitudes. But if the other literary arguments are found convincing, these may add some further plausibility to our general theories of the imitation and parody to be found in the *Satyricon*.

iv. *The Author of the Work*

It was Scaliger in the *Leidensis* manuscript (which was copied probably around 1571) who first positively identified the author of the *Satyricon* with the courtier of Nero whose death is described by Tacitus and who is mentioned by the elder Pliny and Plutarch.[2] Here are the three passages:

T. Petronius consularis moriturus invidia Neronis, ut mensam eius exheredaret, trullam myrrhinam HS $\overline{\text{CCC}}$ emptam fregit...

(Plin. *H.N.* 37.20)

T. Petronius, a consular, when he was going to die through Nero's jealousy and envy, broke his fluorspar wine-dipper so that the Emperor's table would not inherit it. It had cost 300,000 sesterces ...

17. Paucos quippe intra dies eodem agmine Annaeus Mela, Cerialis Anicius, Rufrius Crispinus, ac⟨T.⟩ Petronius cecidere...
18. De [C.] Petronio pauca supra repetenda sunt. nam illi dies

---

[1] See below, pp. 193 ff.
[2] M. Pattison, Pithou's printer, mentioned the possibility of the identification in 1575; see Burman II, pp. 254 and 297.

per somnum, nox officiis et oblectamentis vitae transigebatur; utque alios industria, ita hunc ignavia ad famam protulerat, habebaturque non ganeo et profligator, ut plerique sua haurientium, sed erudito luxu. ac dicta factaque eius quanto solutiora et quandam sui neglegentiam praeferentia, tanto gratius in speciem simplicitatis accipiebantur. proconsul tamen Bithyniae et mox consul vigentem se ac parem negotiis ostendit. dein revolutus ad vitia seu vitiorum imitatione inter paucos familiarium Neroni adsumptus est, elegantiae arbiter, dum nihil amoenum et molle adfluentia putat, nisi quod ei Petronius adprobavisset. unde invidia Tigellini quasi adversus aemulum et scientia voluptatum potiorem. ergo crudelitatem principis, cui ceterae libidines cedebant, adgreditur, amicitiam Scaevini Petronio obiectans, corrupto ad indicium servo ademptaque defensione et maiore parte familiae in vincla rapta.

19. Forte illis diebus Campaniam petiverat Caesar, et Cumas usque progressus Petronius illic attinebatur; nec tulit ultra timoris aut spei moras. neque tamen praeceps vitam expulit, sed incisas venas, ut libitum, obligatas aperire rursum et adloqui amicos, non per seria aut quibus gloriam constantiae peteret. audiebatque referentis nihil de immortalitate animae et sapientium placitis, sed levia carmina et facilis versus. servorum alios largitione, quosdam verberibus adfecit. iniit epulas, somno indulsit, ut quamquam coacta mors fortuitae similis esset. ne codicillis quidem, quod plerique pereuntium, Neronem aut Tigellinum aut quem alium potentium adulatus est, sed flagitia principis sub nominibus exoletorum feminarumque et novitatem cuiusque stupri perscripsit atque obsignata misit Neroni. fregitque anulum ne mox usui esset ad facienda pericula.

20. Ambigenti Neroni quonam modo noctium suarum ingenia notescerent, offertur Silia, matrimonio senatoris haud ignota et ipsi ad omnem libidinem adscita ac Petronio perquam familiaris. agitur in exilium tamquam non siluisset quae viderat pertuleratque, proprio odio.

(Tac. *Ann.* 16.17–20)

17. The space of a few days saw the fall, one after the other, of

Annaeus Mela, Anicius Cerialis, Rufrius Crispinus, and T. Petronius . . .

18. Petronius deserves some further attention. He was a man who spent his days sleeping and his nights working or enjoying himself. Industry is the usual foundation of success, but with him it was idleness. Unlike most people who throw away their money in dissipation, he was not regarded as an extravagant sensualist, but as one who had made luxury a fine art. His conversation and his way of life were unconventional with a certain air of nonchalance, and they charmed people all the more by seeming so unstudied. Yet as proconsul in Bithynia and then as consul, he showed himself active and equal to his duties. His subsequent return to his old habits, whether this was real or apparent, led to his admission to the small circle of Nero's intimates, where he became the Arbiter of Elegance. In the end Nero's jaded appetite regarded nothing as enjoyable or refined unless Petronius had given his sanction to it. Consequently the jealousy of Tigellinus was aroused against him: he saw in Petronius a rival, someone superior to himself in the whole art of pleasure. So he worked upon the Emperor's cruelty, his master-passion, to which all his other lusts were subordinate. Accusing Petronius of being an intimate of Scaevinus, he bribed a slave to give evidence against him. Petronius did not have a chance to reply and Tigellinus threw most of his household into prison.

19. The Emperor at that time happened to be on a visit to Campania. Petronius got as far as Cumae and was prevented from going any farther. He refused to prolong the suspense that hope or fear involved. Not that he was hasty in taking leave of life. On the contrary, he opened his veins and then, as the fancy took him, he bound them up or re-opened them. Meanwhile he talked with his friends, but not on serious topics or anything calculated to win admiration for his stoicism. He listened to their contributions—not discussions about the immortality of the soul or the views of philosophers, but simply frivolous songs and light verse. He dealt out rewards to some of his slaves and floggings to others. He had a good dinner served and slept for a while, so that his death, although forced on him, should appear

natural. Even in the codicils to his will, he refused to put down any of the usual death-bed flattery of Nero or Tigellinus or any of the other courtiers. Instead he wrote out a full description of the Emperor's vicious activities, prefaced with the names of his male and female partners, and specifying the novel forms his lust had taken. This document he sent under seal to Nero. Then he broke his signet ring in case it should be used later to endanger others.

20. Nero's puzzlement as to how his nocturnal ingenuities were known was resolved by blaming Silia. She was a not insignificant person, a senator's wife, in fact, who had been a chosen partner in all the Emperor's vices and also a close friend of Petronius. She was exiled out of personal spite, the charge being her lack of silence about what she had seen and experienced.

19. Καὶ ταυτὶ μὲν ἐλάττονά ἐστιν. ἐκεῖνα δ' ἤδη χαλεπὰ καὶ λυμαι-
νόμενα τοὺς ἀνοήτους, ὅταν εἰς τἀναντία πάθη καὶ νοσήματα κατηγο-
ρῶσιν . . . ἢ τοὺς ἀσώτους αὖ πάλιν καὶ πολυτελεῖς εἰς μικρολογίαν καὶ
ῥυπαρίαν ὀνειδίζωσιν, ὥσπερ Νέρωνα Τίτος Πετρώνιος . . .

(Plu. Mor. 60 d–e)

These are minor faults. Next, however, comes that unscrupulous practice which has such a damaging effect on silly people. This consists in accusing them of tendencies and weaknesses the very opposite of their real failings . . . This may take the form of sneering at reckless and extravagant spenders for their petty-minded and sordid ways–Titus Petronius did this with Nero.

It is clear that these three passages refer to the same man, despite Tacitus' or his manuscript's apparent divergence over the *prae-nomen*. As we stated above, the manuscripts of the *Satyricon* offer us, in different versions, a Petronius Arbiter. Tacitus calls him Nero's 'arbiter of elegance'. This no doubt is the connection which struck Scaliger and has since been accepted by the majority of Petronian scholars. If we exclude those who believe the work to be of later than Neronian date, the sceptics who hold that the two are not the same seem prompted by the idea that the identification is too good to be true. What then are the substantial arguments for the identification? A few reasons may be dismissed at once as too subjective. There have been those who have argued from the psychological resemblance between the work and the courtier to the identification.[1] This is hardly convincing. Others have pointed to the *species simplicitatis* of the courtier (Tac. *Ann.* 16.18.2) which perhaps alludes to the description of the *Satyricon* as *opus novae simplicitatis* (132.15).[2] But this also is highly disputable.

The argument from the coincidence of names is worth something, but there were other Petronii at the time. The only reason of substance lies in the title *arbiter*, given by Tacitus to the courtier and by the manuscripts to the writer. I believe that this can be strengthened if we anticipate the evidence laid out below (pp. 161–213), which suggests that the *Satyricon* is a highly literary work written for a coterie such as Nero gathered around himself, that it is full of allusions to current literature, and even to Roman high society. It is unlikely that Nero's *arbiter elegantiae*, though clearly a man of taste in material things as Pliny's anecdote shows, would have limited his expertise to them. A literary court circle such as Nero's would require more than that from its arbiter. Petronius the courtier would almost certainly be a refined literary critic and, quite possibly, a practitioner of prose, verse or both, with definite literary principles. The *Satyricon* is of course a work composed on explicit principles and contains a good deal of straight or indirect

[1] Cf. e.g. J. Wight Duff, *A Literary History of Rome in the Silver Age*[2] (London, 1960), p. 140: 'Certainly, in the qualities ascribed to Petronius by Tacitus, there is nothing to render it unlikely that the ascription of the fragments in the manuscripts to Petronius Arbiter refers to any other person than the Petronius who is called by the historian the emperor's *elegantiae arbiter*. . . . On the positive side it may be affirmed that the Tacitean portrait of Petronius wears the very features to be expected in the author of a novel depicting low and vicious characters in tones which argue intimacy of knowledge and at the same time the almost cynically detached spirit of a spectator.' Even where such subjective and dangerous deductions are supported by psycho-analytical resemblances between the author and the work, e.g. the apparent scopophiliac tendencies to be seen in both, the argument can hardly be convincing to those who do not accept the premises (see my attempt in *The American Imago* 18 (1961), 353–69).

[2] E. Bickel, *RhM* 90 (1941), 269 ff.; H. Bogner, *H* 76 (1941), 223 ff.; A. Maiuri, *PP* 3 (1948), 103–5; cf. O. Hiltbrunner, *Latina Graeca* (Bern, 1958), pp. 50, 66.

literary criticism, some of it, as we have stated, about such contemporary writers as Lucan.

If this identification of the courtier and the author is accepted, we can deduce from the description in Tacitus a few facts about his life which may help us to decide which, if any, of the various Petronii of Neronian date he plausibly is. The best candidate is Titus Petronius Niger, whose suffect consulship is dated around A.D. 62.[1] His *praenomen* is that given by Pliny and Plutarch. The year A.D. 62 would fit in nicely with Tacitus' narrative; Petronius would have gone to Bithynia as proconsul in 60–1 (or 61–2) and then held the consulship in Rome (*mox consul*). This would allow two years for him to attract the Emperor's attention, rise high in his favour, only to fall with equal speed after he had aroused the no doubt quickly and easily stirred envy of Tigellinus. Petronius' rise, fall and death, and indeed the writing of much of the *Satyricon*, can easily be fitted into this short period. Certainly one of the later books containing the *Bellum Civile* must be dated to no long time before or after the death of Lucan on 30th April, A.D. 65.[2]

These passages tell us little more of relevance to a literary study. The portrait of the courtier is of course interesting and consistent. The refined tastes, as was stated, could hardly have been confined to highly expensive ways of flavouring wine, and Petronius' capabilities as an administrator were clearly matched by his shrewdness in first acquiring, and then for a time retaining, his influence over Nero. Nero, we know, was tolerant of personal criticism, and no doubt more so of *unjustified* taunts—and Suetonius tells us that

---

[1] R. Browning, *CR* 6 (1956), 46 f.; Rose, 220–3 and *Latomus* 20 (1961), 821–5; R. Syme, *Tacitus* (Oxford, 1958), pp. 387 n., 743; cf. G. Pugliese Carratelli, *PP* 3 (1946), 381.

[2] It is not to my purpose here to date our *Satyricon* more precisely, as the arguments are complicated and tenuous. I would suggest 64 and later. Bagnani has argued for 60 (for the Neronia); Rose for 64–5 (*art. cit.*); and the most recent writer on the subject, E. Cizek in *StudClas* 7 (1965), 197 ff., for 61 or later. Apart from the standard arguments he adduces, Cizek places unjustified weight on the possibility that the humane references to slavery in the work (*Sat.* 71.1) indirectly reflect the general debates on the question raised by the assassination of Pedanius Secundus by his household and the severe measures taken against them (Tac. *Ann.* 14.42–5). For a different explanation, see below, pp. 132 ff.

he himself sneered at niggardliness (*Ner.* 30.1). It is also difficult to believe that the political and personal intrigues at court were not paralleled by literary and philosophical divisions on art and the way to live. An epicurean Atticist and classicist might have strong and outspoken objections to the stylistic innovations and philosophizing of the younger Seneca and the anti-Vergilianism of his nephew Lucan, and the criticisms might well be expressed in literary form. Although Petronius was not admitted to the more intimate circle of Nero's sexual partners, his interest in such matters is obvious from Tacitus' account. Nor would the strong emphasis on sexual matters in the *Satyricon* detract from Nero's high opinion of him. Suetonius informs us that Nero firmly believed that no man was pure and that most people simply disguised their vice; those who admitted to such tendencies were forgiven their other failings.[1] Petronius, like his Epicurean friend Scaevinus, had ignored the early Epicurean tenet of living in hiding, and patently interpreted the main axiom of Epicureanism in a thoroughly Roman, if tasteful, way. The references to Epicureanism in the *Satyricon* are not in the tone of a fanatic; the philosophy is utilized humorously and opportunistically. Perhaps only the literary theory as we know it from Philodemus is taken very seriously: that the aim of art is to please, not to instruct.

[1] Ex nonnullis comperi persuasum habuisse eum, neminem hominem pudicum aut ulla corporis parte purum esse, verum plerosque dissimulare vitium et callide obtegere; ideo professis apud se obscaenitatem cetera quoque concessisse delicta (*Ner.* 29).

CHAPTER II

A Reconstruction of
the *Satyricon*

i. *The Surviving Books and the Extent of the Work*

The tenuous external evidence that permits us to deduce the place in the original work of our extant narrative is complicated and unreliable.[1] The portion of the manuscript *Codex Parisiensis lat. 7989 olim Traguriensis*, which contains the so-called *vulgaria excerpta* (*A*) has the inscription: *Petronii Arbitri Satyri fragmenta ex libro quinto decimo et sexto decimo*. These excerpts finish at 137.9 with the subscription: *Petronii Arbitri Satyri fragmenta expliciunt ex libro quintodecimo et sextodecimo*. None of the other manuscripts, not even that part of the above codex which contains the *Cena Trimalchionis* (*H*), offers any further internal clue as to the number of books in the original.

In May 1423, however, the industrious Poggio wrote[2] that he had received a manuscript from Cologne containing Book XV of Petronius. It seems fairly clear that this was 26.7–78.8 and the original part of the *Parisiensis* known in our editions as *H*.[3] Now *H* has no real gaps in it, but there is no need to assume that Poggio would say for certain that he had the *whole* of Book XV: he might simply have known that he had a long and fairly continuous narrative, more or less complete as an episode, with an indication that it was, or came from, Book XV.

On the other hand, the interpolator of the Paris manuscript of

---

[1] See the preface to Bücheler's edition, pp. VI–VII, and Müller, *Praef.* XXIX–XXXI.

[2] *Ep.* 2.3, *Poggii Epistolae*. Ed. T. de Tonelli (Florence, 1832), I. 91, quoted by Müller, p. IX.

[3] See Müller, p. XXVIII f. and the references there.

Fulgentius' *Mythologiae* (see Fgt. VII) informs us that 20.5–7, and, by implication, the rest of the Quartilla episode, belongs to Book XIV. Finally, a ninth-century manuscript originally at the Abbey of Fleury, the *glossarium Sancti Benedicti Floriacensis* (*Codex Harleianus 2735*) has a tenth-century annotation which tells us that the words *sed video te totum in illa haerere tabula quae Troiae halosin ostendit* (the first sentence of 89) are from Book XV.[1]

The work as we have it divides into three or four sections, between which there are no obviously continuous overlapping references: 1–11; 12–26.6, with another possible break at 16; and 26.7 *ad fin.* There are, on the other hand, cross references between 1–11 and 26 ff. (e.g. the quarrel between Encolpius and Ascyltos and the Agamemnon-Menelaus involvement). As will be seen later, the Quartilla episode (12–26.6) is very much out of place, dramatically and temporally, although a great deal of ingenuity has been expended in order to make it fit plausibly in the sequence of events.[2]

If we are to take account of all the external (and internal) evidence, it would seem that our extant narrative belongs to Book XIV (12 or 16–26.6, the Quartilla episode, being misplaced); Book XV (1–11, 26–7 to 99, where Bücheler suggested there was a natural break with the leaving of the *Graeca urbs*); and Book XVI or even beyond (100 *ad fin.*), for the amount of incident which we can discern in the last fragments of the work and the relatively slow and careful development of the longer fragments make this a reasonable assumption. Other theories, such as Müller's, are of course possible, but these often entail denying arbitrarily part of the evidence.

Now Book XV, as far as we can judge, lacks its opening and contains several apparently short lacunae, but it does provide a full

---

[1] See Müller,[2] p. 405, n. 29, where the passage is printed in full.

[2] The latest and most ingenious attempt is that of Ciaffi, p. 37 ff. The most convincing arguments for its misplacement are those of I. Sgobbo, 'Frammenti del libro XIV delle "Saturae" di Petronio', *RAL* 6. 6 (1930), 355–61. See also F. Ribezzo, *RIGI* 15 (1931), 41 ff. The matter would be simpler if we knew how far we could rely on the interpolator of Fulgentius who attributes 20.7 to Book XIV (Fgt. VII).

and fairly connected narrative, once we have removed the Quartilla episode. 1–11 has approximately 1,425 words; the *Cena*, with reasonable allowances for the insignificant lacunae, 12,000; and 79–99 has 4,890: total 18,315. Given the mutilated state of this book, we would have to allow anything from 20,000 to 25,000 words for it in its entirety–by no means an impossible length. If, as is perhaps more likely, the book containing the *Cena* was rather longer and more elaborate than the average book, and we adopt 20,000 words as our standard length and twenty as the number of books into which the work was divided by the author or editors, this gives us 400,000 words as a reasonable size for the original, which is of course ten times longer than the 35,000 words we now possess. This makes the *Satyricon* nearly eight times as long as the other comparable ancient novel, the *Metamorphoses* of Apuleius (51,000). It must be added that on any count it is not much more than half the size of the Bible (750,000) or *War and Peace* (650,000), and falls far short of Richardson's *Clarissa Harlowe* (984,870). Indeed compared to such achievements as the 40,000 lines of William Morris' *The Earthly Paradise* or the 68,000 lines of *The Sacred War–Reduced to a Poem Epike*, to take merely English examples, the *Satyricon* is no impossible feat for even a writer like Petronius, and attempts to reduce its size too drastically are probably mistaken.[1] Of course, if, as Rose has argued, parts of the narrative we possess may be dated to late 64–summer 65,[2] there is no guarantee that the work was ever finished. As will be argued later, the *Satyricon* was probably intended for recitation to the court circle of Nero rather than for publication proper, hence its frequent topicality and perhaps its episodic nature. The reading of the *Cena*, for instance, would last little longer than an hour.

As is clear, much has been lost, but more may be deduced about the plot and incident of the original than is commonly assumed.

---

[1] Cf. e.g. R. Heinze, 'Petron und der griechische Roman', *H* 34 (1899), 495 n. 1; Paratore, I. p. 149; T. Sinko, *Eos* 36 (1935), 385 ff., 408 ff.; E. V. Marmorale, *La questione Petroniana* (Bari, 1948), pp. 31 ff. On the general questions of length, cf. T. Birt, *Abriss des antiken Buchwesens* in I. Müller's *Handbuch* (Munich, 1913), pp. 292 ff.

[2] *CQ* 12 (1962), 166 ff.

A comparison of *H*, which preserves the *Cena* almost entire, with the tradition that offers the longer excerpts (*L*) reveals that *L* gives us 260 lines in Müller's text and *H* 1,450 or so. The excerpts in this instance constitute therefore something between a fifth and a sixth of the fuller account. Moreover the practice followed with the *Cena* by the original excerptor is interesting. He begins with comparatively full extracts and then, about a sixth of the way through the book, bored perhaps by the same theme, he ceases to give samples of the continuing conversation and the dinner party itself, limiting himself now to the verse and to whatever generalities occur. The impression is left of an abbreviator who, once having the flavour of the new book or episode, quickly tires of it and contents himself with poetry and the moralizing or general apophthegms so dear to the medieval and late Latin mind. If this was his usual practice, and the fragments elsewhere lend some support to this conclusion, we may surmise that the excerptor will record the opening of each new episode (which, of course, will not always coincide with the opening of a new book), but he will not see it through to the end, unless there are sudden changes. He will take account instead of abrupt or dramatic incidents and whatever else appeals to him – verse, generalities (whether ironic or not in their original context), and such instructive and self-contained pieces as literary discussions or 'Milesian' tales.

This erratic procedure complicates any attempt at reconstruction. But as far as the narrative runs, we may tentatively expect the beginnings of the major episodes to be preserved in our fragments, even though their development and *dénouement* will be more difficult to define. Moreover, if this is true, then it would seem not only that the amount of incident from 100 onwards is too extensive and varied to fill only one book, but also that the pattern of abbreviation tells against that common assumption.

Purely mechanical deductions are of course out of the question, given the state of our text. We cannot assume that as 260 lines (Müller's text) in *L* represent 1,450 lines of the *Cena* in *H*, then the 303 lines of the Quartilla episode 12–26.6) must represent two-thirds or so of Book XIV, the remaining third relating the events alluded to in the extant narrative–the disturbance of the Priapic rites, perhaps the stealing of the cloak, and so on. The excerptor of *L* may have been more easily bored by the centre-piece of Book XV and he may offer fuller extracts from episodes where the subject matter, because of the preponderance of dramatic incident, or of obscenity, or of verse (consider the survival of the *Bellum Civile!*), caught his fancy. Again, physical accidents to some archetype might explain partially the mutilated way in which the work survived.

ii. *On Reconstructing the Work*

Any reconstruction of the *Satyricon* is bound to contain elements of speculation. Lost episodes may be partially reconstituted from references in the extant text, from the testimonia, and from the unplaced fragments attributed to Petronius, but even when deductions can be made about the missing parts of the plot, any attempt to place them in their proper sequence is inevitably hazardous. No doubt many digressions from the simple plot line, excursuses on literary, philosophical, and social themes, long verse sections, short stories and incidents unconnected with the main narrative, will have vanished without trace. We can only infer their likelihood from the very nature of the work and the very random frequency with which such pieces occur in the surviving text. Consequently a summary of the missing (and extant) episodes gives a misleading impression, the impression merely of a picaresque romance or an adventure story: it cannot do justice to the tone and spirit of the *Satyricon*. It is obviously difficult even to guess at the digressions which might have alleviated this impression and which were part of the author's intentions. In what follows I have merely tried to reconstruct the lost episodes, sometimes in a purely speculative sequence, and to fill in the gaps in the extant narrative; I have deferred for later examination what possible unifying themes and literary motifs may have been used to make what is predominantly a picaresque plot into a sophisticated, if sprawling, work of art. I have stated the events more or less baldly, but the very tentative character of the summary should not be forgotten.

iii. *The Opening*

The narrator Encolpius is what is nowadays called an 'anti-hero': fairly young, well-educated, cowardly, and amoral. In accordance with the accepted theories (and perhaps practice) of imperial Rome, he is sexually ambivalent, a factor around which much of the plot revolves. He is as much a part of the story as the other characters and he is not the omniscient or disinterested narrator familiar to the modern reader from such novelists as Conrad. Apuleius of course uses the same technique in his *Metamorphoses,* and if we grant that he was at all familiar with Petronius,[1] then Petronius presumably offered no better narrative method than a recital addressed directly to his readers or auditors. This differs from the great epic method of plunging *in medias res*, with the hero discovered in a dramatic situation and the beginnings of the story recapitulated by him on some appropriate occasion such as a banquet. The starting-point of the plot has been plausibly set in Massilia, as we shall see, but there is no need to assume that from this starting-point the plot develops in a straight line, with the same emphasis given to each situation from the first to the last and the digressions entering where they may. If the lost incidents were given the same fairly leisurely treatment as the incidents in the extant narrative, then the work would be intolerably long by any standard. Naturally this would be less serious if it was intended only for a serial recitation to a coterie, rather than for general publication. Still, the possibility must be allowed for of an initial rapid summary of certain earlier events, whatever be the occasion or excuse for the recital as a whole, just as in a modern novel a narrator may briefly sketch his antecedents before entering into the particular happenings that constitute the plot proper. Although different from the standard epic technique, where, after all, we are dealing with familiar mythical figures, the method allows the author the same liberty of selecting a limited number of incidents

---

[1] See Collignon, pp. 388 ff., and V. Ciaffi, *Petronio e Apuleio* (Turin, 1960). It is noticeable that many picaresque novels have a first person narrator, obvious examples being Le Sage's Gil Blas, his Guzman d'Alfarache, and (in more modern times) Thomas Mann's Felix Krull.

for full dramatic treatment. It is also possible that certain events referred to in our narrative were given less thorough treatment than is, say, the Circe episode (126-139.4). Indeed, without these possibilities, our generous estimate of the total length of the work would be in danger of being too low.

The evidence we have for the beginning of the plot, whether it was presented fully or summarized by the narrator, is cryptic and difficult to interpret.[1] Servius on Vergil's *Aeneid* 3.57 (Fgt. 1) tells us that in Petronius there was an account of how the inhabitants of Massilia took measures against a plague. One of their poorer citizens would become a voluntary scapegoat; he would be maintained for a whole year at public expense, living on special food. At the end of that time after proper ceremonies to bring the ills of the city down on his head, he would be cast forth. The fifth-century Bishop of Clermont-Ferrand, Sidonius Apollinaris, mentions Petronius in two lists of great Latin writers, the second reference being:

> et te Massiliensium per hortos
> sacri stipitis, Arbiter, colonum
> Hellespontiaco parem Priapo
> (*Carm.* 23. 155-7 = Fgt. IV)

Finally, various passages in the narrative hint that Encolpius is hounded by the wrath of Priapus (*gravis ira Priapi*, 139.2) and there are dark allusions to the nature of his offence against him (133.3).

This cryptic evidence has led to much wild speculation: for instance, that Petronius was a native of Massilia, but the most reasonable interpretation is that the opening of the work was set in Massilia; that Encolpius was involved, on at least one occasion, in the worship of Priapus, who was usually represented by a tree trunk, rough-hewn into a body and a large phallus, which

---

[1] See the discussions by Bücheler, p. 207; C. Cichorius, *Römische Studien* (Leipzig, 1922), pp. 438 ff.; T. Birt, *PhW* 45 (1925), 95; T. Sinko, *Eos* 35 (1934), 407 ff., *Eos* 36 (1935), 385 ff., *Meander* 12 (1957), 79 ff.; R. Pack, *CP* 55 (1960), 31 f.

often stood in gardens (*Massiliensium per hortos* / *sacri stipitis colonum*).[1]

What exactly the offence (*facinus* 133.3 line 9) against the god was is impossible to ascertain. Perhaps the violation and robbery of a temple (133.3 lines 7–8) or the betrayal of some secret (*proditio*, 130.2). Possibly he even impersonated Priapus, for he seems to be well endowed physically (140.13) and the words of Sidonius–*Hellespontiaco parem Priapo*–might allude to this.[2] Indeed his extenuating plea–*non toto corpore feci* (133.3 line 9)–may be plausibly interpreted as a delicate euphemism. Whatever the crime, however, he had been driven to it by poverty, and this suggests that he would be a suitable candidate for a scapegoat in any case.

How the plague in Massilia that necessitated such a victim fits into the story, we do not know. It might be that the work opens with a plague already in progress. This would make the earlier part of the *Satyricon* Petronius' equivalent of the *Iliad*, as the extant narrative relies on the *Odyssey* for the motifs of wandering and the wrath of an offended deity. Petronius would be reversing his admired Vergil's order in his use of the Homeric epics as successive models for the two halves of the *Aeneid*. Petronius would be alluding to the opening of the *Iliad* in the opening of the *Satyricon*, and then continuing with the more suitable Odyssean theme, for the *Reiseroman* would provide more fertile material for the sort of episodes Petronius had in mind to display his literary versatility. Alternatively, the offended Priapus, in the traditional way of angry

---

[1] Priapus of course is the ithyphallic Asiatic god responsible for the fertility of earth and animals, a late deity much prone to syncretism. The cult began in the Hellespont, particularly around Lampsacus, but in the third century B.C. it spread to various parts of the Greek, and later Roman, world. For the Romans, he became more and more a garden god, although he did not altogether lose his more solemn cult. Roman attitudes are best seen in the *Priapea*, a collection of humorous and obscene poems whose ostensible purpose is affixion to his statue. See H. Herter, *De Priapo* (Giessen, 1932), pp. 351 ff.

[2] A suggestion made by C. Cichorius, *Römische Studien* (1922), pp. 438 ff. One may add that *Priap.* 26, 32, 46, 73 and perhaps 25.3 and 48 allude to the sexual misuse of statues of Priapus by women. The possibility that the work, like the *Iliad*, opened with a plague is also feasible. The suggestion is discussed below.

gods, may have sent a plague upon the city that perhaps reduced fertility or sapped potency, and ironically, Encolpius has to become the scapegoat. At the end of the year he would then have escaped or been ejected from the city. The practice of using scapegoats in the Graeco-Roman world is not known only from this fragment. During the *Thargelia* at Colophon, if some form of expiation was in order, after a famine, for example, or a pestilence, a φάρμακος, usually the most hated man around, was chosen and led through the city so that he might take on himself the contamination and then be got rid of (cf. Hippon. Fgts. 4–9). Some of the details of the treatment accorded him are as bizarre as anything in Petronius: he was given bread, cheese, and figs outside the city, and his genitals were whipped with wild fig branches and sea-onions, while a special melody was played on the flute (cf. e.g. Tz. *H* 5.726–761). Similarly, Valerius Maximus (2.6.7 ff.) has enough stories on the rather strange customs of the Massilians to provide the more adventurous-minded with food for further speculation about the incidents set in Massilia.

What is clearer is that the wrath of the god pursues him in his subsequent adventures and provides one of the mainsprings of the plot, much as the wrath of Poseidon dogged Odysseus.[1] The obvious place for Encolpius' escape was Italy and the drift of his movements then seems southwards: he moves in the extant narrative from Puteoli to Croton, after an earlier adventure in Baiae. He has at some point been in Rome (69.9), but we may leave open the question whether any episodes of the work were located there.

iv. *The Law and Giton: Tryphaena and Lichas*

In Italy Encolpius runs afoul of the law. Perhaps it was here that he robbed a temple, his earlier offence against Priapus being something different: his confession at 133.3 is compatible with either explana-

---

[1] E. Klebs, *Philologus* 47 (1889), 623 ff. This has been a much debated point, cf. also K. Bürger, *Der antike Roman* (Berlin, 1892), p. 346 n. 4; F. F. Abbott, *Society and Politics in Ancient Rome* (London, 1923), p. 123; J. Le Coultre, *Mélanges Boissier* (Paris, 1903), p. 328; Paratore, I. p. 165; C. Marchesi, *Petronio* (Rome, 1921), p. 13; for opposing views, R. Heinze, *art. cit.*; E. Thomas, *Pétrone*[3] (Paris, 1912), p. 65 n. 2; A. Ernout's edn. (Paris, 1958), *Introd.*, p. xiv.

tion. Certainly Fgts. VIII, XIV, and possibly XII, hint at a trial scene. If Encolpius was found guilty of temple robbery by night, he might have been condemned to the arena (*ad bestias*, cf. Paul. *Sent*. 5.19). He manages however to escape his obvious fate (*effugi iudicium, harenae imposui*, 81.3, cp. 9.8), possibly thanks to an earthquake or the collapse of an amphitheatre and some quick thinking on his part (81.3, Fgt. XIII). But while he is in the *ergastulum*, where slaves and criminals would be confined, he meets the young, effeminate, and fickle Giton, with whom he falls in love (81.5). Giton escapes with him and becomes Encolpius' lover and travelling companion. All this may or may not take place in Campania, but the next recoverable episodes certainly take place in or around Baiae, the famous Roman watering-place near Naples. Two distinct adventures may be discerned from later references, their sequence a matter of conjecture.

The pair fall in with a notorious courtesan named Tryphaena. Her initial interest in Encolpius is soon replaced by a deeper affection for Giton.[1] Their situation seems very comfortable, but Encolpius' jealousy over Giton forces them to move, although not before they bring about Tryphaena's public disgrace (106.4). This jealousy of Encolpius' for Giton occurs frequently[2] and seems an important plot-mechanism. The situations that lead to it may be part of Priapus' vengeance.

The hero's other entanglement in this area is with the rich merchant-captain Lichas and his wife Hedyle. This adventure may have occurred before the Tryphaena episode. Lichas was on very intimate terms with Encolpius (105.9, 108.6), but the relationship ends with Encolpius' seduction of his wife and the theft of a valuable sacred rattle and robe of the goddess Isis, who is the tutelary deity of Lichas' ship. To add insult to injury, before departing, Encolpius commits some insulting outrage against the captain in the colonnade of Hercules at Baiae (106.2). Hedyle presumably went with the pair (113.2), indeed she may have been the instigator of the robbery, but if she went, she was quickly

---

[1] 100.4, 104.2, 105.7, 108.10, 109.2, 110.3, 113.

[2] It is aroused by Tryphaena, Ascyltos, Quartilla, Eumolpus, and possibly Lycurgus and Hedyle.

shaken off, jealousy over Giton being perhaps the cause of this rupture also.

It has been suggested that the Tryphaena episode and the Lichas episode are part of a larger adventure with the original triangle developing into a hexagonal sexual situation.[1] More probably, however, we are dealing with two successive situations. Tryphaena's presence aboard Lichas' ship (100 ff.) does not tell against this, for Petronius is not averse to dramatic coincidence, witness the encounter in the brothel (7.4), and the heroes' misfortune in choosing Lichas' ship (100.3 ff.). Tryphaena would not normally be with a rich captain except for temporary business, although the similarity of their separate pursuits and success is striking. It would appear from the replacement of Ascyltos as a rival by Eumolpus that Petronius prefers a succession of triangles to an increasingly complex situation and the *recurrence* of characters to their continued presence. Ascyltos and Eumolpus, for example, are never in direct confrontation.

v. *Ascyltos*

Still in the same area, the pair fall in with Ascyltos, an aggressive young homosexual, who may have been living with a certain Lycurgus (81.4). This episode presumably produced another jealous situation, this time involving Giton, Encolpius, and Lycurgus. Lycurgus must have been brutal as well as lecherous, although later, in Encolpius' jaundiced eyes (81.4), he is surpassed in his cruelty by Ascyltos. Accordingly, Encolpius kills Lycurgus by stealth, and the trio rob his villa and escape. The proceeds of this robbery, some gold pieces, are sewn up in a ragged tunic, which is entrusted for safe-keeping to Encolpius. Oddly enough, Ascyltos seems for a time unaware of the nature of Encolpius' relations with Giton. Encolpius, who seems to have had a very temporary sexual encounter with Ascyltos in some charming garden (*viridarium*, 9.10), is perhaps playing a double game. He certainly pretends that his friendship with Giton is innocent, at least for the first few days the three are together (cf. 9.10, 10.7,

[1] Ciaffi, p. 17 f.

11.4). Perhaps Lycurgus made an assault on Giton when his normal sexual partner Ascyltos was absent, and this led to Encolpius' murderous act and his subsequent pose as the protector of Giton's innocence. It should be stressed that Ascyltos is simply a character who appears for a time in the *Satyricon* and then disappears, as Lichas does and Eumolpus undoubtedly will. Giton is the necessary object of Encolpius' jealousy; Ascyltos is merely one of the many occasions for its display. The evidence for his part in the Lycurgus episode is that he feels a proprietary right to the proceeds of the robbery (*turpissima suspicione*, 13.4) and seems aware of Encolpius' murder of his host ('*nocturne percussor*', 9.9).

vi. *Quartilla, the Cloak, and the Graeca urbs*

The next set of adventures overlap with part of the extant text, if the theory mentioned earlier about the displacement of part of Book XIV is correct. It would seem that in the country somewhere near Baiae and the *colonia* in which our narrative opens, the three commit at least one crime. They steal a cloak, although, in leaving the scene of the crime, they are separated and Encolpius loses the tunic with the gold pieces. This is in some deserted country place (*solitudine*, 12.5), and he sees a peasant find it, but the man is presumably one of their pursuers, for Encolpius dares do nothing about it. Then or later, they also witness and disturb some ceremonies in honour of Priapus, which are being held, it turns out later, by the priestess Quartilla.[1] As we shall see, it is not impossible that the stealing of the cloak and this sacrilege are part of the same episode. Quartilla speaks of robbery (*latrocinia*, 17.4) as well as sacrilege.

The cloak and tunic may be discussed first. This episode culminates with an attempt to sell the cloak and the recovery of the tunic with the gold pieces sewn into it (12–15). The three enter

---

[1] It has been suggested that the crypt near which the secret ceremonies were held (16.3) was the *crypta Neapolitana* (mentioned also in Fgt. XVI), which is the tunnel piercing the ridge of hills between Naples and Puteoli. But the tunnel was very busy and public (cf. Sen. *Ep.*, 57.1–2) and this would be an odd place to hold secret ceremonies. Fgt. XVI might not refer to the adventurers at all.

the market place towards evening, but once unrolled, the cloak is recognized and claimed by its original owners or their servants: a peasant and a girl. The peasant is also the man who found the tunic, and it is now over his shoulders. The trio recover their prize in exchange for giving up the cloak, which is confiscated by the surrounding dealers as disputed property (15.4 ff.), and return to their lodgings. The text becomes fragmentary at this point: apparently there is a meal (16.1), then a knock on the door, which heralds the arrival of Quartilla.

The alternatives are these: the selling of the cloak was prompted by the quarrel between Encolpius and Ascyltos (9, 6 ff.), and therefore 12–15 follows soon after 11.4, or the encounter in the market place, which may have been planned by Quartilla, led to her tracing them to their lodgings. Much depends on the identification of the woman accompanying the peasant with the woman who precedes Quartilla into their room. In the manuscripts she is the same, but Müller, following Jacobs, deletes the identifying phrase.[1] But even so, questions remain. Encolpius and Ascyltos do not renew their quarrel or divide the money, and the latter's presence at Trimalchio's dinner suggests that these matters were temporarily forgotten. Quartilla's remarks about *latrocinia* and *a constituta lite* (17.4, 18.5) are strange without the cloak and a possible law-suit over it, although the possibility of a non-technical or metaphorical use of the latter phrase cannot be excluded. Nevertheless, I am inclined to think that 16–26.6 only is a displaced portion of Book XIV and that 1–15 is a more or less continuous narrative and part of Book XV.

On this hypothesis, the Quartilla episode, essentially the consequence of their earlier disturbance of the rites of Priapus, takes place before the encounter with Menelaus and Agamemnon, but probably in the same city, the *Graeca urbs* (81.3), where they had taken lodgings after Baiae and their adventures in the countryside. The identity of the city or *colonia* in which more than half of the extant narrative takes place has been the subject of much misguided and prejudiced discussion, but the case for Puteoli, the

[1] *illa scilicet quae paulo ante cum rustico steterat*: see R. G. M. Nisbet, *JRS* 52 (1962), 227.

modern Pozzuoli, seems unanswerable.[1] It is on the Campanian seaboard (81.1); it is a *colonia* (44.12, 57.9), administered by aediles (44.3), with an amphitheatre (45.4) and a circus (70.13); it has a road to Capua and a road that leads through a necropolis (62.1); its basilica was built within living memory (57.9); it has a fire-fighting crew (78.7) and oriental contacts (38.3); it has a Seviral college (30.2, 65.5, 57.6). All of these conditions are satisfied by Puteoli (and by Puteoli alone) in the mid-first century A.D., and not by the other places put forward such as Cumae, Naples, Pompeii, and Terracina-Anxur. Petronius' realism in the *Cena* will be discussed later, and his accurate knowledge of the area is understandable in one who owned a villa at nearby Cumae. Puteoli may have been named in the lost part of the work, just as Baiae and Capua are mentioned. What has confused the issue is the suggestion made by Paratore and elaborated by Marmorale that it is an imaginary city and not meant to be identifiable. Now, strangely enough, this notion fits better the last part of the extant narrative where Croton is named but is in no way realistically described. In the case of the *Graeca urbs*, even if it were not named, the town in Petronius' mind was clearly Puteoli. Even if he were not striving for any exact and superfluous particularization beyond his dramatic purposes, the identification would be obvious and hardly unforeseeable by him. In more modern instances, a piece of fiction set in some locale named Oxbridge or Bradpool may often be tied down by significant descriptions to the specific town in the author's mind.

From the beginning of our extant text, then, the three are newly lodged in Puteoli, and Quartilla tracks them down at 16. Unfortunately, the difficulties of the first twenty-six chapters are not over when the Quartilla episode is placed before the scene with

[1] The question was basically settled by C. Iannelli, *In Perrotinum cod. . . . Dissertationes Tres* (Naples, 1811), pp. 117 ff. Of more recent discussions, those of Friedländer, Sgobbo, and Rose (esp. *TAPA* 93 (1962), 402 ff.) are the most complete. For Puteoli itself, see J. Beloch, *Campanien* (Leipzig, 1879), pp. 88–144, particularly pp. 108, 116–17, and 134; C. Dubois, *Pouzzoles antique* (Paris 1907), ch. 3; A. Maiuri, *La funzione economica e commerciale di Puteoli nella Campania* (Naples, 1928) *passim*; and R. Annecchino, *Campania Romana* (Naples, 1938), vol. I, pp. 19-43.

Agamemnon (1 ff.),[1] for the text of the episode itself is fragmentary and confused.

After a dinner prepared by Giton, there is a loud knock on the door. Quartilla's maid comes in and, in conciliatory words, informs them that it was Quartilla's ceremony in honour of Priapus that they had disturbed a night or two ago (*ipsa . . . illa nocte*, 17.7). Quartilla enters and rebukes them for their sacrilegious behaviour, but more in sorrow than in anger. She has been told in a dream to seek them out and to cure her fever, which she refers to as malaria (*tertianae*, 19.2), although its real nature is easy enough to guess. She begs them not to ridicule or spread abroad the age-old cult secrets. Encolpius promises, and offers to help her in any way he can. Quartilla's crocodile tears turn to laughter, a change of mood that worries Encolpius.[2] She now reveals that she has taken over the whole inn to have her 'fever' cured without interruption. Encolpius is alarmed, but consoles himself with the thought of their superior forces (19.5). From this point on the problems become more numerous, although the general import of the episode is plain enough. On the one hand, it is another instance of Encolpius' continual brushes with the resentful Priapus; on the other, Quartilla is the first of the strong, libidinous women we meet in our extant narrative, although presumably not the first in the original work. Such women are targets of Petronius' satire and occasions of his sexual realism. Quartilla's motivation is plain: a desire to silence the trio, expiate their sacrilege, and, most importantly, pay her tribute, in her own enjoyable way, to the mighty deity she reveres and serves. Her religious vengeance and her sexual motives are not to be distinguished too pedantically in a satiric narrative about a priestess of Priapus.

In their present order, the fragments offer the following sequence of events. A sudden change from courage to fear (19.6, 20.1); the

---

[1] The temporal problems presented by 9.2 (*prandium*), 10.6 (*hodie . . . ad cenam*), 12.1 (*deficiente iam die*), 16.1 (*cena*), 19.2 (*hodie*), 21.5–7 (*cenatoria, pervigilium*), 26.6 (*noctem*), and 26.7 (*tertius dies*) are at least alleviated.

[2] *omnia mimico* (*v.l. nimio*) *risu exsonuerant* (19.1) suggests that the friends are being tricked. Cf. *quid ergo . . . cessamus mimum componere* (117.4), which refers to Eumolpus' great imposture.

48

maid spreads a blanket on the floor, and someone tries to arouse
Encolpius sexually, but he is impotent (20.2); Ascyltos covers his
head (20.3); the maid ties them hand and foot (20.4). Then,
surprisingly, we have some humorous by-play involving *satyrion*,[1]
of which Encolpius seems to have drunk more than his share
(20.5-7); someone laughs gracefully (20.7); Giton begins laughing,
especially when the little girl kisses him (20.8). We then revert to
a scene where Encolpius and Ascyltos are being forcibly restrained
by Quartilla's maids, *satyrion* being again in evidence (21.2). They
are assaulted by a *cinaedus*[2] until Quartilla calls him off (21.2).
They both swear to keep some horrible secret (21.3). They are
then rubbed down by some attendants and are led to the next
room (*proximam cellam*), where a lavish dinner is laid out. They
almost fall asleep, but Quartilla reminds them that it is a vigil in
honour of Priapus (21.4-7). The next scene shows Ascyltos asleep
and being lavishly smeared with soot and wine-dregs by the maid
whose advances he has apparently scorned. The whole company
in fact goes to sleep, only to be woken by two thieving Syrians
who have entered the dining-room;[3] Quartilla revives the party
(22.1-23.1). After another lacuna, a *cinaedus* enters who, much to

[1] This aphrodisiac, the best-known in classical antiquity, is mentioned three
times in the *Satyricon* and frequently elsewhere. The name derives from the
Greek for *satyr* with its obvious connotations. The plant itself seems to have
been a tuberous root with an erect fleshy stem, having usually purple or red
flowers and belonging to the genus *orchidaceae*. It was alleged to have erotic
properties even when held in the hand. Of ancient references, cf. e.g. Ov. *A.A.*
2.415-16; Plin. *H.N.* 26.96-9; Mart. 3. 75. 4; Dsc. 3.134.

[2] The earliest meaning of *cinaedus* (literally, *one who moves the genitals*) seems
to have been a lover of boys (in a bad sense). The name was then applied to a
dancer of obscene ballet accompanied by highly indecent songs (Plaut. *Mil.*
668, cf. *Sat.* 23. 2-3); see O. Jahn, 'Wandgemälde des Columbariums in der
Villa Pamphili', *Philol. Abh. der Münchener Akad.* VIII, pp. 254 ff. The term
gradually became a nickname for effeminate men who indulged in face-painting
and other feminine arts: cf. *AP* 11.272; Ar. *Th.* 134 f., Men. Fgt. 303 (Körte).
Cinaedic poetry was a grossly indecent genre, whose best-known exponent was
Sotades of Maroneia in Crete (Ath. 14. 620 f.).

[3] I.e. *triclinium*. Does this mean that the scene takes place in Quartilla's house
or is the word used loosely of the temporary dining room laid out in the inn
(*proximam cellam*, 21.5)?

Quartilla's amusement, sexually assaults Encolpius and Ascyltos. This seems part of some practical joke by Quartilla. Giton laughs and attracts Quartilla's attention; at Psyche's suggestion, she arranges a mock marriage between him and the seven-year-old Pannychis; with Encolpius Quartilla watches their childish play through a peep-hole (23.2–26.5). The last fragment has them sleeping without fear for the rest of the night (26.6).

The main problems are, first, the time and the place for all this action; second, the strange movement from terror (19.3–20.4) to laughter (20.5–8) and back to misery (21.1–3), followed by good treatment, even though it is marred by horse-play (21.4–7); thirdly, the monotonous repetitiveness of some of the incidents.[1] Some of these difficulties may be solved by conventional explanations.[2] It has been suggested that the first part of the action takes place at the inn, but that the vigil lasts three nights and we have large portions of the second night, which ends in the mock marriage. This explains Quartilla's taking over the inn for the day (*hodie*, 19.2), the temporary dining facilities (*proximam cellam*, 21.5; cf. *triclinium*, 22.3), the unexpected tiredness of all the participants (21.7, 22.1–2), and the size of the house (26.1) and the household (22.2, 26.1). The suggestion has the additional advantage of explaining the troublesome opening of the *Cena Trimalchionis* (*venerat iam tertius dies*, 26.7), which would refer to the last day of the vigil; the gloom of the hero and his friends (26.8) now becomes understandable and their deliberations on how to avoid 'the coming storm' more natural. It is unlikely that they would be so worried about a free dinner,[3] however much they may later sneer at their host. Encolpius at least is willing to go to some lengths to cadge such invitations (10.2). Dinner with Trimalchio in fact provides an escape: they will be protected against Quartilla.

---

[1] Both *cinaedi*, if there are two of them, behave in much the same way (21.2, 23.2–24.5); Giton burst out laughing twice, yet apparently he attracts Quartilla's attention only on the second occasion (20.8 and 24.5).

[2] See Ciaffi, pp. 31 ff., and the references there to the other literature.

[3] Bücheler's deletion, however, of *id est expectatio liberae cenae* I regard as certain.

But these suggestions do not explain the odd similarity of some of the incidents, even if we assume very large gaps in our present narrative in order to lessen their apparent proximity, nor do they explain the dramatic movement from terror to laughter and back to misery. A radical solution to these problems was first offered by Gaselee;[1] a solution which becomes in principle more convincing now that the interpolations in the text have been more closely scrutinized.[2] Tampering with the text of Petronius may not have been confined to simple interpolation. Gaselee argued that some of the fragments in the Quartilla episode were misplaced and some of them were simply different versions of the same incident, which were due to an interpolator's supplements of sentences dislocated from their original and fuller context. This produces the appearance of confusion and repetitiveness.

Gaselee's own detailed reconstruction, which he admits is fanciful, is of course, like any other, open to criticism, but I believe that his basic theory, or something like it, is needed to explain our text, even if we cannot now work out the mechanics of this wholesale corruption. If his theory is accepted, Ciaffi's linking of the Quartilla episode to the *tertius dies* of the *Cena*'s opening becomes less plausible.

In the light of these considerations, we may now reconstruct the rest of the Quartilla episode as follows. Quartilla has taken over the inn as part of an elaborate plot. Encolpius' initial confidence is soon replaced by mortal fear (19.6), because Quartilla has brought a large retinue with her. Encolpius asks for a speedy dispatch (20.1), but Quartilla has in mind rather the remedy for her 'fever'. The maid spreads a covering on the floor, and someone, the maid or Quartilla, tries to arouse Encolpius' passions, but his impotence defeats this attempt (20.2). Ascyltos naturally covers his head (20.3). Encolpius' inability to co-operate may well have

---

[1] 'Excursus (I) on the Order of Fragments, Chapters 19–26', pp. 1–7. The order he proposed was: 19.5, 20.2 (*sollicitat*), 20.2 (*ancilla*), 21.3, 20.8 and 24.5 to 26.10, 21.4, 21.7, 20.3 and 20.5, 21.1, 20.7, 19.6, 23.2 to 23.5, 20.4, 20.1, 21.2, 22.1–23.1, 26.6. This puts the mock marriage much earlier in the episode, amalgamates the two *cinaedi* and gives Giton only one outburst of laughter.

[2] See Müller, *Praef.* xxxix.

enraged Quartilla, as it will later enrage Circe in the same situation (128.1, 132.2). The harsher treatment this calls for may be hinted at in 20.4, where the maid ties their hands and feet. The next three fragments (20.5–8) seem to be out of place. The ill-treatment the friends are presumably subjected to is reflected in 21.1, where they attempt to call for help. But the inn is empty of possible rescuers and the maids silence the helpless pair with a hairpin and a brush soaked in *satyrion*. The final piece of ill-treatment is sexual assault at the hands–or rather the lips–of a *cinaedus*, until Quartilla intervenes. They then swear to keep the secret mentioned in 21.3 (the nature of the Priapic rites or Quartilla's sexual failure).[1] It is here perhaps that the light-hearted episode involving the *satyrion* should be inserted. They are now released, massaged, and taken into the next room for dinner. They almost fall asleep, but Quartilla reminds them of the vigil (21.4–7). After a perhaps considerable lacuna, Ascyltos is found again falling asleep, followed by Encolpius and the rest of the party. If we accept the suggestion that this scene takes place at Quartilla's house, the similarity between these two incidents, which looks suspicious, now becomes explicable.

After another lacuna the *cinaedus* appears again and makes a further sexual assault on the pair, this time as part of a joke. He is presumably the same *cinaedus* (cf. 26.1). Giton bursts out laughing and attracts Quartilla's attention, apparently for the first time (24.5). With Gaselee we might assume that 20.8, where the little girl kisses him, should be incorporated into this present narrative, for the kisses might well prompt Psyche's suggestion that Pannychis be deflowered by Giton, and hence the mock marriage in the face of Encolpius' jealous protests. What happens after Quartilla's further attempt on Encolpius as they watch the bridal pair through a peephole (26.4–5) we shall never know. The last fragment of the episode (26.6) sees the friends enjoying a no doubt well-earned rest without fear. The strenuousness of the adventure with Quartilla, not to mention the episode in the brothel (7.3 ff.),

---

[1] Fgt. XXVIII might fit somewhere in this episode. The story of Midas' secret has both the right tone and the right subject to fit this aspect of the Quartilla affair.

would still help to explain their bad state at 26.7 (*tot vulneribus confossis*).

This reconstruction can only claim that it gets rid of the strange dramatic movement and the more unconvincing repetitions, without altering the order of the fragments more than seems strictly necessary. Gaselee wished to put the whole sequence culminating in the mock marriage earlier than the incident of the *satyrion*. And it may well be that the disorders of the whole episode go far deeper than our reconstruction assumes, but they will then be beyond any but the wildest speculation. Radical surgery on this body of the text might remove considerable portions as mere summary around extracts from the longer fragments:[1] the first occurrence of Giton's laughter, for example, at 20.8 might be a mere allusive extract and summary of 24.5 ff.; the first *cinaedus* scene (21.2) might be a summary of the second and longer scene (23.2–24.5); similarly, 21.7, where Encolpius and Ascyltos are falling asleep and are aroused by Quartilla, may be a summary of the longer fragment that follows (22.1–23.1), and Quartilla's final remark in the first scene might have been taken from the latter. But such speculation goes beyond the evidence we at present have and such solutions may present more problems than they solve.

vii. *Agamemnon*

How the Quartilla episode ended we do not know, nor whether there were further adventures in the *colonia* before our abrupt opening chapter. But Encolpius and Ascyltos have to eat and we may safely assume that early in the morning they go out into the town, leaving Giton at their lodgings, and make the acquaintance of Agamemnon, who runs a school of rhetoric in the town with the aid of his assistant Menelaus. It is impossible to say how they scraped this acquaintance, perhaps through certain overtures made by Menelaus to Encolpius (cf. 81.1), but typically they are ready

---

[1] The possibility of an interpolator's summaries, or supplementations, of a detached fragment may be suggested for 124.3–4, where *qui statim opes suas summo cum certamine in Eumolpum congesserunt* followed by *certatim omnes heredipetae muneribus gratiam Eumolpi sollicitant* seems suspicious, as Ernout noticed.

to make capital of it. It is doubtful if they are seriously looking for a job as teachers (10.5); this would be out of character. They are posing as men of culture for less reputable purposes: at very least they hope to get a free dinner out of Agamemnon or one of his rich friends (10.1–3). At the school, it is likely that they were treated to a piece of epideictic oratory, perhaps a *controversia* argued by Agamemnon himself (3.1, 48.4). This prompts a seemingly frank outburst from Encolpius against the training methods used by teachers of rhetoric like Agamemnon. At its height our extant narrative opens.

The content of the speech and of Agamemnon's reply will be considered later, but the dramatic function of Encolpius' criticism deserves notice, as some have argued that nothing said by the narrator can have any bearing on Petronius' own views. Encolpius has presumably been asked his opinion of some declamation, perhaps Agamemnon's own. Now he and Ascyltos are trying to get something out of Agamemnon, at least a dinner, as their poverty at the moment is acute (14.3). Instead of the obvious sycophancy which the reader would expect, Encolpius delivers a fairly sophisticated attack on contemporary rhetoric. We know from Ascyltos that Encolpius is not above straightforward flattery (*'qui ut foris cenares poetam laudasti'*, 10.2), so it is possible to conclude that the criticism represents Petronius' own views and that Encolpius is therefore allowed a more subtle form of flattery, the apparent frankness which implies that its recipient is too honest or too intelligent to need flattery. It is reminiscent of Petronius' own way, as described by Plutarch, of dealing with Nero. Here it works also, for Agamemnon compliments Encolpius on his rare good sense and is frank in his turn, confessing that teachers have to play up to pupils and parents in order to live. His excuses are followed by some stern reflections on what the proper method of training would be, and by an impromptu poem of the sort Lucilius was supposed to turn out,[1] in which he describes a literary education which was, no doubt, fairly old-fashioned by Neronian standards.

---

[1] Encolpius may have quoted Lucilius before our text begins or else Agamemnon is alluding to the story that Lucilius could turn out 200 verses an hour 'standing on one foot' (Hor. *Sat.* 1.4. 9–10).

Early in this discussion Ascyltos slips away, bored and hungry (10.1), although he may have had more sinister motives. Encolpius, having by now obtained an invitation to dinner for them all, hurries off after him. Losing his way, he is guided to a brothel by an old woman and there bumps into Ascyltos, who explains that he was unwittingly taken there for immoral purposes by what looked like a respectable citizen. The fragmentary text (8.4) indicates that an attack is made on them by the inhabitants of the brothel, who seem to be under the influence of *satyrion*. The pair beat off at least one troublesome pursuer. In their flight they are again separated and we next find Encolpius, perhaps after further mishaps, rushing to Giton, who is standing in the street (9.1). Back in their room, Encolpius extracts from the boy the information that on his earlier return Ascyltos had tried to rape him. A hot quarrel ensues which throws a lurid light on the past of the participants. As was suggested, Encolpius may have been keeping the nature of his relationship with Giton secret, his experiences having made him suspicious, and his pose is one of altruistic indignation on behalf of Giton's youth and innocence. The quarrel ends in laughter.

Between 10.3 and 10.4 there was perhaps a recital of Encolpius' adventures after the incident in the brothel; they then take the second meal of the day (*prandium*, 9.2). But Encolpius is still aggrieved and wishes anyway to return to his old footing with Giton; he suggests to Ascyltos that they part. The latter, thinking of their invitation to dinner that day, wishes to postpone the break-up until the next day, but Encolpius is adamant. The lost narrative between 10.7 and 11.1 will have described Ascyltos' packing (*lorum de pera*, 11.4) and departure. The suspicious Encolpius follows him in order to see where he was going, but loses him. After scouring the city, he returns and is making love to Giton (11.1) when Ascyltos bursts in and makes certain of Encolpius' hypocrisy. He beats him insultingly with a strap. In his haste to leave, Ascyltos had probably forgotten the valuable cloak they had stolen and has returned to make sure he gets his share of the proceeds.

The obvious solution is to sell the cloak. The next section (12 ff.) finds the pair entering the market-place at the end of the day. The joy following on their recovery of the tunic with the gold pieces no doubt causes their original plan for going their separate ways to be shelved, until Ascyltos' further misbehaviour with Giton after dinner with Trimalchio (79.9) brings about the final rupture.

The time sequence of these early chapters is clear. Encolpius and Ascyltos are at Agamemnon's school reasonably early in the morning, as Agamemnon would follow the usual Roman practice of very early school hours.[1] Encolpius asks Giton about lunch (9.2) after his adventures in the brothel and perhaps elsewhere. The quarrel and what follows brings us to the later afternoon, and it would not be impossible for them to take up their invitation to dinner with Agamemnon (10.6) in the missing part of Book XV, for Ascyltos cannot have meant dinner with Trimalchio.

The Agamemnon episode must have been quite lengthy, particularly if our text was preceded by a description of Agamemnon's performance in the school (cf. 3.1), for Petronius does not stint himself when it comes to parody or imitation. Encolpius' criticism of contemporary rhetoric was certainly longer than what we now have. His introduction to Agamemnon, with the possible preliminaries involving Menelaus, would require describing. Much has been lost from the brothel and quarrel scenes, particularly if the hypothesis is accepted that the excerptor gives lengthy extracts from the beginning of a new scene and then reverts to mere *disiecta membra*.

viii. *The Cena Trimalchionis*

The literary qualities of the *Cena* will be discussed elsewhere and as our text is substantially complete the episode needs but brief summary and no reconstruction. Essentially this description of a dinner with a *nouveau riche* freedman is, like so many other parts of the *Satyricon*, a digression from the main story, a massive set-piece which sheds some light on the character of Encolpius and his new friend Ascyltos, but does not further the immediate action,

---

[1] Cf. e.g. Mart. 9.69.

which is the break-up with Ascyltos, or the basic plot, the wrath of Priapus against Encolpius. There is however one immediate problem which requires attention. As was mentioned earlier, the episode opens with the words:

> venerat iam tertius dies [id est expectatio liberae cenae], sed tot vulneribus confossis fuga magis placebat quam quies. itaque cum maesti deliberaremus quonam genere praesentem evitaremus procellam, unus servus Agamemnonis interpellavit trepidantes . . .
>
> (26.7–8)

It was now the third day, but we were smarting from so many hurts that we wanted to run rather than rest. We were mournfully discussing how to avoid the storm that was upon us, when one of Agamemnon's slaves broke in on our frantic debate . . .

This passage has caused difficulty because it has been frequently assumed that Agamemnon would have invited them to Trimalchio's dinner during his long conversation with Encolpius. This in turn produces a confusion about the dinner to which Ascyltos says they have been invited that very evening (*hodie*, *noctem*, 10.6), which could scarcely be with Trimalchio. It has also been assumed that the *tertius dies* must refer to the date of the dinner.[1] But if the dinner was the *procellam* the trio are worried about, this, as was mentioned above, is very much out of key with their normal eagerness for free dinners. Arguably they are being summoned *ad hoc* to accompany Agamemnon as uninvited guests (*umbrae*), and they are apparently willing (26.10).

If this is so, then the *tertius dies* refers to the length of their stay in Puteoli, the first night being taken up by Quartilla, the second by the quarrel, and possibly a dinner with Agamemnon, although they may not have gone through with this. But they have not been particularly lucky: apart from fighting among themselves, they have been involved in sexual assaults in a brothel and a very

---

[1] Ciaffi argued (p. 34) that they were expecting the last day of Quartilla's *three-day* vigil in honour of Priapus, two days having been already occupied by the events of 16–26.6.

exhausting and painful orgy. No wonder they feel they are in a storm and are thinking of moving on (*fuga*), rather than resting.

A humorous and satiric example of symposium literature, which owes a great deal to certain literary predecessors, notably Plato and Horace, and also to a subtle observation of contemporary language and life, the *Cena* avoids the monotony which is the danger of this static genre by dramatic surprises and careful changes of pace. Trimalchio's entrance proper (32.1) is prepared for by the description of his house, its appurtenances, and certain hints about his character and behaviour, emphasizing in particular his pretentiousness, a note which Trimalchio himself immediately strikes on taking his place at the table. He is impolitely late and insists on finishing his checker game. This note of pretentiousness is also struck in the various courses presented to the guests. Roman food tended to be heavily disguised, but Trimalchio carries this tendency to an absurd degree. Many of the courses become dramatic *tableaux*, and such uninitiated guests as Encolpius are kept in a state of puzzlement about the food set in front of them and the scenes and jokes built around it. These novelties, surprises, and farcical incidents comprise one of the targets of Petronius' satire, but the theme is carefully varied in a number of ways.

Once presented with Trimalchio himself and a sample of the dinner, we are given from the lips of Hermeros a description of Trimalchio's wealth, his wife and his circle of friends (37.2–38.16). Trimalchio's boastfulness about his wealth, the reality of which has been confirmed by Hermeros, has by this time been displayed in the incident of the fallen silver dish (34.2–3) and the serving of the fake Opimian wine;[1] now his ignorance and superstition are

---

[1] L. Opimius was consul in 121 B.C. and the vintage that year was famous and long-lived (Cic. *Brut.* 83); not, however, long-lived enough for Trimalchio to serve it to his guests. Not only would Opimian be older than the 100 years on the label, but it would also be undrinkable (cf. Plin. *H.N.* 14.55). One does not affix a label telling how many years old a wine is, but the date it was produced. Trimalchio has been cheated by his vintner or, more probably, he is pretending to have genuine Opimian to impress his guests.

satirized in his disquisition on the symbolism of the Zodiac dish.[1]

At 41.9 Trimalchio excuses himself and an intermezzo follows, in which the conversation of Trimalchio's friends provides a vivid and well-observed picture of the life and values of the *petits gens* of a Campanian town. At 47.1 Trimalchio returns and his vulgarity is satirized. The dinner continues with variations on the culinary theme and the humorous scenes that accompany the dinner. The conversation and incidents which punctuate the courses continue to reveal Trimalchio's ignorance and ostentation, but a diversion comes with Hermeros' quarrel with Ascyltos (57 ff.), and a further diversion with the two ghost-stories (61.10–63.10).

The entry of Habinnas, clearly modelled on Alcibiades' drunken entry in Plato's *Symposium* (212 c ff.), opens the third phase. Although the familiar culinary theme is not dropped, our attention is now dominated by Trimalchio's private life, particularly his relations with his wife, Fortunata, and his household. His tastelessness, however, remains a target for satire, notably in the instructions he gives Habinnas about his tomb (71.5 ff.), and the impromptu bath he and his guests take (72.3 ff.). The climax comes in the quarrel with Fortunata. This is followed by Trimalchio's portentous account of his career, culminating in his mock funeral (77.7 ff.). The party breaks up in the confusion caused by the arrival of the fire brigade.

ix. *Eumolpus*

After leaving Trimalchio's house, the three finally find their way back to their lodgings (79.6), which, being locked, they enter with some difficulty. Ascyltos has now accepted the relationship between Giton and Encolpius, and a short poem depicts Encolpius' present bliss. An ironic touch, for during the night Ascyltos takes advantage of Encolpius' drunkenness to transfer Giton to his own bed. Encolpius' jealousy at the discovery of this almost leads to murder, but he contents himself with ordering Ascyltos out. After

[1] See J. G. W. M. de Vreese, *Petron 39 und die Astrologie* (Amsterdam, 1927), although many of his statements are highly dubious.

they divide up their loot, Ascyltos, perhaps harking back to an agreement made when they first met, now suggests dividing the boy up. A bloody fight is averted through Giton's pleas, and Ascyltos suggests that the boy himself choose between them. Encolpius' confidence that their long relationship has become as strong as ties of blood is abruptly shattered when Giton chooses Ascyltos. Abandoned by the pair, Encolpius moves to a place by the seaside to avoid any further dealings with Menelaus. After a miserable two days, Encolpius arms himself with a sword and goes looking for revenge, but he runs into a soldier, who disarms him (82.2–4).

The short poem about Tantalus (82.5) and the sententious dictum that one should not trust one's plans too much, as Fortune has a way of her own (82.6), offer little clue as to their context. They could be part of an Encolpian soliloquy. Encolpius is ultimately relieved that the soldier has taken his sword (82.4), and some philosophical reflections would be in order. The poem's theme is that people may starve in the midst of plenty. Encolpius may have been consoled with the thought that there are plenty of opportunities for him to make his way in life or love, if he would look for them and not be distracted by fear or stubbornness. The point of the philosophical apophthegm may be that Encolpius should be flexible and take advantage of what turns up rather than rely too much on settled expectations and plans.

To distract himself, he visits an art gallery, where he rhapsodizes over famous Greek paintings of the past. Some of the subjects are familiar mythological topics involving love, which excites him to further self-pity. He is joined by an elderly man of shabby but intellectual appearance. This is the poet Eumolpus, another of the companions Encolpius picks up in his wanderings. The conversation begins with Eumolpus explaining why he is so threadbare. It is because the rich not only neglect, but actively persecute, lovers of literature (84.3). The text becomes fragmentary once more, and Eumolpus presumably makes the point that poverty is the sister of high-mindedness.

The next fragment makes it clear that Encolpius tells Eumolpus his troubles (84.5). Possibly he dwells on Giton's unscrupulousness (cf. 79.9–11); this would provide a good opening for Eumolpus' amusing tale of the Boy of Pergamum, which illustrates the astuteness, mutability, and immorality of boys. Encolpius turns the conversation to art and the causes of contemporary artistic decadence. Eumolpus blames materialism and sensuality, which he contrasts unfavourably with the altruistic attitudes of the scientists and artists of bygone days. Noticing Encolpius' interest in a painting on the Fall of Troy, he recites, apparently impromptu, a poem of 65 lines on the subject. The poem is a free reworking of part of Book 2 of Vergil's *Aeneid* in iambic *senarii*. Strollers in the colonnade throw stones at Eumolpus and he rushes down to the sea, followed by Encolpius, who invites him to dinner, provided he promises that he will forbear reciting poetry for that day at least. The innkeeper is asked to get a meal prepared (90.7), while Eumolpus and Encolpius follow the usual Roman custom of going to the baths before dinner.

There Encolpius finds Giton standing miserably against the wall, obviously in attendance on Ascyltos. The two are reconciled: Giton's motive had been fear of Ascyltos' superior strength. They escape from the baths, leaving Eumolpus reciting poetry and Ascyltos' clothes unattended (cf. 92.7). Eumolpus finally joins them at Encolpius' lodgings. To Encolpius' dismay, the poet is very much taken with Giton. Ascyltos, he tells them, had been vainly searching for Giton and his clothes, but his superior sexual equipment had brought him aid in the shape of a notorious homosexual who had taken him home.

Encolpius is suspicious of Eumolpus' intentions and pretends to know nothing about Ascyltos. The conversation over dinner seems guided by the poet, who again attacks the vices of the age, this time the modern contempt for what is natural and lawful and the perverse desire for what is exotic, dangerous, and expensive. But he has broken into verse and Encolpius, worried about the effect on the neighbours, insists that he stop. Out of apparent politeness, Giton tries to keep the peace and moderate Encolpius' irritation. This serves to increase Eumolpus' attentiveness and, consequently, Encolpius' anger. He warns the poet to leave, but as Giton has already gone on some errand about the house,

Eumolpus bolts the surprised Encolpius in his room and goes after the boy (94.7).

Encolpius in despair tries to hang himself, but is frustrated in this by the return of Giton and Eumolpus. Giton melodramatically seizes a practice razor from Eumolpus' hired man, who is now there, and pretends to commit suicide. The shouting that takes place during this scene attracts the attention of the landlord of the block, Marcus Mannicius (?), who, seeing the disorder of the room, suspects that they are drunk or runaway slaves who may be trying to avoid paying their rent. Eumolpus has a fierce argument with him and pursues him from the room. Encolpius thereupon locks him out, and leaves him, despite Giton's appeals, to the mercy of the servants in the house. The fray is interrupted by the manager of the lodging-house, Bargates, who happens to be a friend of Eumolpus'. He takes him off for a quiet talk, as he wishes him to write some insulting verses to keep his woman in order.

At this point (97), a town crier arrives with Ascyltos and announces a reward for the return of Giton, whose description is given. Giton and Encolpius are still in their room, and the latter has been watching events through a crack in the door. Giton hides himself under the bed. The house is searched and Encolpius' locked doors arouse Ascyltos' hopes. Encolpius however tricks him, and presumably Ascyltos goes away without causing further trouble. This is left to Eumolpus, who threatens to betray Giton for the reward. Encolpius continues to pretend that Giton is not there, but the boy's sneezing gives the trick away.

Giton mollifies the indignant poet and binds his wounds. He throws himself on Eumolpus' mercy. A mere scrap remains of Eumolpus' no doubt lengthy remarks. It is to the effect that he has always lived as though each day was to be his last. This is to explain perhaps his contempt for danger and his desire for the pleasures of the moment. Eumolpus and Encolpius are reconciled: they decide to join forces and travel together. A sailor arrives to warn Eumolpus that his ship is about to leave. The three and Eumolpus' servant pack and embark (99.6).

x. *Lichas and Tryphaena Again*

On board ship and bedded down in the hull, Encolpius tries to minimize to himself Eumolpus' patent attraction to Giton. After all, he argues philosophically, the good things of life are enjoyed by everyone. It is natural that Giton should be admired by others, and Eumolpus is too old to get up to any real mischief. Although not too convinced by this reasoning, he is attempting to sleep when two familiar voices are heard from the poop deck. Giton and Encolpius wake the drowsing Eumolpus, who confirms their fears. The ship belongs to Lichas and he is conveying Tryphaena to Tarentum, his home port.[1] Giton explains their danger. After rejecting a number of plans of escape, they settle on the subterfuge of shaving their heads, tracing brandmarks on their foreheads with ink, and pretending to be recaptured runaway slaves. Unfortunately they are spotted by a seasick passenger named Hesus (?) while they are cutting their hair off, and he is horrified by this unlucky omen (103.6).

Next morning, Lichas and Tryphaena are found discussing their dreams. Lichas has been informed by Priapus that Encolpius is aboard his ship and Tryphaena has dreamed that the statue of Neptune at Baiae told her that she would find Giton aboard also. Eumolpus is with them and tries to ridicule these visions by invoking the doctrines of Epicurus, who believed that dreams were never veridical but simply stray images of the day.[2] Lichas is not convinced and suggests searching the boat to avoid any suspicion of impiety,[3] when the text breaks off. No doubt Encolpius and

[1] Although Lichas and Tryphaena probably belong to different episodes originally, they have met and are now jointly on the look out for the culprits (but see Ciaffi, p. 11).

[2] See W. Headlam, *Herodas* (Cambridge, 1922), p. lii; Fgt. XXX is an exposition of Epicurean theory on the subject with examples and would be appropriate here. Neptune may have been chosen to give warning to Tryphaena because of his role in the *Odyssey* as a persecuting deity, although Tryphaena would naturally have prayed to him before embarking on her voyage (cf. Sen. *Ep.* 85.33). His Petronian equivalent, Priapus, reveals Encolpius' presence on board to Lichas.

[3] Fgt. XXVII (on the fear of the gods) would fit here as Eumolpus' answer to this.

Giton are flushed out, but their appearance is for the moment convincing until Hesus (?) identifies them as the men whom he saw shaving their heads in the moonlight (104.5). Lichas takes this very seriously and has the culprits brought forward. Eumolpus unsuccessfully tries to explain it away, but, to expiate their offence against the ship's protecting deity, the unfortunate pair are ordered forty lashes. Giton's cries are identified by Tryphaena's entourage and the punishment is interrupted. Lichas then recognizes Encolpius and the deception practised upon Tryphaena and himself.

Punishment is still in order for their earlier misdeeds. Eumolpus intervenes and attempts to reconcile the opposing parties. But his factitious pleadings are useless against Lichas' hard-headed objections. Eumolpus, in his irascible way, intends to prevent, by force if necessary, any further harm to Encolpius and Giton. Things are moving towards physical violence when peace is restored by Giton's feigned attempt to castrate himself and Encolpius' pretence of cutting his throat. In a parody of tragic verse Tryphaena pleads for a cessation of hostilities. Eumolpus lays down terms. Lichas and Tryphaena are to abstain from any unwanted attentions or further revenge under pain of financial penalties. The quarrel ends in general merrymaking, enlivened by Eumolpus' ludicrous poems on the pair's baldness, which Tryphaena's maid eventually conceals by producing wigs for them both.

Eumolpus continues to hold the floor: he jokes about woman's fickleness and tells the famous story of the Widow of Ephesus. Like all the short tales in the *Satyricon*, this has dramatic point, and here the inspiration was no doubt Tryphaena's changeability. Lichas is annoyed because it reminds him of his wife's infidelity and desertion. Meanwhile Tryphaena's forward attentions to Giton are making Encolpius very jealous. He feels miserable and neglected.

The text now becomes very fragmentary and perhaps we have lost a whole night of amorous adventure and intrigue. It would seem that Lichas attempts, without his usual arrogance, to get into the gay circle of Tryphaena, Giton, and Eumolpus, from which Encolpius is still excluded (113.10). The next fragment (113.11) is puzzling:

'si quid ingenui sanguinis habes, non pluris illam facies quam scortum. si vir fueris, non ibis ad spintriam.'[1]

'If you have any decent blood in your veins, you won't regard her as anything more than a whore. If you're a man, you won't go to such a perverted creature.'

The manuscripts attribute this to Tryphaena's maid addressing Encolpius. Maids are not necessarily blind to their mistresses' character, and she may be trying to win Encolpius for herself or, as Ciaffi suggests, for Lichas. But Encolpius has no further sexual interest in Tryphaena and is jealous of her besides. It would fit the situation best if it were Encolpius speaking to Lichas.[2]

The next two fragments concern Eumolpus (113.12–13). Encolpius is afraid that Eumolpus will discover something (*quicquid illud fuerat*), perhaps what had happened with Lichas or Tryphaena, and take revenge for Encolpius' earlier injuries to him by composing poems on the subject. Perhaps he pleads with the poet and Eumolpus' solemn oath (113.13) is a promise to let the past stay buried.

A storm interrupts the conversation. It is generally assumed that the ship by this time is in the dangerous Straits of Messina, between Sicily and Italy, although to judge from 116, where they have only a short way to go before they reach Croton, the more obvious location of the shipwreck is in the Gulf of Squillace, not far from Cape Rizzuto. But this is the sort of unimportant detail that Petronius might well ignore; his realism works on quite a different level. Lichas pleads with Encolpius to save the ship by returning the stolen rattle and robe of Isis, but he is suddenly swept overboard. Tryphaena's servants get her into a small boat and save her. Encolpius and Giton, now reconciled, tie themselves together to die in each other's arms, while the rudderless ship drifts helplessly

---

[1] *Spintriam* is the plausible emendation put forward in Tornaesius' edition of 1575. The word (from σφιγκτήρ) was also the name of a kind of flexible bracelet. The speciality of *spintriae*, a neologism according to Tacitus, was copulation with several people at once (Tac. *Ann.* 6.1, Suet. *Tib.* 43, Lamprid. *Heliogab.* 33; cf. Mart. 12.43.8 and Auson. *Epig.* 119.3).

[2] The MSS attributions of fragments in the narrative are not always to be trusted, cf. below, p. 70, n. 1 on 132.1.

in the waves. Apparently it comes close to shore and fishermen, enticed out by hopes of profit, stay to help. They drag it to ground on the beach. Encolpius and Giton hear groaning and find Eumolpus tucked away in the cabin, writing a poem. They pull him to land and, after plundering the vessel (if that is the meaning of *hoc opere tandem elaborato*, 115.6), they make a frugal supper from the spoilt ship's stores and pass a dismal night in a fisherman's hut. Next day, while they are debating where in the world they are, Encolpius sees the corpse of Lichas floating shorewards and he indulges in various compassionate reflections on the uncertainty of human life. They build Lichas a funeral pyre, but the epigram that Eumolpus is trying to compose for the occasion is presumably lost (115.20).

xi. *The Road to Croton*

They take the road that they had decided on, and soon, from a mountain top, they see not far off a town on a commanding height, which they discover from a countryman is the ancient city of Croton, once the most powerful state in Italy.[1] The countryman further informs them that the only occupation of its inhabitants is legacy hunting and that all the townspeople belong to one of two classes, those who have fortunes to leave and those who are scheming to inherit them. Encolpius doubtless wishes to give the city a wide berth but the more resourceful Eumolpus (*prudentior*, 117.1) produces the scheme of passing himself off as an extremely rich and ailing old man who has been shipwrecked while travelling to forget the death of his only son. The others pledge him their fidelity in this imposture and all their resources, which include a robe and the money stolen from Lycurgus.

As they journey towards the city, after a farcical farting scene (117.11–13), in which Eumolpus' hired man, Corax, reveals his discontent,[2] Eumolpus treats the company to a disquisition on

---

[1] On Croton, see T. J. Dunbabin, *The Western Greeks* (Oxford, 1948), *passim*.

[2] This sort of scene is common enough in comedy (cp. Ar. *Ra.* 8 ff.) and J. van Leeuwen's ed. (Leyden, 1896) *ad loc.* but the dramatic point here is somewhat obscure. It may be simply an imitation of Aristophanes. If it reflects on the criticism of Lucan that follows, as Rose suggests, pp. 170, 199, perhaps we

poetic style past and present. He shows himself a traditionalist with an admiration for Homer, the Greek lyric poets, Vergil, and Horace. Historical epic must be highly literary and must not be treated as history. The Vergilian machinery of gods and prophecies is vital. Epigrammatic glitter must be subordinated to an even stylistic texture. This is clearly a criticism of Petronius' great contemporary Lucan, and the long poem that follows in fact rehandles Lucan's treatment of the beginning of the Civil War and its causes (see below, pp. 170–82).

xii. *Croton and Circe*

It is Petronius' practice to interweave two or three sub-plots in each episode, if we except the *Cena Trimalchionis*, although even this may be seen as part of the Agamemnon episode. Certainly the Ascyltos-Quartilla-Agamemnon books move easily between different focal points, as do the Ascyltos-Eumolpus and the Eumolpus-Lichas-Tryphaena episodes. So too at Croton: the first sub-plot, Eumolpus' imposture, is interwoven with the Circe episode, which again brings to the fore the primary plot of the *gravis ira Priapi*, which has been recurring in both the Quartilla and the Tryphaena-Lichas scenes. Circe provides a digression from the legacy-hunting theme, as the Quartilla and Trimalchio episodes provide a digression from the Ascyltos-Giton theme.

On arriving in Croton, the four put up at a small inn, and next day, while pretending to look for a more suitable home, they fall in with a crowd of legacy hunters, who are immediately taken in and compete with each other in putting their wealth at Eumolpus' disposal (124.3). No doubt the missing narrative that followed described the tactics of the legacy hunters in ingratiating themselves with Eumolpus, as is hinted by 124.4. This description may or may not have been of considerable length, but the next fragment (125.1) indicates that no short time (*magno tempore*) has elapsed, and Eumolpus' good fortune is going to his head. He

should compare the anecdote in Suet. *Vita Lucani*. There certainly seems a hint that Corax may be a threat to the whole imposture (cf. 125.3) and possibly, in the later missing narrative, he plays some small part in the exposure of their schemes.

believes that he and his friends can do whatever they wish. Typically, Encolpius is more worried, despite the affluent circumstances. He is afraid that the legacy hunters will investigate Eumolpus' claims or that Corax will betray the plot. They will then be reduced to their former miserable and lawless existence. Having thus prepared us for the steps Eumolpus will take when we return to the theme of the legacy hunters, Petronius now introduces the Circe episode (126–39).[1]

The beginning of this chapter of the story is lost and a number of problems face us. We first find Chrysis, Circe's maid, explaining the nature of her mistress' strange passion to its object Encolpius, whose slave name is one of Odysseus' titles, Polyaenus, 'the greatly famed', no doubt in order to stress the Homeric allusions. The meeting-place is clearly a park or promenade in which stands a plane-tree grove and a temple of Venus (128.4). Whether this was Encolpius' usual spot for walking or whether he was brought there by Chrysis or by an anonymous letter, we cannot know. If the former, it might explain how Circe caught sight of him. At any rate, it continues to be their place of rendezvous (131.1).

Chrysis has presumably made her proposal, but Encolpius-Polyaenus, in his role as slave, has deprecated such an honour (cp. 126.5), particularly as he has not yet seen the lady. The maid takes this as a conceited attempt to bargain (126.1–4). But his conversation with the maid, once he has verified that it is not she who is in love with him, proceeds in quite a good-humoured, indeed humorous, way (126.12), and he suggests that Circe be brought to the nearby plane-grove. Circe is waiting in a laurel grove next to the path; her appearance provokes an ecstatic description of her beauty (126.14–18). For the first time, Encolpius despises his old passion for some mysterious Doris. His opening remarks, or his astonishment, please her and she, modestly and unconditionally, asks him to become her lover. Encolpius is reciprocally humble in his acceptance and offers to give up Giton. Circe has obviously made inquiries about Encolpius; she knows about his close relationship with the boy and she is suitably impressed. She

---

[1] This might easily occupy a whole book. For the difficulties and some suggested solutions, see Ciaffi, pp. 106 ff.

tells Encolpius her name and comments on the appropriateness of the pairing of a Circe and a Polyaenus. They lie down on the grass and in an atmosphere charged with epic burlesque (127.9), they begin to make love. Encolpius turns out to be impotent, for the next fragments show us Circe waxing sarcastic about her own attractions and the malign influence of Giton. The miserable Encolpius suspects that he is bewitched. Apparently she summons Chrysis and reassures herself about her charms. She then hastily vanishes into the nearby temple of Venus.

Encolpius wonders if it may not be all a bad dream and the poem that follows speaks of the longing of the awakened heart for the joys and illusions of the night (128.6).

He returns home and sleeps in the same bed as Giton, for in the next fragment Giton ironically thanks him for showing him the same respect that Socrates showed Alcibiades when he spent the night with him.[1] Encolpius distressedly admits his impotence: his former great powers are gone (129.1). The next fragment suggests an interruption, for Giton, afraid of causing scandal, runs off into an inner part of the house. The cause is the imminent arrival of Chrysis, who enters with a letter from her mistress, the gist of which is a sardonic disclaimer that Circe is thinking only of herself or that she is offended. Encolpius will be cured of his dangerous disease if he sleeps without Giton for a couple of days.

Chrysis is consoling and she also suspects witchcraft. She recommends that Encolpius send a mollifying letter to her mistress, who is extremely upset. In the letter he confesses that he has been wicked in various ways and that he is willing to be punished, but he argues that his equipment, not he himself, was guilty of this recent offence and he asks for a chance to make amends. The gap in the narrative between 131.6 and 131.7 may have contained Encolpius' confession of his continued impotence with Giton[2] and the promise of a strenuous attempt to restore his powers (*eiusmodi pollicitatione*). Chrysis leaves and Encolpius, obviously expecting a fresh chance, puts himself on a diet and goes to bed alone. Next

[1] 128.7, cp. Pl. *Smp.* 219 b–d.
[2] Hence Proselenus' knowledge of Encolpius' impotence with both male and female partners (134.2, 134.8).

day he returns to the plane-tree grove and waits for Chrysis. She appears with an old woman, Proselenus, who tries magic on him to restore his virility with some, clearly temporary, success. Encolpius is now taken to Circe again and a romantic poem describes the place, which is either in the same plane-tree grove, despite its ill-omened associations, or, more probably, in Circe's own private garden. Circe is waiting and, after a little humorous banter, they begin kissing. The next fragment (132.1)[1] describes the growing warmth of their love-making, but Encolpius' ultimate failure and Circe's furious reaction are wanting. The narrative resumes with the terrible, if appropriate, penalties inflicted on Encolpius by Circe's servants. He is humiliatingly ejected from the house and returns home, where he tries to hide his injuries and discomfiture by shutting himself up in his room.

There he vents his anger on his offending parts and we have a mock-epic description of his attempt at self-castration, followed by an indignant speech against the recalcitrant member. Encolpius is overcome by a feeling of shame at this unseemly behaviour, but he defends what he is doing by comparing the ways other people, including tragic heroes, address different parts of their bodies. As for the indignity of the object, he justifies this in a poem which reads like the author's own *apologia pro opere suo*, as it defends the tone and many of the subjects of the whole *Satyricon*.[2] It is a realistic work, dealing with ordinary everyday matters, including sex, in a simple, new, and straightforward style. On Epicurean principles, sex is a vital element of life and there is no cause for censure (132.15). The poem may have been followed by a more elaborate defence in prose, but if so, all that survives is a sententious fragment to the effect that there is nothing more misleading than silly beliefs and nothing sillier than moral hypocrisy (132.16).

[1] This fragment is preceded in the MSS by the annotation, *Encolpius de Endymione puero*. It has been suggested that the whole fragment is misplaced, or that Endymion means Giton, and that Encolpius has alluded to his previous ineffectual night with him. My own view is that there was here a parallel drawn or a comparison in verse made between Encolpius and Endymion, who, being asleep, was therefore impotent, cf. *AP.* 5.165 (Meleager); Cic. *Tusc.* 1.38; App. *Met.* 1.12.4.

[2] For a full discussion of the poem, see pp. 98–102 below.

* Having relieved his feelings, Encolpius calls for Giton and asks him whether Ascyltos, when he took him to his bed that night (79.9), stayed awake to molest him or spent the night with him chastely. Giton ambiguously swears that Ascyltos offered him no violence (133.1–2). The motive for reverting to this earlier event is obscure. A modern reader might speculate that Encolpius' failure with Circe would give rise to doubts about his virility in general, and that this would lead by an obvious psychological progression to more suspicion and jealousy. But perhaps the question serves a dramatic purpose.[1] Encolpius is trying to discover the reason for his impotence. Was it for some crime, perhaps a punishment for interrupting Quartilla's rites in honour of Priapus? In that case Ascyltos should have been impotent also, and Giton's answer gives him hope that he may have been.

Encolpius, after his second failure, decides to call on divine aid. He knows which deity he has offended, and he goes to what is obviously a shrine of Priapus, perhaps near the scene of his crime and near the shrine of Venus to which Circe retreated (128.4).[2] There, in verse, he confesses and excuses his past offences, not adverting to the Quartilla incident specifically. His committing murder and his violation of the temple were due to desperate necessity, not wilfulness. He promises lavish sacrifices for the god's forgiveness. At this point Proselenus enters with torn hair and ragged clothes and pulls him outside, upbraiding him for getting her too into trouble. She perhaps decides on a final test, and takes him to the adjoining room of her friend, Oenothea, yet another priestess of Priapus. After an initial refusal, which is probably overcome by her arguments, Encolpius is pulled in without further resistance. Proselenus throws him on the bed and beats him severely, until they both burst into tears. Oenothea now arrives and asks the reason for their tears. Proselenus describes Encolpius' impotence and the priestess claims that she alone can cure it, but it will involve the young man's spending a night with her. A lacuna prevents our knowing what would happen if she doesn't

[1] See Paratore II, p. 420 and Ciaffi, p. 114.
[2] Shrines of Venus were frequently near shrines of Priapus; cf. Herter, *De Priapo*, pp. 310–12.

restore Encolpius' virility, but she boasts in verse of her great magical powers (134.12). Encolpius is terrified.

Encolpius now expresses his amazement at the ingenious shifts of poverty, and Oenothea's humble home is described in Ovidian verse. The magical ceremonies then begin and Oenothea insists that both of the others follow her instructions (135.2). Proselenus has been given some money by Encolpius to go off and buy the necessary supplies. While she is gone, the fragment suggests that Oenothea tries an obvious way of testing his virility. Foiled in this attempt no doubt, she begins her preparations for the ceremonies. Encolpius is set to work shelling beans, a vegetable appropriate in this context because of its supposed venereal associations. An accident puts the fire out and Oenothea goes off for some fresh flame.

Encolpius moves to the door, but suddenly some geese, sacred to Priapus, as we subsequently learn, turn up for their midday meal and attack Encolpius. His vigorous defence ends in the death of their leader. Fearing a possible rebuke, he decides to leave, but Oenothea's return foils him. Encolpius tells her what he has done and offers her the dead goose as consolation. Oenothea is horrified: this was Priapus' pet and the punishment for killing it could be crucifixion. Her house has been polluted by the blood-spilling and now any enemy who wishes can have her expelled from her priesthood. Facetiously, Encolpius offers her an ostrich in exchange. Proselenus returns and is equally distressed. Encolpius thereupon offers financial compensation and this changes their attitude. Oenothea apologizes and says she will try to keep the matter a secret. Encolpius must ask for heaven's forgiveness himself. A few satirical verses on the power of money follow (137.9).

The magical ceremonies continue and the succeeding fragments (137.10 ff.) show Oenothea trying to foretell the future for Encolpius, first by means of nuts floating or sinking in wine–a method of which Encolpius is sceptical–and then by using the liver of the dead goose. The goose is now cooked and, ironically, Encolpius finds himself served a splendid meal. Wine flows freely.[1] The original purpose of Encolpius' visit is now taken up, and various ways of restoring Encolpius' virility are tried, including a dildo,

[1] It has been suggested that Fgt. XXI would be appropriate here.

herbal remedies, and urtication.[1] All this may have been too much
for Encolpius or, more probably, he anticipates certain demands
that he might be unable or unwilling to fulfil; he escapes, pursued
by the drunken and libidinous old women in full hue and cry
(138.4).

The narrative so far, despite considerable gaps, has been reasonably continuous. Perhaps the exciting nature of the events held
the excerptor's interest, but now, towards the obvious end of the
Circe episode, the fragments become more puzzling and the story
more disconnected.[2] We may distinguish three or more situations.
Encolpius finally returns home (139.1), but there, or on the way
back, he encounters someone, presumably Chrysis herself, who
informs him that she 'who had hated your former station in life,
intends to share it even at the risk of death' (138.5). Chrysis has
learnt of Encolpius' real status and also of the possible penalties
he may pay for his sacrilegious slaying of the goose. But the
glowing description of a woman's beauty which we find in the
next fragment must refer to Circe. Encolpius will forget all that
she has done to him, if only he can get back into her good graces
with his virility restored. The next fragment continues this theme
with Encolpius lying restlessly in bed, distracted by images of his
lost love (139.1).

The poem that follows reverts to the causes of his impotence
and his failure to win Circe. The anger of Priapus is responsible.
He consoles himself with the thought that the wrath of angry
deities has pursued such famous heroes as Hercules, Laomedon,
Pelias, Telephus, and Ulysses. The poem has been taken, not
without some justice (cf. Fgt. IV), as a key to the plot. Encolpius
knew of course of Priapus' wrath (133.3), but perhaps now he
decides to turn elsewhere for help. At what point or how such
help is invoked, with the desirable results shown at 140.12–3, we
cannot say.[3]

---

[1] This is hardly the place for details of this subject, but it may be mentioned
that Oenothea seems well aware of the connection between genito-anal irritation and erethism, the principle of such drugs as *cantharides*.

[2] See Ciaffi, pp. 118–19, and the references there.

[3] Ciaffi (p. 120) believes that Encolpius invokes Mercury here and that a

We next find Encolpius talking to Giton. Because of his various adventures Encolpius, although he may have been sleeping at home, has been absent during the day; indeed, we gather he has been neglecting his duties for two days (139.5). Giton informs him that an attractive lady had called yesterday and finally said that Encolpius was very much to blame and would be punished as a slave should be, if he persisted in his resentment. Was this Circe or Chrysis? Probably Chrysis. She would learn from Giton after her threat that Encolpius was not really a slave and this would kindle the latent attraction that Encolpius suspected (126.8).[1] Chrysis would be less worried about his impotence than about his servile state. Encolpius no doubt tells Giton something of what has happened to him. Before he has finished, Chrysis arrives; throwing herself into his arms, she declares her undying passion (139.4).

The fragment following takes us back to the other sub-plot of the Crotonian episode: Eumolpus' machinations against the legacy hunters. One of the new slaves, unaware of Encolpius' real status, informs him that Eumolpus wants him urgently and probably has a whipping in store for him because of his long absence (139.5). The Circe episode now passes from our ken and we can do no more than guess at the dénouement. The logic of the plot dictates that it cannot have ended happily, even if the restoration of Encolpius' virility is more than temporary (140.12–3). My own guess would be that Circe's desire turns to hatred because of Encolpius' imagined slight, and she joins the legacy hunters in their attempted vengeance on Eumolpus and his accomplices. Chrysis, who is now in love with Encolpius and, like some of the other maids in the Satyricon, a rather sympathetic figure, may then have helped the hero and Giton escape.

nekyomanteia for Encolpius' dead member is the next (missing) episode. I would prefer to put any such scene later, because at 140.11, Encolpius is still impotent. Ciaffi wishes to account thus for the two missing days (biduo, 139.5), but these may be explained by assuming Encolpius' absence by day and his return each night. See also Paratore, II, p. 436.

[1] Ciaffi, p. 123. It is perhaps going too far to suggest that she represents spiritual as against purely sensual love. The point is that she, like Tryphaena's maid (110.5), is more humane than her mistress and serves as a foil for, not the object of, Petronius' satire.

The narrative however has reverted to Eumolpus and the legacy hunters. A self-contained anecdote (140.1–11) gives us a sample of Eumolpus' haymaking while the sun shines–his seduction of the daughter of Philomela,[1] who had been left with him by her mother for that very purpose, as the best way she knows of ensuring a legacy. The wit of the prose, as seen in the play on *bonitas*, and the farcical nature of the scene, effectively distance the initially startling nature of the subject.

Encolpius tries to take advantage of the same situation with Philomela's son, but his divine enemy frustrates him as before. The next fragment (140.12) finds him restored to his great powers,[2] thanks to Mercury. We may assume then some episode in which Mercury, the god of thieves, guide of the dead to and from the underworld, and Odysseus' protector against another Circe,[3] has been invoked and has cured the hero. Whether or not there was some sort of comic *nekyomanteia* along the lines of *Odyssey* 11, we cannot tell. The next fragment is equally puzzling (140.14). It is a sentimental excerpt, of the sort favoured by the abbreviator of the text, to the effect that Socrates never looked into taverns nor trusted crowded assemblies: one should talk only with wise people. The context is irrecoverable, although it sounds like the conceited Eumolpus (cf. 83.8), who may be flattering himself on the success of his imposture. He may have enlarged upon his own cleverness and the folly and greed of the legacy hunters, for the next piece of text is a concession from the doubtlessly worried Encolpius that what Eumolpus says may be true, and that people who are after another's property fall most easily into traps. The fragment following continues this drift of the conversation and Encolpius points out that none of Eumolpus' promises or claims are being fulfilled. The legacy hunters are becoming less liberal, and it looks as though their own fortune is once more going to take a turn for the worse.

---

[1] The Philomela of myth killed her children for revenge.

[2] Encolpius is sexually well-endowed, what the Romans described as *mutoniatus* (cf. 129.1, 140.13, and perhaps 105.9). Doubtless this played a significant part in the earlier part of the story and makes his present impotence so much the more humorous.

[3] See Hom. *Od.* 10. 275–308.

This conversation is obviously the prelude to fresh action on Eumolpus' part. The last pages of the *Satyricon*, as we have it, offer a fragmentary sketch of his new scheme.

To keep the legacy hunters on the hook, Eumolpus pretends to be dying.[1] But in order to discourage them without endangering himself and his accomplices, he has his will read out before he is actually dead.[2] The condition which he hopes will be unacceptable is that all named in the will, except his freed slaves, must eat his dead body in order to collect their inheritances (141.2). Unfortunately for the scheme, the reading of the will is followed by a fragment to the effect that the great reputation of Eumolpus' fortune blinded the audience, and that one Gorgias was prepared to carry out the conditions (141.5). If the last fragment belongs to Eumolpus, then he hypocritically encourages him by citing nations who eat their dead instead of burying them, and describing the diet of those who are besieged in time of war.[3] The *dénouement* of the episode is lost, for the text breaks off finally with the would-be encouraging picture of mothers in captured Numantia holding half-eaten children to their breasts. No doubt Eumolpus ends his connection with the hero in the way Lichas ended his – by death – while Encolpius and Giton, with Chrysis' aid perhaps, survive for further adventures.

xiii. *The Ending of the Work*

What these further adventures were can only be guessed. If our estimate of the original size of the work and the assumption that 100 onwards consists of the remains of two (or more) books are correct, then not much more could be fitted in before the presumed resolution of the main plot, the Wrath of Priapus, which alone would end Encolpius' wanderings. That Priapus was appeased and Encolpius allotted some suitable destination seems likely, whether we look for our analogies to the *Odyssey*, the

[1] He has been feigning ill-health all the time of course (117.9, 140. 6–7). Ciaffi (p. 126), following Sinko, suggests that he did in fact die.

[2] Not the utterly strange notion it seems to us: Trimalchio does it (71.4).

[3] Cannibalism is a not uncommon subject in Roman literature, cf. the references in J. E. B. Mayor, *Thirteen Satires of Juvenal* (London, 1888), vol. 2, pp. 355 ff.

Greek novel proper, the *Reiseroman*, or even the only comparable Latin work, Apuleius' *Metamorphoses*. Some vague suggestions may be offered. Isis might well play a comic role in the final resolution (cf. *deum matrem*, 117.3; 114.5), as she plays a serious part in Apuleius. And although there are alternative explanations of the allusions to Egypt,[1] the possibility cannot be excluded that one episode, perhaps the last, took place in Egypt (Fgt. XIX), where scenes in later Greek novels were often set. The presumably genuine fragments (I–XXX) cannot help us beyond this.[2]

If however some of the other poems and fragments attributed to Petronius could be trusted, further hints might be gleaned. This of course is a delicate matter, particularly as many of the poems attributed to our author, even some of the more attractive poetically, such as *Lecto compositus* (Bücheler XXXXVIII) and *Foeda est in coitu voluptas* (Ernout LIV), cannot possibly be genuine on stylistic grounds. On the other hand, some of the poems attributed to Petronius by Scaliger do not seem self-subsistent poems, but rather *poèmes d'occasion fictive*, belonging clearly to a context such as the *Satyricon*. Could a case be made for the authenticity of such pieces as XXXVII, LI, LII (Bücheler), we might find in them more clues to the postulated beginning and end of the *Satyricon*. XXXVII is clearly a prophecy, which would be appropriate to Encolpius; it speaks of leaving one's native shores for foreign lands, of extensive wanderings, and alludes clearly to a greater Ulysses.[3] LI,

---

[1] Ciaffi, for instance, suggests (p. 16) that Fgt. XIX might be connected with ceremonies on board Lichas' ship in honour of his tutelary deity Isis, and he is even willing to bring Fgt. XX into connection with this on the grounds that Diana-Trivia may be identified with Isis.

[2] Müller prints no more than these, not without some justice. But his principle seems to be that the attribution of a poem to Petronius, even by Scaliger, let alone the untrustworthy Binetus, must be disallowed unless it is confirmed by other evidence, such as its being quoted by Fulgentius or its following a genuine verse fragment from the *Satyricon* itself (see his apparatus to Fgts. XXVI–XXX).

[3] Ciaffi (p. 120) even suggests that it was uttered by Mercury in the missing narrative after 139.2. But it clearly refers to some occasion before the addressee, whoever he is, has left his native shores.

which contains another reference to Ulysses and whose style is reminiscent of Seneca's epigrams from exile and certain Petronian verse mannerisms, reads like a typically high-flown lyric that might be part of a happy ending. The subject is a return to familiar places and an apostrophe to a happiness that can never be taken away. Unfortunately such speculation could be endless, particularly as there is the possibility that the *Satyricon* was unfinished when Petronius committed suicide.

xiv. *Other Fragments and Allusions*

Finally, a word should be added about the fragments and the allusions from the *Satyricon* itself which cannot be given any context, despite much profitless speculation. Some of the fragments have been preserved simply for their grammatical or idiomatic interest (Fgts. II, III, V, Vb, IX, X, XI, XII, XIII, XIV, XV); for their metrical and poetic value (Fgts. VI, XIX, XX, XXI); or for the light they throw on literary or historical facts (Fgts. VI, XVI, XXV). And if we deduce from these that female bath-attendants, raging women named Albucia, Cerberus-like lawyers named Euscios (?), and drunken old ladies with trembling lips appeared as characters, and that some scenes involved the pangs of envy, legal trials, public addresses, the discovery of valuable stolen property, molestation by mosquitoes, and hiding in public lavatories, we shall be neither surprised, given our knowledge of the extant narrative, nor eager to deduce too much from these arbitrary survivals. It is tempting of course to think that the woman with the dangerously bitten finger-nail of Fgt. III must be the disappointed Circe, but it might equally well be Tryphaena or anyone else. The Albucia, who is tamed by satire (Fgt. VI), might well be Bargates' mistress (96.7), but the *Satyricon* was long and much is lost. Even in the text that has survived there are many threads that are difficult to tie up. We are reasonably sure that Lichas' wife was named Hedyle (113.3); we are not positive. But who was Doris, the old lover of Encolpius (126.18)? Perhaps she was involved in the episode set in Massilia, but we cannot know. We are not even sure that Quartilla's *virguncula* of 17.1, 18.7 and 19.5 is the Pannychis to be deflowered by Giton at 25.1.

xv. *Survey of the Satyricon*

The distribution into books of the events alluded to in our narrative and the fragments is a very hazardous undertaking. If our
evidence is to be trusted, the episodes involving Agamemnon and
Menelaus, Trimalchio and his circle, and the abandoning of
Ascyltos for Eumolpus (1–99 and earlier) belong to Book XV;
the Quartilla episode, the stealing of the cloak and the loss of the
valuable tunic come from Book XIV. It is reasonable then to infer
that the meeting with Ascyltos, who is, after all, a comparatively
new friend (10.7), the encounter with and murder of Lycurgus,
and the robbery of his villa, should be put in Book XIII. The
Tryphaena affair and the adventures culminating in the seduction
of Lichas' wife and the plundering of his ship might reasonably
occupy Books XI and XII. All of this seems to have taken place
in Campania, in Baiae and its environs, and in Puteoli and the
district around. Encolpius seems to have been somewhere or other
in Puteoli about a week (26.3, 26.7, 79.4, 81.2, 90.4). The many
other events referred to, the plague and Encolpius' year as scapegoat, the offence against Priapus, the robbery of a temple, the
trial, the escape from the arena, the meeting with Giton, the affair
with Doris–all of these may be fitted easily into the first ten books,
whose locale would move from Massilia to southern Italy; indeed
events in Rome and the adventure, if there was one, in Egypt, are
not automatically excluded. If 100 marks the approximate opening
of Book XVI, it also marks the departure from Puteoli by sea to
the neighbourhood of Croton. This book would seem of reasonable length, if it embraced the events on board ship, of which
many are lost, Eumolpus' story of the Widow of Ephesus, and
various poems of his, including the long *Bellum Civile*. The initial
adventures at Croton might open a new book or terminate Book
XVI, but the Circe episode would also provide a plausible beginning for a new book. This might very well run on until the end
of our extant narrative, as it is clear from 139.3–4 that the Circe
affair is by no means over, even after Encolpius' harrowing experiences at the hands of Proselenus and Oenothea, although the
focus of interest has shifted in the concluding chapters back to

Eumolpus and the legacy hunters (139.5 ff.). Book XVIII would then perhaps end with the departure, or rather escape, of Encolpius and Giton from Croton. This would leave two books, or possibly six, for further adventures, perhaps ranging as far as Egypt, and culminating in the appeasement of Priapus and the release of Encolpius from his miserable existence, whether now returned to Massilia or settled in some appropriate place.

What the books would contain apart from mere plot is even more difficult to guess. The extant narrative has satire on religion, women, freedmen, the poet-reciter, intellectual hypocrisy, Stoic philosophizing, legacy hunting, and superstition, not to mention criticism of literature and rhetoric, and lengthy imitations of tragic verse and historical epic. We might guess at a parody of a declamation just before the opening of our text; we might imagine that the obvious opportunities in the opening books for religious satire and legal parody (cf. Fgt. XIV), perhaps even political parody (cf. Fgt. XXII), were taken. Indeed the survival of some phrases from Petronius in the grammarians, if these come from our Petronius and not from other authors of that name, makes one ponder the likelihood of satire on scholarship and pedantry of the sort indulged in by the Emperor Claudius. Obvious occasions for further satire and parody would occur after the close of our narrative. Egypt would offer golden material, not least for further religious satire, and the likely death of Eumolpus might produce a parody of a death scene. All this of course is pure speculation and no doubt the fertile imagination of Petronius in fact did much better.

CHAPTER III

The Choice of Form

---

i. *The Literary Background*

The Neronian Age, perhaps through the encouragement of the emperor and the early presence in the court circle of Seneca, was a period of intense literary activity, comparable in quantity, if not in quality, to the Augustan Age.[1] Certainly it produced four recognized classics: Seneca, Persius, Lucan, and Petronius. As is common in a literary renaissance, there was a great deal of revolution–and reaction–in the air. Lucan's new anti-Vergilian epic, which dispensed with the divine machinery of tradition in favour of more Stoic elements, might have been matched, on his own admission, by the earlier linguistic experiments of Persius in the writing of satire.[2] Strangely enough, Petronius, as will be seen, was in many ways a reactionary and a traditionalist: as Collignon says, '*sceptique en morale, Pétrone est en littérature un homme de foi et de tradition*' (p. 68). In the light of his principles, one might have expected from him something rather conventional or 'classical', perhaps along the lines of the pastoral poetry of Calpurnius Siculus. What he produced instead was a highly original work, unparalleled in ancient literature, which seems comparable only to such individually unique productions as *Tristram Shandy* and *Ulysses*.

---

[1] Many of the statements in this section are documented and discussed more fully below.

[2] cf. *Vita Persi de Commentario Probi ap. A. Persi Flacci et D. Iuni Iuvenalis Saturae* (Ed. Clausen) lines 20–2: Sed Lucanus mirabatur adeo scripta Flacci, ut vix se retineret recitantem a clamore: quae illius essent vera esse poemata, se ludos facere.

This last provides a useful analogy to explain the *Satyricon*. If we contrast such works as *Ulysses* and *The Waste Land*, so revolutionary in their time, with other professedly revolutionary works such as Dos Passos' *U.S.A.*, William Burroughs' *The Naked Lunch*, or Allen Ginsberg's *Howl*, we notice a major difference in that Joyce and Eliot are profoundly traditional in certain ways, whereas Burroughs and Ginsberg are, insofar as they can be, resolutely anti-traditional. The structure of *Ulysses* is taken from an interpretation of the plot of the *Odyssey*, and the whole work is steeped in English, Irish, and other literatures. Something similar may be said of *The Waste Land*.

So with Petronius. However strange and new the mixture, the principles of organization and style, the elements of the work, even the intentions, rely heavily on literary tradition. Not only does the narrative form, the *mélange* of prose and verse, belong to the well-established genre of Menippean satire, which goes back through Varro to the third century B.C., but many of the satiric and dramatic incidents are overtly based on Greek and Latin literary exemplars. The plot itself utilizes the motif of a comic *Odyssey*; the *Cena Trimalchionis* is an example of symposium literature which owes much to Plato's *Symposium* and more to Horace's *Cena Nasidieni* (*Sat.* 2.8); many of the satirical subjects, aggressively lecherous women and legacy hunters, are familiar to us from earlier authors, and elegy, epic, and philosophy are all put under contribution.

Yet even when this is pointed out, the *Satyricon* impresses the reader as a curiously 'modern' work. As T. S. Eliot said of John Donne, 'There are two ways in which we may find a poet to be modern: he may have made a statement which is true everywhere and for all time . . ., or there may be an accidental relationship between his mind and our own'.[1] The latter is the case with Petronius: it is not just that he has left us the nearest ancient approximation to our most flourishing art form, but his tone and techniques strike us as 'modern' too. It is not easy, of course, to define exactly the elusive but certain feeling of modernity that

[1] *The Nation and Athenaeum* 33 (1923), 331. See also G. S. Fraser, *The Modern Writer and His World*[3] (London, 1964), pp. 12 ff.

impresses the English reader of Petronius.[1] An interest in the past and in literary tradition is naturally not incompatible with modernity, witness Pound, Joyce, and Eliot, and Petronius has like them a critical, rather than a reverential, attitude to his predecessors, even though he is in a way a literary conservative. One is tempted to say that he is using his traditional materials in a very untraditional and original way. Some adventitious resemblances to certain areas of modern literature are also noticeable: the protagonist of the work is an 'anti-hero', an emotional and pessimistic Felix Krull; there is the bizarre invention of the plot, the strangeness of which is heightened by its fragmentary nature; the helplessness and self-pity of the hero in many modern novels may be paralleled by Encolpius' attitude to death and his feelings of unjust persecution;[2] and for the vein of realism, even of morbid sexuality, in the work, it would be idle to cite recent parallels.

This feeling of modernity however may be too seductive for the critic. It may lead him to accept Petronius without explanation, because of his contemporary appearance, and consequently he may fail to appreciate his real qualities and originality, and may at the same time undervalue him as a mildly unsatisfying precursor of realistic fiction, who lacks firm control over his spasmodic naturalism, his tone and atmosphere, and his characters; a writer who can tear the veil of verisimilitude with an inappropriate aside to the reader (132.15), or by the excessive use of coincidence, and even through the introduction of verse into his prose. So for a proper understanding of the work Petronius has to be set against his literary and historical background.

If the evidence is valid, we may say that the *Satyricon* was written for recitation to Nero's sophisticated and highly literary court circle. Whatever Nero's moral failings, he was an emperor

---

[1] R. G. Collingwood's words come to mind: '. . . writers (at any rate, good writers) always write for their contemporaries, and in particular for those who are likely to be interested; which means those who are already asking the questions to which an answer is being offered; and consequently a writer very seldom explains what the question is that he is trying to answer.' *An Autobiography* (Oxford, 1951), p. 39.

[2] *Sat.* 115. 8–19; 91. 2–6; 94.8; 101.1; 125.2–4; 133.3; 139.2.

as interested in literature proper as any since Tiberius, and his motives, being the personal motives of an interested practitioner, were perhaps purer, if no less self-centred, than those of the great propagandist, Augustus.[1] Tacitus does not mention Petronius' writings, just as he barely glances at Seneca's, but it is unlikely that Petronius gained his position as Nero's Arbiter of Elegance by confining his taste to decisions about the correct serving of *becafica en cocotte*. And we know from the fate of Silia that he did not play the part of master of the revels in Nero's less literary debauches.

Over against this encouragement, and the confidence of an almost captive audience, must be set certain disadvantages. Under the Empire, as Ovid had found under Augustus and as Juvenal later pretended to fear, literature which was unacceptable for whatever reasons to the régime could be dangerous. Whether because of Nero's jealousy of a fellow practitioner or, less probably, because of political suspicion, Lucan was forbidden to publish his work in the usual way and this may have contributed to his involvement in the Pisonian conspiracy and to his death.[2] Petronius' literary and social position did not save him either: he was forced into suicide, because he was about to be accused of misprision of treason. This was all part of the not infrequent periods of terror and arbitrary injustice under the Julio-Claudians. Now much nonsense is talked about the state of art under constricting religious, political, or social conditions. It is often regarded as a bonus of civil liberty that art too flourishes under freedom; in fact, great literature has been produced in all sorts of societies where the extent and quality of civil liberty have been much diminished. Indeed the restriction of literary activity and publication is not always attended by poverty of artistic creation. It seems however a fair empirical observation, confirmable by ancient and modern instances, that the quality of life and literature is not improved by such restrictions, as censors sometimes think. Much

[1] For Nero's literary and artistic interests, see K. Heinz, *Das Bild Kaiser Neros* (Bern, 1948), pp. 52 ff., where the evidence from Pliny, Martial, Tacitus, Suetonius, Dio, and Philostratus is collected.

[2] On the difficulties of the orthodox theory of Lucan's relations with Nero, see G. K. Gresseth, *CP* 52 (1957), 24 ff.

depends upon the source and nature of a literature's strength, and it is arguably unfortunate for Roman literature that so much of its intellectual endeavour went into oratory (and one might include history as a branch of rhetoric), the one art form which would be open to obvious limitations in the political conditions of the Principate. The Augustans had the advantage of bridging two worlds; educated in the traditions of one, they wrote successfully in another, and if sometimes the strain is apparent, as is the case perhaps with Propertius, Horace, and even Vergil, such strain may be turned by a good poet into true literary tension. A half-century after Augustus' death, things were different.

A number of critical cross-currents may be detected in the literary theory and practice of the Neronian age. Some of these were new, some went back to the Ciceronian and the Augustan age. In oratory, and in prose writing generally, the Atticists and the Asianists continued in conflict, the ramifications of their quarrel taking in the pointed, poetic, and mellifluous styles encouraged by the ever growing practice of epideictic declamation and the increasing ingenuity and unreality of contemporary rhetorical training. Subsidiary disagreements concerned the use of archaisms, the status of Cicero, literary decorum, and the relation of style to subject matter. These questions were taken seriously: the younger Seneca, we are told, when he was Nero's tutor, discouraged his pupil from the study of earlier orators in order to reinforce the young man's admiration for his own style, a style which, as Quintilian and Tacitus were to point out, lacked classical restraint as much as did his nephew Lucan's poetry.

The poetic situation was even more complicated, and critical lines were sometimes eclectically drawn. There were, on the one hand, the upholders of the Latin (one is tempted to say the *Italian*) tradition of down to earth realism. Plain, blunt, sometimes archaic, language, and rugged unmellifluous verse were its aims, and its heroes were Ennius, Plautus, Lucilius, and Horace (particularly in his satires). The obvious example of this position–one can hardly call it a group–is Persius, and his very choice of satire[1] is

[1] The *Vita* informs us (lines 44-6) that in his boyhood he wrote a *Roman* play (*praetexta*) and, if Pithou's emendation is accepted, a book of poems about

a critical as much as a literary decision, for this was the most unabashedly Latin genre of substance, as Quintilian's famous boast indicates: *satura quidem tota nostra est.* Although there is more than a hint here of the fallacy of expressive form, the style of satire was meant to conform to its subject matter, and behind the genre was a more or less coherent literary theory. Its most succinct expression, if we exclude Juvenal's puzzling *quidquid agunt homines* (1.85-6), is to be found in Martial, who may be regarded as an honorary satirist:

> quid te vana iuvant miserae ludibria chartae?
> hoc lege quod possit dicere vita, meum est.
> non hic Centauros, non Gorgonas Harpyiasque
> invenies: hominem pagina nostra sapit.
>
> (10.4.7-10)

Or, as Buston turned it,

> No centaurs here, nor Gorgons look to find,
> My subject is of man, and humankind.

This and Martial's slighting remark about Callimachus' *Aetia* (10.4.12) is a vulgarization of Persius' more complex literary *credo* in his first satire. He sets his face against the mythological subjects, the verse forms, the neoteric spondaisms and Hellenizing language, of Alexandrian or, more specifically, Callimachean theory.[1] That he is not against Greek literature as such is clear from his praise of Old Comedy, which, on Horace's showing, was regarded as the ancestor of Lucilian satire. Like Horace, who called for important subjects in poetry, for an *os magna sonaturum*, rather than delicate and polished miniature epics and elegies of the first and second generation Neoterics, Persius may be regarded as accepting the Hellenic, rather than the Hellenistic, classics and as anxious to return to the earlier Roman classics, who were in his eyes unaffected by decadent Alexandrian theory. There is much misapprehension in this critical standpoint, but it was a tenable

---

journeys, which suggests that Lucilius and Horace were even then his models.

[1] Cf. lines 34 (*Phyllidas, Hypsipilas*); 51 (*elegidia*); 70 (*nugari solitos Graece*); 93 ff. (*Berecyntius Attis, Appennino, Mimalloneis . . . bombis*) etc.

position. The quarrel between the two views was waged most fiercely in the Augustan period, and indeed left its imprint on later Latin literature. The 'classics' seem to have won at that period; Horace became a text book despite his very qualified assent to the merits of Lucilius and despite the Alexandrian polish he put on his own non-Alexandrian poetry; Vergil abandoned his earlier neoteric position, wrote epic in despite of Callimachean–and perhaps his own–principles, adding various Roman elements and allusions to such poets as Ennius, and so became a classic in his own right. Persius enlisted both these Augustans on his side (cf. 1.96 and 116).

It follows however from Persius' criticism, which has many points in common with Petronius', that Alexandrian theory and practice was more the Neronian orthodoxy, as we might expect from the emperor's admiration for all things Greek and his association in various ways with contemporary Greek literature. This seems still to have been dominated by Alexandrian principles. Greece, like Greek literature, had come down in the world since the great classical days and lacked the self-confidence that Roman literature had acquired. A glance at the record of Nero's own productions does nothing to dispel this impression and the work of Calpurnius Siculus or the Einsiedeln Eclogues, although Vergilian enough in inspiration, might provide further evidence, if we could be sure that they were not simply inert imitations of an established Roman classic.

There are some tenuous signs that these literary preferences were tied to philosophical positions, although this must not be pressed too far. Satire professes utility, whatever the real motives for its composition and the true causes of its occasional success. The slogan of the great-grandfather of the arch-saint of Stoicism, Cato, *rem tene verba sequentur*, might be seen as a description of its no-nonsense style. Literature was regarded by the Stoics as a way of helping man in his progress to philosophical virtue; hence allegorical interpretation and the monumental moral effusions of Seneca. Epicurean theory, on the other hand, as we know from the scraps of Philodemus that have survived, held more properly that the aim of art *qua* art was pleasure and this would obviously encourage, not of course exclusively, the more ornamental, and gem-like, productions of Alexandrianism and neo-Alexandrianism.

Epic was banned by Callimachean theories and no doubt its moral strenuousness and seriousness, its classic nature, its lofty and inspiring subjects, made it anyway a more admirable and sympathetic form to both the followers of Stoicism and the supporters of the Latin literary tradition, particularly as there was now the sheer *fact* of Vergil's pre-eminence as *the* central Roman classic. Lucan shared Persius' admiration for Vergil–he certainly knew him well–even though he thought he could improve on his precursor in certain Stoic ways: for instance, by choosing a more historical subject, the Civil Wars; by making the younger Cato, who had inherited the mantle of Stoic sainthood, almost the hero;[1] and by more or less abolishing the Homeric divine machinery that Vergil had continued to use in favour of a supernaturalism that was philosophically more acceptable.

Where does Petronius fit into this literary scene? Largely because of his death and his friendship with Scaevinus, it has been argued that he is to be grouped with Lucan and Persius as a sort of artistic opposition to orthodox Neronian theory.[2] But his Epicurean moral and literary position and his criticism of Lucan and Seneca, indeed the evidence of the *Satyricon* itself, surely are against this. There is no sign indeed that he was unhappy with his situation at Nero's court, and Tacitus' account specifies Tigellinus' jealousy, not his own complicity, as the cause of his downfall.

Not unexpectedly in an arbiter of elegance, Petronius seems something of an eclectic. His views on the function of art are Epicurean, but he is no Alexandrian in the technical sense, although he has an admiring word for Callimachus[3] and is intimately familiar with the work of the Roman elegists. He is an Atticist of sorts, to judge from his style when straight narration with no parodic intention is involved, although he can for his purposes

[1] It is interesting to compare his uncle's praise of the same man (Sen. *Ep.* 104. 29 ff.).

[2] See e.g. M. A. Levi, *Nerone e i suoi tempi* (Milan, 1949), pp. 51 ff., although the idea goes back at least as far as G. Boissier.

[3] If we may accept Junius' decipherment of *Bachineas* as *Battiadae* at 135.15.

move on a variety of stylistic levels. His tastes in both Latin and Greek literature are classical; his criticism of Lucan and the *Bellum Civile* itself indicate that he is an orthodox admirer of Vergil's poetic practice. His own *oeuvre* moreover has to be placed firmly in the Latin tradition, the tradition of satire and its related genres, in all respects but one, namely, the lack of a professedly moral or utilitarian standpoint. Petronius adopts its realism; defends it on Epicurean grounds; but he gives it a new and original function.

ii. *The Choice of Menippean Satire*

If the *Satyricon* was a work directed primarily at a coterie, the exigencies of the circle, as well as purer literary principles, might determine to an extent the choice of literary form. As arbiter of a literate court, Petronius would presumably take on the function of critic as well as the role of experimental practitioner. The vehicles of ancient literary criticism were satires (e.g. Hor. *Sat.* 1.4 and Pers. *Sat.* 1), epistles such as Horace's *Ars Poetica*, or the more technical treatise. For recitation to a circle the epistle is too artificial a genre, and as Petronius' critical techniques included parody and imitation, common enough in ancient criticism of the informal sort, the treatise form was equally unsuitable, even if we disregard the fact that Petronius was himself a practising poet and prose writer. The choice of satire, even apart from other considerations, seems appropriate. As his critical interests took in contemporary rhetoric and philosophy, an equally obvious choice was the free mixture of prose and verse called Menippean satire, a well-established form in Roman literature because of Varro and, to judge from Seneca's *Apocolocyntosis*,[1] still flourishing in Neronian times.

---

[1] The so-called *Ludus de morte Claudii* is almost certainly the *Apocolocyntosis* of Seneca, referred to by Dio (60.35). The motivation fits no one better than Seneca and the language may be explained by the genre. The difficulty, that there is no mention of a 'gourd' into which Claudius is transformed, is removed if we do not take the joke in the title as intended to parallel exactly the word *apotheosis*. The traditional English translation, *Pumpkinification*, is misleading; the meaning would be better represented by something like *The Deification of Claudius the Clod*.

Menippean satire owed its origins, according to tradition, to Menippus of Gadara, who lived in the early third century B.C. The form may have begun with a more and more lavish use of quoted or parodied verse in Cynic diatribes and other popular philosophical sermons; parody and literary burlesque seem to lie at the root of the genre.[1] Once established by Varro in Roman literature, its attractions, for certain purposes, must have been apparent; its disadvantages, mainly the temptations to artistic self-indulgence and formlessness, the connotations of the genre, and the manifest problems of tone, may have been less evident. At any rate, it began a tolerably distinguished, if intermittent, career, counting among its many exponents besides Varro, Seneca, Macrobius, Boethius, Martianus Capella, and, by no means least, Petronius, all of whom used it in quite different ways.

This choice of literary form may explain further features of the *Satyricon. Satura* is a flexible form in Roman literature and may deal with such subjects as the poet's education, a journey to Brundisium, or its own origins, subjects which our narrower definition would not regard as satire at all. Nonetheless there were many topics used by satirists from Lucilius onwards which do conform to our definition. It is from these, and their growing preponderance in the originally more flexible Roman tradition of *satura*, that the later notion of 'satire' evolved. It is this later concept, not *quite* settled for Horace but self-evident to Juvenal, that we have inherited. Once the quality is more or less isolated, the critic may look back and discover satire of a sort in genres quite different from *satura* or even claim, as Horace did, the dependence of certain types of *satura* on quite different literary forms.[2] Given the choice of Menippean satire, various traditional themes, which were subjects of satire in the proper sense, might then suggest themselves to Petronius as appropriate to his form and his purposes. However original a Roman writer might be, he was still more conscious than any modern of tradition and literary *decorum*, of the appro-

---

[1] See R. Hirzel, *Der Dialog* (Leipzig, 1895), I, pp. 373, 381–2; cf. II, pp. 37 ff.; E. Norden, *Die antike Kunstprosa* (Leipzig, 1909), pp. 755–6. On Menippean satire in general, see *RE s.v. Menippus* (R. Helm).

[2] *Sat.* 1.4.1. ff. where the influence of Old Comedy on Lucilius is cited.

priate subjects and treatment in each literary genre. Nor would the expectations of the audience be entirely neglected in the adoption of a given form. Originality could still operate within these boundaries. Petronius in some ways is not as revolutionary as Lucan or Persius. Petronius' touchstones were the familiar ones in literary genres other than his own: Homer, Vergil, Horace, Demosthenes, and Cicero (5, 118.5); and his reactions to Lucan were patently unfavourable (118.6). Consequently, the rehandling of earlier satirical topics in a partly traditional and partly original way need occasion no surprise: the rich and vulgar freedman, the legacy hunters, the high-born lady with a taste for slaves, importunate poets and reciters, are familiar to us from earlier (and later) Greek and Roman literature; and on the literature of the past Petronius draws freely. When all reservations are made, he is not the least important example of the continued vitality of the satiric impulse through the first two centuries A.D.

iii. Parody and Imitation

As stated earlier, Menippean satire was closely linked with parody from the beginning. And as long as the form was used for satiric purposes proper and not for philosophical purposes, as with Boethius, or for purely literary ends, we would expect this association to continue. Seneca, for instance, in a work whose basic purpose is to satirize Claudius, turns aside at one point to parody the high-flown periphrases used by poets to specify time (*Apocol.* 2.1–4). Parody after all is just a particular way of satirizing a literary style, genre, or work. And the element of parody bulks noticeably large in Petronius. Parody however is not always malicious or tendentious. Although a literary attack is often launched most successfully with the weapons of humorous imitation–or exaggeration–and ridicule, some parody is intended simply as humour or a display of versatility and conveys no sense of disrespect or lack of admiration. Parody of the former sort certainly occurs in Petronius[1] and more no doubt was to be found

---

[1] An example is the *Troiae Halosis* (89), which imitates Seneca's style in his tragedies; another set of examples is the various philosophical reflections reminiscent of Seneca's *Epistulae Morales* which are incongruously put into the

in the lost parts of the work. But in adopting as a mainspring of his plot the *gravis ira Priapi*, a motif which clearly alludes to the Wrath of Poseidon against Odysseus in Homer's *Odyssey*,[1] Petronius' aim is burlesque and the humour of incongruity, the comparison of low events with lofty themes, or the clothing of trivial and sordid happenings and ideas in epic or tragic language. Plato's *Symposium* is drawn upon for the structure of the *Cena Trimalchionis*, as Horace's *Cena Nasidieni* (*Sat.* 2.8) is used for characterization and some incident, but no disrespect seems intended. Such uses may be regarded as 'affectionate' or humorous parody, as the intention is not in any way critical.

The large amount of parody, imitation, and allusion in the *Satyricon* has led scholars to the conclusion that for the work *as a whole*, as well as for separate incidents, episodes, interludes and characters, there must be a model which is imitated or closely parodied by the basic plot. The validity of this view depends very much on what we are to regard as a structural parody or imitation and also on what we construe to be Petronius' deliberate intention, that is, what Petronius had in mind as a model which he intended his audience to recognize. It is easy in such questions to take accidental likenesses as deliberate resemblances. Two theories have been suggested and each has found its adherents.

iv. *Epic or Novel Structure?*

Klebs first propounded the view that the whole work is a sort of parody of the *Odyssey* and epics like it, and he concluded that Petronius' intention was '*eine prosaische Travestie zu den Gesängen vom Zorn Poseidons oder Junos zu schreiben*'[2] and he was able to cite the evidence of Fgt. IV and the lines:

mouths of Petronius' disreputable characters (e.g. 71.1, 84.2–4, 99.3, 115.9–19, 140.15). The whole question is discussed more fully below in Chapter V, pp. 186–213.

[1] For Petronius' admiration of Homer, see 5 (line 12), 118.5; for the frequent allusions to the *Odyssey*, which remind the reader of a basic motif, see 97.5; 98.5; 101.7; 105.10; 127.5; 127.6–7; 132.13.

[2] *Philologus* 47 (1889), 630.

me quoque per terras, per cani Nereos aequor
Hellespontiaci sequitur gravis ira Priapi

(139.2)

Over land and grey Nereus' sea I am hounded
By the mighty rage of Priapus of Hellespont.

This relation to the *Odyssey* is underlined by the frequent references mentioned earlier to Odyssean themes. Examples are the
comparison of Giton under the bed to Ulysses under the sheep or
the whole Circe episode, where there is even a theme of magic
common to both Homer and Petronius. Of course, given a picaresque plot with the hero persecuted and wandering over the face
of the earth, it would be difficult for an ancient reader or writer
not to think of the *Odyssey*. But Klebs' general point is moderate
and correct: clearly the Wrath of Priapus *is* a humorous imitation
of the Wrath of Poseidon, and the *Satyricon*, with all due qualifications, may be reasonably described as a 'comic Odyssey'. Half
the humour of the plot depends upon our keeping the *Odyssey* in
mind when it is relevant, and Petronius' other Homeric allusions
ensure that we do so. But Klebs' thesis must not be taken too far
or misunderstood. It is simply the *motif* of the wrath of a deity
pursuing a homeless wanderer and one or two supporting incidents
which are derived from the *Odyssey*; we must not look for further
correspondence than this. Petronius is free within this broad
framework of the Wrath to introduce scenes, episodes and digressions quite different from those in the carefully structured plan of
the *Odyssey*. Despite the great differences, Joyce's *Ulysses* is much
more of a close and affectionate parody of the *Odyssey* than is the
Satyricon.

The other theory about the structural model adopted for the
work is that the framework into which the other episodes and
incidents fit is a sort of parody of the conventional Greek
romance.[1] As we know it from the surviving works of Iamblichus,
Xenophon of Ephesus, Longus, Heliodorus, Achilles Tatius and
Chariton, the plot of such romances centres around a pair of lovers
who are torn from each other, undergo various temptations and

---

[1] The theory was first adumbrated by R. Heinze, *H* 34 (1899), 494 ff.

93

dangers, and are finally reunited. There are variations on this theme, and the additional elements and digressions vary from author to author, but substantially this outline may be regarded as the paradigm of a doubtlessly large class of sentimental works of fiction, whose popularity in later classical times may be inferred from the number which has survived, but the slightness of whose merit, with the exception of the atypical Longus, is self-evident.

The theory, which has recently been restated, is that the *Satyricon* 'is not only in its frame and many of its episodes a parody of the novel, but that within this Petronius intended a whole series of parodies of the most diverse works'.[1] The features of the standard Greek novel which are allegedly taken over and parodied in the *Satyricon* are as follows: the boy and girl theme is parodied by the homosexual liaison between Encolpius and Giton; the usual chastity of the heterosexual pair, invariable for the girl, is parodied by the infidelities of Encolpius and Giton; the homosexual attempts on some of the heroes of the Greek novels are parodied in Encolpius' sexual diversions with Doris, Tryphaena, Hedyle, and Circe; Ascyltos and Eumolpus are parodies of the faithful friends who accompany the heroes of the Greek novels; the rhetorical lamentations of the heroes of the Greek novel are parodied by the ridiculous contexts of Encolpius' declamatory bewailings of his fate; and, finally, the upper class milieu of most of these novels is debased by transferring the action of the *Satyricon* to a set of disreputable, lawless characters moving in a lower class ambience. Suicide attempts, far-flung wanderings, descriptions of works of art, trial scenes, storms and shipwreck, are offered as further points of resemblance between the Greek romance and Petronius.

The theory is at first sight attractive because it would help to explain why so much of the extant plot revolves around the relationship of Encolpius and Giton and concerns itself with the emotional interactions of the main characters. Nor would the low critical esteem in which such trivial fiction was held be an objection to the thesis, given Petronius' willingness to draw on mime for much of the incident in the *Satyricon*. But although, pending fresh papyrus discoveries, we cannot entirely exclude the possi-

[1] E. Courtney, *Philologus* 106 (1962), 86.

bility, there are many objections to it. To begin with, although the Greek novel in the developed form we know is no longer to be dated as late as was thought, that is, to the period of the Second Sophistic,[1] there is no evidence for the paradigmatic Greek novel which the theory requires. The Ninos romance,[2] for example, seems more of an historical novel with a romantic motif and is in fact reminiscent of that most sentimental and moving episode in Xenophon's *Cyropaedeia*, the story of Panthea and Abradatas.[3] Now it is important for a parody that it should be recognizable, and it has to be said that the large number of subordinate parodies in the *Satyricon* would soon blur the satiric outlines needed for some parts of the thesis under discussion to hold. For instance, if Eumolpus is a parody of the faithful friend, then his other dramatic and literary roles very soon hide this function. He is much more likely to impress the reader as a parody of the hypocritical philosopher or the importunate poetaster. Again, the Greek novel, as we know it, and notwithstanding Heliodorus, usually revolved around the motif of involuntary separation; Giton and Encolpius are separated in our extant narrative for a very short time and there is nothing to frustrate the reunion but lack of inclination. It is highly improbable, moreover, that Giton was with Encolpius from the beginning, whereas the plot of the typical Greek romance begins with the hero and the heroine as the focus of attention.

Most important of all, Petronius keeps us in mind of the epic

[1] See E. Rohde, *Der griechische Roman und seine Vorläufer*[3] (Leipzig, 1914), in particular the *Anhang*, and R. M. Rattenbury, 'Romance: the Greek Novel' in *New Chapters in Greek Literature: Third Series* (Oxford, 1933), pp. 211-57, who says: 'the sentimental love-story was exploited at least as early as the first century B.C.' (p. 223). For the early prevalence of non-Greek, but no doubt influential, narratives of the relevant type, see J. W. B. Barnes, 'Egypt and the Greek Romance' (*Akten des VIII. Internationalen Kongresses für Papyrologie*, Wien, 1955), *Mitteil. aus d. Papyrussamml. d. Öst. Nat.-Bibl.*, n.s. 5 (1956), 29 ff. Greek novels often have an episode set in Egypt, but whatever the possibilities presented by Fgt. XIX, this is not evidence of any *parody* of the Greek novel.

[2] This has been dated to the first century A.D.; see U. Wilcken, *H* 28 (1893), 161-93 and *Archiv. f. Papyrusforsch.* 1 (1901), 255 ff.

[3] *Cyrop.* 6.1.45,48; 3.36; 4.2; 7.1.32; 3.4,10,11,13 etc. See also the other fragments of novels in B. Lavagnini, *Eroticorum graecorum fragmenta papyracea* (Leipzig, 1922).

parody by his frequent references to the *Odyssey*, and indeed most of the significant features of the plot as we have it can be easily attributed to the parody of epic, as can many of the minor resemblances between the *Satyricon* and some of the Greek novels. After all, the Greek romance also is not without its debt to epic, as well as to tragedy and New Comedy, and it is just as plausible to suggest that the similarities between Petronius and the Greek novels are due to the direct influence of the original sources as to an intention to parody the novel. Storm and shipwreck are features of the *Odyssey* and the *Aeneid*; the picture-gallery episode has its epic parallels in the Shield of Achilles and Vergil's description of the scenes decorating Dido's temple; Encolpius' diversions from his liaison with Giton are reminiscent of Odysseus' dallying with Calypso and Circe–and moreover in the latter case we have direct Homeric allusions in the names. As for the lower class milieu of the *Satyricon*, this may be seen as humorously parodying the heroic ambience of epic rather than the upper class ambience of the novel, particularly as epic references are to be found in the most unheroic situations (cf. in particular, the Vergilian cento to describe Encolpius' impotence, 132.11). Nor is it clear that Romans, particularly at the court of Nero, would regard homosexuality as a parody of heterosexuality: Petronius, like most of his contemporaries, no doubt regarded all men as potentially, if not actually, bisexual.[1]

To conclude, most of the subsidiary proofs of an elaborate parody in the *Satyricon* of a standard Greek romantic novel turn out on inspection to be inconclusive and many of the resemblances may be traced to that commonest of sources, epic. We might with as much reason suppose that the whole erotic sub-plot of the work is an expansion of some shorter 'Milesian' tale or Greek novella, just as Apuleius' *Metamorphoses* is an expansion of the Pseudo-Lucian Λούκιος ἢ "Ονος, or that the main plot is directly based on some Alexandrian *Reiseroman*, or that it burlesques that common literary genre, the *Periplous* or Circumnavigation. It is better, in my view, to look to the ancestor of all ancient *Reiseromanen*, the *Odyssey*, for the structure. This is not to say that fictitious romantic narrative of some sort had no influence on Petronius' handling of

[1] See below, Chapter VII, pp. 232–53.

the 'subjective' parts of the *Satyricon*, the relationship between Giton and Encolpius and between Encolpius and Circe. It is a fair assumption that Petronius intended to parody sentimental relationships and erotic situations as seen in various literary genres, whether elegy or prose narrative;[1] Eumolpus' little stories of the boy of Pergamum and the Widow of Ephesus (85 ff., 111 ff.) are cynical about both sides of the sexual coin.

Another attempt to link the *Satyricon* to the tradition of the novel is more easily disposed of. It has been claimed that in Petronius we have the first European example of the realistic erotic novel.[2] Now there is a strong strain of 'realism' in Petronius, and this strain is not accidental, but part of Petronius' literary intentions. But the realistic love novel to which we are accustomed in later European literature springs from quite different principles of realism from those which operate in the *Satyricon*. The modern realistic novel is simply carrying to certain, originally unpopular, conclusions the tradition of naturalism, whose most obvious exponents are, in their very different ways, Flaubert and Zola. In an attempt to depict life as it really is, without moralizing or romanticism or concealment, the realistic novel tries to depict love and sex as it conceives it must be. An impossible aim ultimately, of course, even when techniques other than apparently inartistic and non-literary narrative are used, as witness *Ulysses*. But one important principle of the realistic novel in the proper sense is that it aims at verisimilitude: Petronius does not. Not only is there an aside to the reader,[3] various expressions of the author's own taste and views, and large elements of fantasy (e.g. 85-7, 141), but moreover the realistic elements themselves are placed in a highly literary framework which makes free use of traditional models for its particular purposes. Even the choice of Menippean satire militates against our regarding the work as a realistic novel, for the latter

---

[1] For the variety available to him, see S. Trenkner, *The Greek Novella in the Classical Period* (Cambridge, 1958), particularly Index of Motifs, pp. 189-90. Cf. also A. Hausrath, *NJA* 33 (1914), 441-61.

[2] See F. F. Abbott, *CP* 6 (1911), 257-70; C. W. Mendell, *CP* 12 (1917), 158-72; B. E. Perry, *CP* 20 (1925), 31 ff.

[3] The ironic *apologia pro opere suo*, 132.15.

usually employs a transparent narrative prose. If Petronius were working for verisimilitude, the only acceptable way of introducing verse would be by means of reported quotation, as is the case with Eumolpus' effusions.

v. *The Realism of Petronius*

Now if Petronius is not a realistic novelist in the sense with which we are familiar, then it is important to define exactly the nature of the realism that is surely one of the most obvious features of the *Satyricon* to the modern reader. The best way into the problem is through an examination of the key passage for our understanding of the *Satyricon*–132.15. This is a mere eight lines of verse, an aside of the author to his audience, explaining part of his intentions and principles in a defence of the subjects of the *Satyricon* and his literary treatment of them. The passage in fact raises several significant issues, but for our present purposes we may concentrate on the issue of realism. The passage runs:

> quid me constricta spectatis fronte Catones,
> damnatisque novae simplicitatis opus?
> sermonis puri non tristis gratia ridet,
> quodque facit populus, candida lingua refert.
> nam quis concubitus, Veneris quis gaudia nescit?
> quis vetat in tepido membra calere toro?
> ipse pater veri doctos Epicurus amare
> iussit, et hoc vitam dixit habere τέλος.

A translation of this would not be very helpful, and the following paraphrase is an attempt to bring out Petronius' meaning:

The work you are now hearing no doubt provokes the usual strictures from the more censorious who believe that, in accordance with Stoic principles and literary theories, a work of art should be instructive and moral, not least in the narrowest sense of that term. Such critics will condemn this work, which is a reaction against our present modes of writing and old-fashioned puritanism, and has its own literary and stylistic intentions. Its pure latinity has one end: to charm you, not to instruct you.

My subject is human behaviour and the narrative is realistic, although *honest* might be a better way of describing it. No one is unaware of the important place sex has in ordinary life. Does anyone take a moral stand against harmless and natural sexual enjoyment and comfort? As an Epicurean, I could even invoke philosophical principles in their defence and point to Epicurus' doctrines about its supreme importance.[1]

The context is important here, as the poem must not be taken as embracing all the aspects of the *Satyricon*; its highly *literary* quality, for instance, is ignored. Encolpius has proved himself impotent with Circe and now, back in his room, after chiding his weak member, he suddenly feels ashamed of himself for his behaviour. His defensive analogies from tragedy and elsewhere are to the effect that other parts of the body may be addressed by their owners, but this is not yet enough to justify the indecency of his particular subject; hence the poem, and the lines are meant to defend the large areas of sexual matter in the work. That the *Satyricon* was a work very much occupied with sexual matters is,

---

[1] For similar programmes, see Mart. 3.85, 4.49, 8.3, 11.15 and for general discussion H. Stubbe, *Die Verseinlagen im Petron, Philologus Supplbd.* 25 (1933), 150 ff. On the more significant points of the interpretation: for *Catones* and Cato's symbolic function in Latin literature, see Cic. *Ad Att.* 16.1.6; Sen. *Ep.* 97.8,10; Mart. 1 *Epist. ad lectorem,* 1.1, 5.51.5, 9.28.3, 11.39.15, 12.6.8., 2.89.2, 11.2.1–2, 11.15.1, 11.15.6, 10.19.21; Juv. 2.40, 11.90; Val. Max. 2.10.8; on *simplicitas,* cf. Mart. 1. *Epist. ad lectorem (absit nostrorum iocorum malignus interpres)* and 11.20.10 (the *Romana simplicitas* of Augustus' obscene epigrams); for the stylistic implications of *simplicitas,* see E. T. Sage, 'Atticism in Petronius', *TAPA* 46 (1915), 47 ff., and G. M. A. Grube, *The Greek and Roman Critics* (London, 1965), p. 202; for *nova* as opposed to *prisca simplicitas,* which was associated with the Stoic admiration for the good old days of Republican hardihood and frugal living (cf. e.g. Sen. *Ep.* 86 on Scipio Africanus), see K. Borszák, 'Die *Simplicitas* und römische Puritanismus', *EPhK* 70 (1947), 1 ff. That it could have literary connotations is clear from Juvenal's *illa priorum scribendi . . . simplicitas* (1.151–3); for Epicurean teaching on the subject of sex, cf. H. Usener, *Epicurea* (Leipzig, 1887), Fgt. 67 οὐ γὰρ ἔγωγε ἔχω τί νοήσω τἀγαθόν, ἀφαιρῶν μὲν τὰς διὰ χυλῶν ἡδονάς, ἀφαιρῶν δὲ τὰς δι' ἀφροδισίων κτλ. (the quotation is in fact from the περὶ τέλους); and cf. Fgt. 68 and Varro, *Sat. Men.* Fgt. 402 (Büch- eler); further details in C. Bailey, *Epicurus* (Oxford, 1926), p. 390, and N. de Witt, *Epicurus and his Philosophy* (Minneapolis, 1964), pp. 292–3.

I think, clear from the original title, *Satyricōn libri*,[1] from my reconstruction in an earlier chapter, and from Macrobius' evidence, which will be discussed below. Our impression of the fragmentary work we now possess may be misleading because of the length and merits of the *Cena Trimalchionis*. However much he may offend our sensibilities and however much he overlooks important elements in the *Satyricon*, Hadrien Turnèbe was at least partially correct is his judgment: *Petronius Arbiter venustatem orationis suae inquinavit spurcissimis amoribus.*

The factors determining Petronius' realism are several and it is unnecessary, perhaps even a mistake, to decide upon their actual or logical priority. If the choice of Menippean satire, as the most suitable form for Petronius' intentions and talents, came first, then there were certain laws, topics, and connotations of the whole satiric genre which would affect the work. The realism of satire had its association with the seamier side of life, the low sexual elements which were studiously avoided in the more elevated literary forms of epic and tragedy–the mind boggles at the thought of a realistic description of the cave scene in *Aeneid* IV–although realistic violence in the battle scenes of epic was more acceptable. I suspect however that the rules of satire should be invoked only to explain the possible *acceptability* (in literary terms) of some of Petronius' themes. Satire after all had developed a long way from its rude stylistic beginnings, according to Horace (*Sat.* 1.10.64 ff.), and some further explanation is needed of the extensive use by the Arbiter of Elegance–at Nero's court, it is true–of gross, though delicately handled, sexual material, often of a somewhat bizarre nature. And it should be remembered here that the deployment of these themes is humorous and not satirical, as with Juvenal.

Petronius' complaints against the artificiality of some contemporary literature may be invoked: he attacks, for instance, the unreal topics of the rhetorical schools (1 ff.), pirates on beaches dangling chains and tyrants ordering children to cut off their fathers' heads, but this criticism is fairly specialized, and it is not

---

[1] Viz., *Book of Satyric Matters*. The early modern habit of deriving *satura* from *satyrus* led to some confusion in editors' minds, hence Bücheler's *Saturae*, the French *Satiricon*, and even Highet's *Satirica*, which tries to redress this emphasis.

the resolutely down to earth position of Martial, who is against anything that does not relate directly to life (cf. Mart. 10.4). Petronius opposes such training in declamation because it does not lead to good oratory and is useless for fitting young men for their ultimate sphere in life: politics and the bar. On the other hand, he rebukes Lucan for his rather historical approach to epic, and recommends more mythological machinery (*ambages deorumque ministeria*, 118.6).

To understand this juxtaposition of the gross and the highly sophisticated we ought perhaps to look more closely at the conditions of the age and the audience. The pages of Tacitus, Suetonius and Dio offer a vivid and scarifying picture of Neronian society. For all its material luxury and literary sophistication, it is a society which another age than our own might classify as decadent and depraved. Of course societies which combine a high degree of literary culture and civilization with immorality and decadence are common enough: one thinks at once of the eighteen-nineties in England and the Continental equivalents. J. K. Huysmans' *A rebours* and Oscar Wilde's *The Picture of Dorian Gray* are typical literary products of such societies. In these, as in Petronius, amid all the exotic culture, we find clearly delineated what has been aptly called *la nostalgie de la boue*. This seems to have been a characteristic of Nero's circle too. Quite apart from the sexual excesses described, perhaps exaggerated, by the historians, we know from Suetonius that the Emperor liked to wander through the less reputable parts of Rome and play the mohock with respectable citizens.[1] Given the society, this is not psychologically surprising, and we may conjecture that this interest is mirrored in the *Satyricon*, not only in the realistic portrayal of a highly vulgar milieu in the *Cena Trimalchionis*, a sort of literary 'slumming' which goes far beyond the more impressionistic requirements of satire, but also in the episodes involving Quartilla, Eumolpus,

---

[1] Cf. Suet. *Ner.* 26; Tac. *Ann.* 13.25; Dio, 61.8.1. Capitolinus (*Verus* 4.6) mentions Caligula and Vitellius as also addicted to the habit, and Suetonius says the same of Otho (*Otho* 2.1). Cf. also Lampr. *Com.* 3.7. Messalina's brothelgoing (Juv. 6.115) and Claudius' fondness for gladiatorial shows (Suet. *Claud.* 21) may betoken the same attitude.

Ascyltos, and so on. Such sections would no doubt titillate the tastes of the court circle, much as information about the sexual proclivities of the Emperor was interesting to Petronius (Tac. *Ann.* 16.19). The rather peculiar *type* of sexual themes is of less specifically literary interest and a discussion of them may be deferred (see Chapter VII). If, however, this was the unconscious motive in Petronius, he would be able to defend his choice of subject-matter on literary grounds and from literary precedent.

The determinants of Petronius' literary decisions are not of course the end of the matter. Their choice of the novel form does not explain the differences between Henry James, Franz Kafka, and D. H. Lawrence. The willingness to gratify certain expectations in a coterie, to conform to the rules of a genre or the example of precursors in a tradition, even to make use of sexual fantasy, cannot explain finally why the *Satyricon* is what it is as a work of art. The less tangible decisions taken by an artist are what finally produce the work of art, and these may only be explained, if they can be explained at all, in the context of the work and in the light of its own dynamics. All we have done so far is explain and so render less strange the external features of Petronius' work, the mere preliminaries of his achievement. In the succeeding chapters some attempt will be made to repair this deficiency, but first, the critical problems of realism deserve some attention.

vi. *The Limitations of Realism*

The concept of art as some sort of imitation (*mimēsis*) was, from Plato's time on, highly influential in ancient critical theory, although, like many critical concepts, it had fortunately less effect on practitioners of the arts. Its influence may be seen in such things as Aristotle's famous definition of tragedy as 'a representation of an action, worthy of serious attention, complete in itself, and of some magnitude' or in such later slogans as *ut pictura poesis*. Form and style become the means appropriate to the subjects represented. The theory of course is by no means as crude as this, and it was capable of highly subtle formulation, as Aristotle's *Poetics* shows.[1]

---

[1] On *mimesis*, see E. Auerbach, *Mimesis* (New York, 1953) particularly pp. 31–40; for Plato's and Aristotle's views, see Grube, *op. cit.*, pp. 51 ff., 66 ff.

Nor was the relationship between life and the work of art a simple one. To take an obvious example, the well-known dictum that Sophocles portrayed men as they ought to be and Euripides as they are gives us some insight into the basis of the common charge against Euripides that he degraded tragedy by introducing beggars in real rags and so on. This was offending against the rules of literary decorum. We, of course, if we were to criticize Euripides on some such grounds (and in this case we would not), would speak not of 'degrading tragedy', but of 'doing the dirt on Life', as D. H. Lawrence puts it.

Petronius subscribed to this critical view at least in relation to the pictorial and plastic arts. Encolpius in the picture-gallery (83.1 ff.) admires 'sketches of Protogenes, so life-like that they were a challenge to nature herself' (*Protogenis rudimenta cum ipsius naturae veritate certantia*), and says of the lines of the paintings that they 'were so subtly realistic that you believed they were expressing the subjects' very souls' (*tanta enim subtilitate extremitates imaginum erant ad similitudinem praecisae, ut crederes etiam animorum esse picturam*).[1] His literary theories are more complex, but they are not uninfluenced by the twin critical concepts of *mimesis* and *decorum*. The statement, *quodque facit populus, candida lingua refert* (132.15), claims that the *Satyricon* is an honest representation of human behaviour and the *apologia* that follows is a defence on Epicurean and commonsense grounds of the aspects of that behaviour selected for literary imitation, the simple style chosen for the representation being perfectly in accord with the demands of literary decorum. Indeed the *sermo plebeius* used to depict the conversation of the plebeian circle of Trimalchio, which reproduces the Grecisms, vulgarisms, solecisms, and banalities of the speakers, shows how far Petronius was prepared to carry his theories of literary propriety. If his usual style is the *genus tenue*, as his own description *purus* perhaps implies, a style elaborated after ordinary everyday speech,[2] then in the conversation of Trimalchio and his friends

---

[1] For the influence of the theory on popular art criticism, see e.g. *AP* 6.56.5–6; 9.761, 713 and ff.; 16.54, 57, 58, 97; Mart. 3.35, 3.41, 4.47 etc.

[2] Cf. e.g. Cicero's characterization of the basic style (*Orat.* 76): *summissus est et humilis, consuetudinem imitans, ab indisertis re plus quam opinione differens. itaque*

we often have what is positively the *genus humile* (or ταπεινόν).
Satire in general (and satirical epigram) is also governed by these concepts. The satirists commonly claimed that they wrote of life as it was, and although they might feel impelled to defend that choice of subject on grounds of utility or indignation,[1] the defence was, we may assume, often as factitious as that other claim put forward by any poet who wrote on sexual topics, that 'jocund his Muse was, but his Life was Chaste'.[2] It followed not only that the appropriate style for the everyday topics used was a *sermo pedestris*,[3] but also that for the more scabrous themes, equally scabrous language might be appropriate. The real motives for such writings might be less avowable. At best, they might be predominantly artistic, as is perhaps the case with Juvenal,[4] who saw in satire with its traditional subjects the art form most attractive to his particular talents; at worst, they are, as one suspects with Martial, the prurient or self-seeking motives of the popular pornographer.

Now the critical objection to certain forms of realism in literature, which applies to some areas of satire and to erotica – for the latter too may profess realism as their literary principle – is that the work is not so much a depiction of the real, for our moral instruction or the expansion of our experience, as a 'denigration of the

eum qui audiunt, quamvis ipsi infantes sint, tamen illo modo confidunt se posse dicere; nam orationis subtilitas imitabilis illa quidem videtur esse existimanti, sed nihil est experienti minus. This may be glossed by Steele's remarks in the *Guardian* (no. 15): 'So true it is, that simplicity of all things is the hardest to be copied, and ease to be acquired with the greatest labour.' Although Petronius' prose is much more artistic in its clausulae, it is interesting to compare with it the early example of the plain style in *Auct. Her.* 4.10.14 ff.

[1] Cp. Martial's *sed non vis, Mamurra, tuos cognoscere mores,* / *nec te scire* (10.4. 11–12) and Juvenal's *difficile est saturam non scribere: . . . facit indignatio versum* (1. 30, 79).

[2] Cf. such *apologiae* as Cat. 16.5–6; Ov. *Rem. Am.* 361–2, 385–6; *Trist.* 2.353 ff.; *Priap.* 2. 49; Mart. 1. *Epist. ad lectorem,* 1.4.8, 11.2.1–2, 11.15.1–4,7–9.

[3] Hor. *Sat.* 2.6.17. Cf. also *sermoni propriora* (*Sat.* 1.4.42) and *sermones repentes per humum* (*Ep.* 2.1.250). The descriptions of course do not imply any lack of art, as Horace's criticism of Lucilius' carelessness makes clear (*Sat.* 1.4.9. ff.). Petronius' self-avowedly simple style is highly artistic and rhythmical.

[4] See H. A. Mason, 'Is Juvenal a Classic?' in *Critical Essays on Roman Literature: Satire.* Ed. J. P. Sullivan (London, 1963), pp. 93 ff.

real'. The phrase is Mary McCarthy's and there is a revealing paragraph in one of her short stories that throws some light on the idea. A young man in hospital hears what he thinks are the screams of a cancer patient:

> He knew immediately that he was not meant to hear; these shrieks were being wrung from a being against its will; yet in this fact, precisely, lay their power to electrify the attention. 'A dying woman screaming in the night', the young man repeated musingly, as the cries stopped, at their very summit, as abruptly as they had started, leaving a pounding stillness, 'this is the actual; the actual, in fact, is *that which should not be witnessed*. The actual', he defined, pronouncing the syllables slowly and distinctly in a pedagogical style, 'under which may be subsumed the street accident, the plane crash, the atrocity, is pornography.'[1]

This 'denigration of the real', or, as it may be described in its subtler manifestations, 'doing the dirt on Life', is a temptation for the satirist, particularly if his motives are mainly cerebral and literary. The temptation and the consequent artistic failure, in the deepest sense, are avoided if the writer has a genuine moral centre from which he can deploy, sensitively and intelligently, his moral positives. It is of course a commonplace that the whole difficulty of satire as a genre is the close connection in it of art and morality, and different satirists may be criticized from these different sides. Only occasionally do we find supreme works of art in satire, works which deserve truly the honorific title of *poems*: The Dunciad, The Vanity of Human Wishes, and Don Juan are such rare works. In the case of Juvenal, his moral positives seem more perfunctory than his witty denigration of marriage, old age, and a mother's prayers for her daughter.

Similarly, with Petronius, we find his chosen realism and his satire, such as it is, impose on him certain limitations. It has been frequently observed that there is not a single admirable character in the work. His themes, or a large proportion of them, have

---

[1] From the story 'The Old Men' in *Cast a Cold Eye*.

scandalized readers for centuries.[1] Any elevated literary or moral criticism we find in the work has been suspected, sometimes needlessly, because of its provenance, a narrator who is a self-confessed murderer or a hypocritical old fraud of a poet. Even the carefully observed satire of Trimalchio is undercut, not necessarily unintentionally, because the 'centre' from which it comes is Encolpius, whose own moral and aesthetic positives clearly leave much to be desired. How far Petronius the artist managed to transcend these self-imposed limitations of his theory and his chosen genre, or how far the *Satyricon* as a work of art is necessarily and in fact flawed by these limitations, must be the subject of later discussion (see Chapter VIII).

vii. *Petronius: Artist or Moralist?*

So far I have tried to outline the genesis of the *Satyricon* in the light of its historical ambience and the Latin literary tradition. But it will have been noticed that underlying the explanation there is the assumption that Petronius is above all an artist of great versatility, culture, and originality; that in producing this significant work of art, his intentions and achievement were literary, in the proper sense, and not philosophical. There have been scholars, however, who were not content with this, and, disgruntled by the

---

[1] The reader may like to add one or two out of the way criticisms to his own. In 1679 John Oldham spoke of:

> Nero's learned pimp, to whom we owe
> What choice records of lust are extant now.

Lecky, in his *History of European Morals*, described the *Satyricon* as 'one of the most licentious and repulsive works in Roman literature'. G. Civitelli said 'Il *Satiricon* è un romanzo che non si può leggere senza nausea' (*Sirene e Satiri*, Naples, 1897, p. 13); Fr. P. Masen, s.J., in the fly-leaf of his copy, now in the library of Nancy, describes the work as one 'qui in eodem cum suo auctore rogo flagrare debuit, non alia luce dignior'. The *Satyricon* has of course often received short shrift from such legal authorities as the Croydon magistrates. Charles Nodier perhaps summed up this attitude best: 'Le livre de Pétrone ... C'est tout bonnement la débauche d'esprit d'un libertin élégant qui possède l'art d'écrire à un degré très élevé ... le *Satyricon* est du nombre des écrits dont la connaissance peut à peine être avouée par un honnête homme' (*Questions de littérature légale*, Paris, 1872, p. 13). For others, see *Arion* 5 (1966), 401 ff.

bad reputation Petronius enjoyed when regarded simply as an artist, they have argued that Petronius is primarily a moralist and that his artistic abilities and his choice of characters and themes are subordinate to, or at the service of, his didactic purposes. Possibly such scholars are dissatisfied with purely literary achievements, if any important work of art can·be described as *purely* literary, or, being misled by the connotations of the word *satire* as a sort of artistic moralizing whose chief aim is the castigation of vice and the encouragement of virtue, they wish to look for some larger, non-literary aim of this sort in Petronius also.

The thesis that Petronius is fundamentally a moralist has been best elaborated by Highet,[1] who argues that .

> the themes and moral intentions of Petronius are those of a true satirist, working within the tradition of earlier and contemporary satire, and criticizing the world from the point of view of Epicurean morality. His purpose in writing the *Satirica* is shown to be identical with that which governed the most famous and characteristic actions of his life.

The purpose of satire to the Romans, says Highet, was to correct or chastise social, aesthetic, or moral anomalies by ridicule or reproof. He finds in the *Cena Trimalchionis* a 'monumental exposé of the revolting and ludicrous aspects of bad manners'; for him the literary criticism in the discussions with Agamemnon and Eumolpus involves direct social criticism and an attack on false taste by means of parody or a rival attempt. The episode of the legacy hunters, for all its admitted humour, is taken equally seriously; Petronius can use farce for his serious satiric purposes. What might be a weak point in this thesis, the behaviour of the protagonist and his friends, is in fact further satire. Only their failures, dangers and fears are depicted: 'to show their repulsiveness, to describe their constant danger and guilt, without ceasing to be interesting, is to be a moralist and a satirist.' The sexual situations are all painful or ridiculous: Petronius, following the *true* Epicurean views on sexual morality, is showing the reader what should be avoided, and this

---

[1] *TAPA* 72 (1941), 176 ff.

makes the work a moral work. The wages of folly are contempt, ridicule and discomfort: the ideal state is Epicurean *ataraxia*. The lack of open moralizing is no objection to this view; Petronius' attitude is still one of moral seriousness, for other satirists such as Juvenal also use exposition rather than open comment. According to Highet, the satire has relevance to the way of life of Nero and his court: there is a close similarity between Nero's goings-on and the fictional adventures of Encolpius and his friends. Petronius' amused superiority to his characters is thus an implicit criticism, social, aesthetic and moral, of the life he found around him.[1]

Now I have no wish to deny that Petronius was an Epicurean of a sort; his manner of dying was almost an Epicurean parody of a Stoic death scene. Petronius does write satire on traditional themes and is quite prepared to use, sometimes humorously or ironically, the Epicurean tenets on nature, religion, and life as his dramatic positives,[2] just as he uses his acute sense of what is proper and tasteful in literary and social matters for his criticism and satire in the discussions of rhetoric and poetry in the *Cena Trimalchionis*. Petronius' method, to anticipate a later discussion, is opportunistic, but occasionally it may be described with justice as *ridentem dicere verum*, in Horace's phrase. Moreover, having chosen satire as his literary form, he obeys the rules of that form, even though he may be regarded as interpreting those rules in a spirit quite different from the great classics of satire. Nor is Petronius always as dissociated from his material as Highet claims. The amused superiority is not always in evidence, particularly in the case of Trimalchio where a real artistic involvement, indeed sympathy, begins to emerge, whatever the original motives for the choice of theme (see below, pp. 151 ff.). Furthermore, the large element of obscenity in the work, which is hardly like Swift's use of obscenity in the Fourth Voyage of *Gulliver's Travels*, would present a real danger of the reader's losing sight of what Highet claims is Petronius' main object.

There are more concrete objections to this view, quite apart

---

[1] This thesis turns up in different forms, see e.g. R. H. Crum, *CW* 45 (1951), 161 ff., 197 ff.

[2] See O. Raith, *Petronius ein Epikureer* (Nuremberg, 1963), pp. 6–19, 28–50.

from the dubiety of the assumption that Roman satire is always moralistic in the full sense.[1] To begin with, Epicurean philosophy proper and its teachers took little interest in art. There are of course exceptions—Lucretius is obviously one and Philodemus another. But there is not the Stoic interest in making everything subservient to a philosophic purpose with its consequent bad results for literature: the overt moralizing in poetry; the allegorical method of interpretation; and the acceptance of the common assumption that all good poetry has a didactic purpose. Philodemus indeed is quite positive on this point. A poet *qua* poet does not *have* to have a specifically moral and educational purpose, nor does a poem *have* to have any clear relation to truth.[2] Consequently there was not the temptation for an Epicurean, as there was for a Stoic, to approach literature and his own writing in a philosophical spirit, or to see literature predominantly as a pleasing way of purveying philosophical doctrine.

That this was more Petronius' attitude seems evident from 132.15, which not only contradicts Highet's view that all the sexual episodes are meant to be painful or ridiculous but also describes the work in terms much nearer those of Philodemus than those of the standard literary theories of *miscere utile dulci*. The work is described as an *opus novae simplicitatis*, which seems at least to deny a deeper philosophical content, and the line

sermonis puri non tristis gratia ridet

is obviously professing charm, humour, and a good literary style. Were any philosophy at issue, the defence against the censorious

[1] In remarking that Petronius' mere depiction of his characters' loose behaviour may nevertheless be satirical, Highet adduces Juvenal's portraiture of the pervert Naevolus in the ninth satire. But this seems a peculiar mode of the intentional fallacy. Satire is moralistic, therefore any use of this form must imply moralizing. This and the biographical fallacy do much to vitiate Highet's *Juvenal the Satirist* (Oxford, 1956). On the nature of Juvenal's art, see H. A. Mason, cited above (p. 104, n. 4), which is an implicit refutation of Highet's views on Juvenal as a 'moral' satirist.

[2] See C. Jensen, *Philodemus über die Gedichte, fünftes Buch* (Berlin, 1923), pp. 7 f., 110 ff.; L. P. Wilkinson, *G & R* 2 (1933), 144 ff.; A. Rostagni, *Scritti Minori* I (Turin, 1955), pp. 394 ff.; and Grube, *op. cit.*, pp. 193 ff.

would become much easier. Petronius invokes Epicurean principles only to defend his choice of subject matter: sex. And although the poem is humorous and is not meant to characterize the work in its every aspect, if it cannot be interpreted as a statement of the author's intentions, then it becomes rather pointless.

There are other pieces of evidence that may be adduced to establish Petronius' literary views. To take one relevant example, we find in the criticism of historical epic at 118 that Petronius recommends the retention of divine machinery and all the Vergilian apparatus, this despite a number of Epicurean criticisms of religion and superstition throughout the work,[1] nor is allegory offered as a defence, although Petronius is familiar with that method and seems quite prepared to use it for some of his poems (cf. 82.5 on the Tantalus story and Fgt. XXV on Prometheus). This implies surely a literary view akin to that of Philodemus, whereby poetry's own laws, the rules and precedents of each genre, are more important than philosophical or, in this case, historical truth.

Of course the chief objection to the theories that Petronius is in some way or other a genuinely philosophical or strenuously moral satirist is the sheer difficulty of reading the work in that way. For any critical interpretation to be convincing, it must fit the literary facts, which here point in just the opposite direction. So however difficult a pill it may be for some to swallow, we must conclude that Petronius' refined style, acute observation, and, it must be added, sexual interests, are not there to sugar an exposition of his Epicurean philosophy, but to achieve his literary and artistic ends. Indeed he was not unwilling to use Epicurean philosophy itself for his local dramatic purposes, as when Eumolpus invokes the divine Epicurus to throw scorn on the unfortunately veridical dreams of Tryphaena and Lichas, which have revealed the presence aboard ship of Encolpius and Giton (104.3).

All this is merely to stress that Petronius, whatever his deficiencies, is an artist and not a moralist; that the *Satyricon* is a work of literature and not an Epicurean tract, a political pamphlet, or an elaborate parody. And there is more to the *Satyricon* than this. Those who wish to assimilate him to de Sade as a wicked, if

[1] Cf. e.g. 104.3, Fgts. XXVII and XXX and see Raith, *op. cit.*, pp. 12 f.

sophisticated, pornographer, amorally overturning accepted values; those who try to see him as a Swiftian satirist, vividly describing what he condemns; and those who regard him as a Neronian T. S. Eliot, sketching the sterility, barbarism and futility of the waste land about him,[1] are not without some justification for their views. It is clear that the work is not only a product of its times and its tradition, but also the product of an imaginative and critical talent. The theories of the work outlined above are perhaps attempts to get at the unifying vision, the attitude to life, that most readers of the *Satyricon* sense is there, whether they notice particularly the morbid attitudes of Trimalchio to death, the lecherous attitudes of other characters, or the unreasonable *Angst* of Encolpius. My own views on this question may be deferred,[2] as our present concern is Petronius' choice of form. But a misapprehension of this, or a limited appreciation of the possibilities open to him, is bound to lead to critical misunderstanding. Parody has many purposes and *satura* is not always satire.

viii. *The Testimonia*

The scanty ancient evidence must now be examined to see whether the light it throws on the nature of the *Satyricon* contradicts the description of the work offered above.

Macrobius, who flourished around 400, in discussing the type of fiction which may be used in philosophy, distinguishes two classes:

Fabulae, quarum nomen indicat falsi professionem, aut tantum conciliandae auribus voluptatis aut adhortationis quoque in bonam frugem gratia repertae sunt. Auditum mulcent, velut comoediae, quales Menander eiusve imitatores agendas dederunt, vel argumenta[3] fictis casibus amatorum referta, quibus vel

---

[1] See e.g. H. H. Bacon, *Virginia Quarterly Review* 34 (1958), 262 ff. No doubt Eliot's use of 48.8, Trimalchio's story of the Sibyl, as his epigraph to *The Waste Land* has contributed to this view.

[2] See Chapter VIII.

[3] Cf. Quint. *Inst.* 2.4.2, who opposes *argumenta*, plots which are false but resemble life, as in comedy, and *fabulae* such as those of tragedy and poetry, which are obviously unlike life.

multum se Arbiter exercuit vel Apuleium nonnumquam lusisse miramur.

(Comm. in Somnium Scipionis 1.2.8)

Tales, which are, as the name indicates, the retailing of falsehood, are found in two classes, those which give only pleasure to the hearer and those which also provide their audience with encouragement for good works. The hearer is merely *pleased* by such examples as the comedies which Menander and his imitators put on the stage, and the plots packed with the fictitious adventures of people in love, a genre to which the Arbiter applied himself a good deal and with which, to our surprise, Apuleius sometimes trifled.

It seems clear from this that the *Satyricon*, if this is the work to which Macrobius is referring, impressed the ancient public as a tale of predominantly sexual adventure–more so than Apuleius' *Metamorphoses*, for instance–a conclusion which the extant narrative does little to dispel and the reconstruction of the missing episodes much to support. Macrobius' linking however of Petronius with Apuleius gives some support to the view that a predominantly erotic plot at least does not entail that the *Satyricon* is modelled on, or a parody of, the standard Greek romance. The *Metamorphoses* is an expansion of a short adventure story, *Lucius* or *The Ass*, and has never been assimilated to the Greek romantic novel. Whatever the inspiration or kernel of Petronius' work, humorous *Periplous* or epic parody, Macrobius seems to take the narrative, however different in tone and intention, as comparable to the later tale of connected and frequently amorous adventures, and of no moral import whatsoever.

Marius Mercator, who died some time after 431, in his attack on his Nestorian opponent, says of Julian's language:

Erubesce, infelicissime, in tanta linguae scurrilis, vel potius mimicae, obscenitate. Vulgares tu dignus audire acclamationes: . . . namque Martialis et Petronii solus ingenia superasti.[1]

(Liber subnotationum in verba Juliani, IV. 1. Migne)

[1] The learned editor, Baluzi, going on no more of Petronius than we have, comments:

You should blush, you unfortunate wretch, for the vile obscenity of your language, the language of a low comedian or rather a mime. You deserve to get the acclamation of the groundlings: . . . for you alone have surpassed the 'talents' of Martial and Petronius.

This of course tells us nothing except that obscenity, and perhaps perversion, bulked largely in the work, a conclusion already obvious. A little later, Marius says:

Eleganter, scurra, loqueris more tuo et more quo theatrum Arbitri Valeriique detristi. Constat in illis prosatoribus generis humani fuisse libidinem insitam eorum naturae, quam quidem divinae scripturae, non ut tu vis, libidinem solent, sed carnis concupiscentiam nominare . . .

(ibid. V. 1)

Your style is elegant, you clown, after your fashion and the fashion in which you have run the performances of the Arbiter and Martial into the ground. It is a shared assumption of those human writers that lust has been implanted in human nature–an impulse which in fact the Holy Scriptures are accustomed to name, not lust, as you prefer, but carnal concupiscence.

Theatrum is being used metaphorically here by Marius[1] and is intended to connect Julian with the obscenity of the mime;[2] obviously this is the worst form of obscenity Marius can think of,

Ille epigrammata, ille satiram scripsit; uterque flammis digna opera: ut mirum sit ex hoc stercore colligi gemmas a Christianis, famam eruditionis ex eo conquiri, unde morum sanctitas violatur. [The one wrote epigram, the other satire: both producing works that deserve to be committed to the flames; so it is surprising that jewels are picked out of this dung by Christians and that from it a reputation for learning should be sought which violates the sanctity of morals.]

[1] Baluzi wrongly sees in this an allusion to Martial's epigrams on the amphitheatre, *Liber de spectaculis:* cf. *theatrum nostrum* Mart. I, *Epist. ad lectorem.*

[2] For the obscenity of the mime, cf. e.g. Val. Max. 2.10.8; Minuc. *Oct.* 37.12; Lactant. *Inst.* 1.206 and *n.b.* Mart. 8. *Epist. ad lectorem (mimicam verborum licentiam).*

and it is therefore for him an apt characterization of the tone of these three authors. Again, we glean no more information about Petronius than that his work was of a grossly sexual nature.

Lastly, the sixth-century Byzantine writer, Johannes Lydus, says in a discussion of ancient satire and comedy:

Τοῦρνος δὲ καὶ 'Ιουβενάλιος καὶ Πετρώνιος αὐτόθεν ταῖς λοιδορίαις ἐπεξελθόντες τὸν σατυρικὸν νόμον παρέτρωσαν.

(De Magistratibus Populi Romani 1.41)

But Turnus, Juvenal, and Petronius, by making abusive attacks in this sort of writing, injured the satire form.

It is quite possible that Johannes Lydus had not even read Petronius, but even his hearsay at least links Petronius clearly with satire, as is proper, although the assumption underlying his remarks is that Trimalchio and the other characters in the Satyricon are real people. This is almost certainly a mistake, although it is a tribute to Petronius' liveliness and realism.

None of these testimonia then add to our knowledge, although they help to confirm what has been already surmised from clues in the fragments still extant.

CHAPTER IV

Satire in the *Satyricon*

___

i. *Petronius as Satirist*

The examination of Petronius' intentions and of the literary form of the *Satyricon* should have made clear the idleness of the controversy as to how the work is to be described, whether it is to be called the first realistic novel, a picaresque novel, a satire (in the modern sense), or a parody with further parodies imbedded in it. All of these descriptions have a grain of truth in them, for they point to certain obvious elements of the work. None however can claim to be an all-inclusive description: the *Satyricon* is a new use of older forms. Even to call it, as some critics have done, a *Kreuzung der Gattungen*[1] is not particularly useful, for Petronius did not so much deliberately cross the genres available to him as expand the already existing possibilities of Menippean satire by choosing the loose *Reiseroman* plot, set in motion by the *gravis ira Priapi*, which would accept whatever tones and topics he desired for his particular purposes.

The Menippean tradition was well established: Petronius' predecessors in the form had established subjects and treatment and shaped the expectations of the audience. Satirical themes therefore loom large in the work, although Petronius, as will be seen, is not a satirist in the classic sense. His subjects are often the traditional subjects of satire, but his treatment of them is often more akin to that of a novelist. Our own conception of satire is a very refined one: in it the artist appears as a moralist in a very recognizable way. We speak of a moral centre from which the artist works, of positive and negative standards, with a critical preference for the

___

[1] H. Stubbe, *Die Verseinlagen im Petron, Philologus Supplbd.* 25 (1933), 1.

first. We are, or should be, wary in this genre of the intentional fallacy, when the moral content is not fully presented as art; and for our touchstones we invoke the great moral and literary satires of Pope, Swift, Johnson, and Byron. From these the concept is extended to cover satirical elements in the novel and other genres, just as Horace recognized in earlier Roman satire elements attributable to Attic Old Comedy. By these exalted and refined standards the credentials of certain ancient satirists become suspect. Even Juvenal's classic status as *the* ancient satirist may be questioned: besides Pope and Johnson, Juvenal, it is suggested, is more a great *verbal* artist writing in a traditional art-form, but not the elevated indignant moralist, as was formerly and with difficulty claimed. And by this standard Petronius too is not, in the strictest sense, a great satirist, although different claims may be made for him.

ii. *The Satiric Vehicle – Encolpius*

Satirical topics in Petronius are numerous: there is satire on religion, superstition, legacy hunting, bad taste, and love; there are satirical sketches of libidinous women, corrupt and drunken priestesses, a lecherous and importunate poet, and of course the great portrait of Trimalchio. But whatever the *ad hoc* positives invoked for the particular episode, there is nowhere in evidence that central moral concern which is one prerequisite of the true satirist. One might indeed remark rather on the lack of it; there is instead a sceptical and artistic detachment, an equal interest in literature and life, a strong, if often ironic, sense of humour – which would not of course be incompatible with Epicurean moral or literary principles. I have no wish to deny that Petronius has views on various subjects or standards that he might look to, but rather to say that the views are expressed and the standards invoked *sine ira et studio*. The author deliberately dissociates himself from the narrator, and Encolpius' volatile and subjective reactions are merely the correlative of the author's own objectivity, and are subtly but firmly placed.

The function of the narrator is complicated, and we shall have to take up the question at various later points, but here some specific comments on him may help to clarify the question of Petronius' satirical methods and merits. We do not know, unfortunately, how Encolpius was introduced or under what circumstances his narrative is being presented. His name, like most of the other names in the *Satyricon*, has point, Encolpos, a collateral form, being the name of a favourite catamite in Martial and Aelius Lampridius;[1] and a Peacockian translation might be Mr. Encrotch, an appropriate choice for the protagonist of a predominantly sexual story. Although much of the plot concerns Encolpius himself, who is satirized for his enthusiasms, pretensions, despairs, mishaps, and general behaviour as much as anyone else in the work, he has to be the moral repository, as it were, of whatever satiric values are invoked, for the events are seen through his eyes and what moral comment there is must come from him. As will be seen in the examination of the *Cena Trimalchionis*, the judgments of Encolpius on Trimalchio and the other satiric targets are subtly but surely undercut by his being a target for satire himself. This is clearly deliberate on Petronius' part, and it has the effect of dissociating the author from the satiric criticisms and any values that they may imply. Similarly, by satirizing some of the mannerisms and behaviour of Eumolpus, who is his vehicle for the longer poems, Petronius can avoid making any great claims for them. Nevertheless, just as Petronius is willing to direct our attention away from the hero to literary discussions by Agamemnon and Eumolpus, or to Trimalchio, so he is ready to speak through Encolpius *in propria persona*, when he explains his literary purposes at 132.15.[2] This is why it is more important to see Encolpius as the narrator rather than as a realistic hero. Even though he himself is often the subject of the plot and the humour, our interest is not focused on him as a person, but as the occasion for sexual adventures, parody, and burlesque. Petronius' interests, it must not be forgotten, are literary rather than psychological. That is why any use of the term *realism* in connection with the *Satyricon* must be severely limited. There is, for example, a lavish use of coincidence in the description of Encolpius' dealings with his

[1] Mart. 1.31; Lamprid. *Alex. Sev.* 17.1, 48.7.
[2] On the whole question, see P. Veyne, *REL* 42 (1964), 301 ff.

environment: it is by coincidence that the tunic with the gold is recovered; that Agamemnon's assistant is named Menelaus; that Encolpius chooses the name Polyaenus before he meets Circe; that characters from the lost part of the novel fall in with him again on board ship; that he accidentally bumps into Ascyltos and Giton, the friends who have left him or lost him; and so on.

Encolpius is not always brought in as a moral commentator or as a vehicle for parody. Sometimes only his presence is required, while his interests are elsewhere. In the Croton episode, for instance, the traditional theme of legacy hunting is presented dramatically. Petronius is not interested in it as a moral problem, but only in the additional twists which he can give it—the tricksters tricked, Philomela's fruitless prostitution of her children, and even cannibalism, another satiric topic which is found also in Juvenal's fifteenth satire. There is no moral comment and none is needed. The theme is simply milked for its humour, which varies from the farcical to the obscene; there is no bitter indictment of the practice. Consequently the only moral standard present is the reader's, and we are not invited to feel more than the stock disapproval which attaches to the subject from its previous use in satire. One doubts indeed if the Roman attitude to the practice was really much more lively and responsive than ours. Both Horace and Petronius deal with the topic in a very external way, and the general atmosphere of the Croton episode is hardly more real than Ulysses' dialogue with Teiresias in the underworld in the Horatian satire on the subject.[1]

As a consequence of all this, Encolpius, as far as we can judge from the extant fragments, is very far from being an artistic and rounded creation. In this respect he is inferior to Trimalchio. We see much of him, but because of Petronius' aims, he has to be an ambiguous figure, and indeed some of the scenes and subjects that cry out for a consistent and unwavering observer may acquire a

[1] Cf. *Sat.* 2.5 and W. J. N. Rudd, *The Satires of Horace* (Cambridge, 1966), pp. 224 ff. The subject admittedly occurs in Seneca, Pliny, Martial, Juvenal, and Tacitus, cf. D. Schmid, *Der Erbschleicher in der antiken Satire* (Tübingen, 1951), but I cannot help finding in the *loci classici* a certain externality of treatment, inviting a more or less stock reaction.

similar ambiguity, which can be resolved only with great patience and much hesitation. Only when Encolpius more or less removes himself from the action, as in the *Cena*, does the action offer us something beyond amusing erotic farce and fairly sophisticated literary burlesque. Farce can stand inconsistency; comedy requires something more. Encolpius' character, unlike Trimalchio's, is disorganized and fragmentary, not because he is at odds with himself or suffering from a spiritual instability that the author is interested in exploring, but because he is the structural and narrative link for the different themes that Petronius has chosen, as well as the victim of certain comic and satiric situations. The character of Encolpius, alternately romantic and cynical, brave and timorous, malevolent and cringing, jealous and rational, sophisticated and naïve, is composed of *those traits, even if contradictory, which are appropriate responses to the demands of the particular episode.* The comparison recently made of Encolpius and his changing entourage to the spiritual drifters in certain picaresque twentieth-century novels, such as those of Jack Kerouac, turns out on inspection to be illusory. Petronius' intentions are far less ideological.

iii. *Quartilla, Circe and Others*

One of the main targets of Petronius' humorous satire is the libidinous and aggressive female, who occurs in several different guises in the work. The subject is familiar in earlier and later literature, and the variety of examples presented by Petronius offers us some insight into his literary techniques. The main examples are, in order, Quartilla, Tryphaena and Circe; to this list may be added certain subsidiary characters: Psyche and Chrysis, who are both ladies' maids, but who are, in their different ways, as sexually forward as their mistresses; the two old women, Proselenus and Oenothea; and possibly the Albucia of Fgt. VI. No doubt, in an age of sexual permissiveness such as the Neronian, women like these were common enough–the historians present vivid portraits of such termagants as Agrippina, who had a slave lover, and such nymphomaniacs as Messalina.[1] But the literary

---

[1] See J. P. V. D. Balsdon, *Roman Women* (London, 1963), pp. 97 ff.

antecedents of Petronius' women are also plain. In particular, the trait attributed to Circe by her maid has an interesting ancestry:

'nam quod servum te et humilem fateris, accendis desiderium aestuantis. quaedam enim feminae sordibus calent, nec libidinem concitant, nisi aut servos viderint aut statores altius cinctos. arena aliquas accendit, aut perfusus pulvere mulio, aut histrio scaenae ostentatione traductus. ex hac nota domina est mea; usque ab orchestra quattuordecim transilit, et in extrema plebe quaerit quod diligat.'

itaque oratione blandissima plenus 'rogo', inquam, 'numquid illa, quae me amat, tu es?' multum risit ancilla post tam frigidum schema et 'nolo' inquit 'tibi tam valde placeas. ego adhuc servo numquam succubui, nec hoc dii sinant ut amplexus meos in crucem mittam. viderint matronae, quae flagellorum uestigia osculantur; ego etiam si ancilla sum, numquam tamen nisi in equestribus sedeo.' mirari equidem tam discordem libidinem coepi atque inter monstra numerare, quod ancilla haberet matronae superbiam et matrona ancillae humilitatem.

(126.5–11)

'You say you're just a poor slave, but this is only exciting her desire to boiling point. Some women get het up about absolute scum, and can't feel any passion unless they see slaves or bare-legged messengers. The arena sets some of them on heat, or a mule-driver covered with dust, or actors displayed on the stage. My mistress is one of this type. She jumps across the first fourteen seats from the orchestra and looks for something to love among the lowest of the low.'

I said in a voice full of sweetness: 'Tell me, the lady that is in love with me, is that you?'

The maid laughed heartily at such an affected way of putting it. 'Don't flatter yourself,' she said. 'I have never yet gone to bed with a slave, and heaven forbid I should ever see a lover of mine crucified. That's for ladies who kiss the whip-marks. Even though I'm a servant, I've never sat anywhere except in the lap of knights.'

I couldn't help some surprise at such contrasting sexual

desires. I thought it very strange that a maid should cultivate the superior outlook of a lady and the lady the low taste of a maid.

Such women are alluded to briefly elsewhere in the *Satyricon*: Glyco's wife (45.7) and Trimalchio's former mistress (75.11) share Circe's tastes. The most familiar classical example is perhaps in Herodas' *Mime* 5, in which a lady berates her slave lover for his suspected infidelity, but other references are not hard to find in earlier and later literature.[1] Indeed the character-type is not uncommon in modern literature, turning up recently as Madame Philibert in Thomas Mann's *Bekenntnisse des Hochstaplers Felix Krull*. Having once delineated her character, and allowed Encolpius to comment on the lady's low taste by comparison with her maid's superior attitude, Petronius now develops her as a character and the satiric impulse is subordinated to the depiction of an individual. Circe is not a sympathetic figure, but then what character in the *Satyricon* is? But the motives at work seem rather artistic than satirical. The portrait is now elaborated in various ways. She is contrasted with her maid, who despises slaves and prefers gentlemen (126.10). When Chrysis discovers that Polyaenus is not a slave, then she too falls in love with him, despite his impotence (139.4); Circe however is only interested in him as a sexual object, as her complete lack of sympathy, savage irony, and furious wrath prove when she is faced with his repeated fiascos (128.1–4, 129.4–9, 132.2–4). By contrast with the bold demeanour of the maid's approach to Encolpius (126), Circe is presented initially as demure and almost virginal in her coy advances:

> delectata illa risit tam blandum, ut videretur mihi plenum os extra nubem luna proferre. mox digitis gubernantibus vocem: 'si non fastidis' inquit 'feminam ornatam et hoc primum anno virum expertam, concilio tibi, o iuvenis, sororem. habes tu quidem et fratrem, neque enim me piguit inquirere, sed quid prohibet et sororem adoptare? eodem gradu venio. tu tantum

[1] Other references are: Hdt. 1.173; Ar. *Th.* 491, Fgt. 695; Muson. *ap.* Stob. 6.61; Ael. *NA* 7.15, 8.20; Luc. *D. Meretr.* (*passim*); Philostr. *VS* 2.25; D. Chr. 2.446; Mart. 12.58; Juv. 6.279; Tert. *Spect.* 22.2.

dignare et meum osculum, cum libuerit, agnoscere.' 'immo,'
inquam ego 'per formam tuam te rogo, ne fastidias hominem
peregrinum inter cultores admittere. invenies religiosum, si te
adorari permiseris. ac ne me iudices ad hoc templum Amoris
gratis accedere, dono tibi fratrem meum.' 'quid? tu,' inquit illa,
'donas mihi eum, sine quo non potes vivere, ex cuius osculo
pendes, quem sic tu amas, quemadmodum ego te volo?' haec
ipsa cum diceret, tanta gratia conciliabat vocem loquentis, tam
dulcis sonus pertemptatum mulcebat aëra, ut putares inter auras
canere Sirenum concordiam.

(127.1–5)

She was delighted and smiled so sweetly I thought the full moon
had shown her face out of a cloud. Modulating her voice to her
gesture, she said: 'If you don't find a lady distasteful, one who
had a man for the first time only this year, let me recommend
myself as your sister, young man. Of course, you have a brother
too–I wasn't ashamed of making inquiries, you see–but what's
to stop you adopting a sister as well? I come on the same footing. You have only to agree to put up with my kisses as well,
whenever you like.'

'On the contrary,' I replied, 'I must beg you, you beautiful
creature, not to disdain to take on a poor stranger as one of your
adorers. You will find him devoted if you permit him to worship
you. And don't imagine I am entering this temple of love without making an offering. I shall sacrifice my brother for you.'

'What?' she said. 'Are you making me a sacrifice of the boy
you cannot live without, the lips you cling to, the one you love
the way I want to love you?'

As she said this, there was such charm in her voice, such a
sweet sound caressed the enraptured air that it was as though
the song of the Sirens sang through the breezes.

But her delicately feminine behaviour soon changes, as does
Quartilla's after her first appearance (17.2 ff.). None of the women
in the *Satyricon* seems patient when frustrated or crossed.

Quartilla's character is also based on a satiric type, this time the
hypocritical woman who masks sexuality beneath the guise of

religion, a theme which is repeated in the other priestess of Priapus, Oenothea, who is even more cynically corrupt in her religion, as Encolpius finds when he tries to bribe her into overlooking his slaying of the sacred goose (137.6). Quartilla too moves from feminine tears (17.2 ff.) to hypocritical altruism and religiosity (17.6,8), before she throws off the mask to reveal her amorous intentions, and hint at force unless they are gratified (18.5). Quartilla's characterization however now leaves the plane of satire and becomes a character study of a strong, lecherous woman, with a keen sense of humour and a good deal of wit, although she lacks Circe's fine irony. Her speech is given an individual flavour by her favourite catch-phrases, 'Ita' and 'Itane est?', which occur five times in the very fragmentary narrative (20.7, 21.7, 24.4, 25.1, 25.3). Of course she is just as forward as Circe in her sexual advances.

Interestingly enough, Petronius gives us no physical description of Quartilla, presumably because Encolpius' subjective reaction to her is one of fright, and therefore irrelevant to the sexual development of the scene. This point of course cannot be pressed in view of the fragmentary nature of the work. She may have been described during the initial encounter, which is lost.

Tryphaena fits the general type, but her development as an individual is more difficult to discern, as her first appearance in the work is also lost. Nor is there much to say about the witch Proselenus or Oenothea, who combines magic with her priestly duties. They are more conventional sketches and appear to be based on the traditional picture of the bawd that we find in New Comedy, mime, and elegy. Herodas, Plautus, Propertius, and Ovid all offer examples of disreputable old procuresses, who are usually characterized by drunkenness, an acquaintance with the magic arts, and an hypocritical religiosity.[1] Normally they are procuring

---

[1] See Herod, *Mime* 1; Plaut. *Curc.* 96 ff. (Leaena); Prop. 4.5 (Acanthus); Ov. *Am.* 1.8 (Dipsas); Luc. *D. Meretr.* 3; App. *Met.* 9.15. Cf. also Webster, *The Malcontent* V.1. Oenothea's being a priestess is no objection to the thesis; such creatures are frequently pious in all appearances as in Herod. *Mime* 1; cf. Burton's *One Thousand and One Nights*, 1.60, 12.39, 3.133. Clement of Alexandria also links drunkenness and the magic arts in his *Paedagogus* (269–70).

a girl for a man; in the *Satyricon* they are trying to revive Encolpius' virility to gratify Circe. These sketches of course are not drawn from the horrendous reality of such imperial figures as Messalina, Agrippina, Junia Silana, or even Petronius' friend, Silia; they are to be attributed rather to Petronius' choice of low life and low characters for the milieu and the people in the *Satyricon*, and the consequent availability of literary prototypes for him to develop.

A study of these two basic types and their elaboration by Petronius will provide some insight into his technique, but it might be appropriate at this point to stress once again the complete absence of any favourable reference to women in the *Satyricon*. Even in the *Cena*, where the sexual aspect is less in evidence, a similar, rather cynical, picture of women emerges: not only are there references to wives having affairs with slaves, but the one favourable observation on a woman, offered by Niceros, is immediately cancelled. Niceros explains that he fell in love with Melissa, not in a purely physical way, but because of her good nature (61.6), but his conventional, and perhaps overemphatic, protestation loses its force when we appreciate that she was the faithless mate of a fellow slave. Her brusque treatment of Niceros described at 62.11 does not alleviate our misgivings. The portraits of Fortunata and Scintilla do even less to dispel this general impression. Indeed, it might be said that the attitude to women presented in the *Satyricon*, while not as captious as that of Juvenal's sixth satire, is best represented by Eumolpus' comment on the frailty of woman and the story he tells to illustrate it, the tale of the Widow of Ephesus (110.6 ff.). But it must also be observed that this gloomy picture is not simply the product of the satiric impulse, but may also be explained by Petronius' 'realism' as defined earlier. Certainly we cannot deduce from it anything about Petronius' own attitude to women, or about contemporary moral attitudes in this matter. Indeed, if we accept the identification of the courtier with the writer, we may surmise from his friendship with Silia that his satirical postures were not prompted by any high moral indignation.

The development of satirical themes beyond the limited aims

of satire, which is hinted at in Petronius' treatment of these ladies, is of course far more observable in the best of his creations, Trimalchio, where the elaboration of character for its own sake, rather than an effort to pin down undesirable qualities for purely satiric comment, is most obvious.

iv. *Trimalchio: the Literary Sources*

The *Cena Trimalchionis* is generally acknowledged to be not only the best of the satiric episodes that have survived of the *Satyricon*, but also the peak of Petronius' achievement. The elaboration of art lavished upon what was, from the point of view of the plot, almost an isolated digression, a mere interlude in the trio's arduous experiences, perhaps indicates that Petronius also was aware of this. The literary sources of the work are correspondingly rich, their use complex, and the introduction of contemporary material particularly striking, although the important thing is the extent to which Petronius has gone beyond the limits of literary burlesque, parody, and conventional satire into true comic creation by an imaginative fusion of his various materials. The episode is an example of so-called symposium literature, a popular and traditional literary genre found with many variations, serving a number of literary and non-literary purposes, and occurring both in isolation and in larger frameworks such as epic.[1] Although its roots are in Homer, so far as we can judge, the most famous and influential example of it is the *Symposium* of Plato, which has its effect upon the structure of the *Cena*. The successive conversational monologues of Trimalchio's guests lack the formality and singlemindedness of the speakers in the *Symposium*, but Alcibiades' description of Socrates (*Smp.* 215A ff.) is paralleled by Trimalchio's sketch of his own life and character (75.5 ff.), just as the dramatic entry earlier of the inebriated Habinnas (65.3–8) is clearly modelled on Alcibiades' drunken entrance in the *Symposium* (212C ff.).[2] It

[1] See J. Martin, *Symposion, die Geschichte einer literarischen Form* (Paderborn, 1931) and *RE s.v. Symposiumliteratur*.

[2] Petronius' familiarity with the work is further evinced at 128.7, where Encolpius' impotence with Giton is compared to Socrates' self-restraint with Alcibiades. See also 'A.L.', *PhW* 20 (1900), 926.

may also be suggested that the wildly inaccurate information purveyed by Trimalchio to his guests may be a parody of the encyclopaedic compilations cast in the form of a Dinner or Banquet. Earlier examples from the Hellenistic age are lost, but from Athenaeus' *Deipnosophistae* and Macrobius' *Saturnalia* we have a good idea of what they may have been like.

Petronius' direct and obvious model, however, within this familiar genre was Horace's brief *Cena Nasidieni* (*Sat.* 2.8), a satire on a contemporary middle class upstart, Nasidienus, who has been entertaining Maecenas, Fundanius, and other friends of Horace. Petronius' use and expansion of this theme illustrates his structural methods and deserves a little attention here.[1]

Horace's satire is in the form of a dialogue between himself and Fundanius, and most of it is taken up by the latter's description of, and comment on, the dinner, interrupted by brief questions and remarks from the poet.[2] Fundanius lists the guests, describes the lavish and expensive foods and wines served. Both of these constitute large elements of the *Cena Trimalchionis*.[3] Nomentanus, a crony of Nasidienus, points out the things the other guests might miss (25-6), which Fundanius finds boring (32-3). In Petronius Trimalchio does most of this himself (34.7, 50.2, 67.8 etc). When one of the guests, Vibidius, demands larger cups, the host is perturbed, either because of the possible social consequences, or because his wines will not be properly appreciated (35-8). With the next course, however, Nasidienus becomes the boastful connoisseur, a role which Trimalchio plays throughout the dinner; he is interrupted dramatically by the collapse of the awning in a great cloud of dust (54 ff.). This is an obvious model for the fall of the young acrobat on Trimalchio (54).[4] Nasidienus is very dis-

---

[1] See J. Révay, *CP* 17 (1922); 202 ff.; L. R. Shero, *CP* 18 (1923), 126 ff. The obvious influences may not be exhaustive, cf. W. Süss, *H* 62 (1927), 349 ff., on the possibility of Varro's *Convivium Granii* (Book XX) being a model.

[2] For the most recent discussion of the Horatian satire, see Rudd, *op. cit.*, pp. 215 ff.

[3] On the importance of food to the Greeks and Romans, and its popularity even in literature, see T. H. Corcoran, *CJ* 58 (1963), 204 ff.

[4] Oddly enough, the change from awning to acrobat may have been suggested to Petronius by a conscious or unconscious verbal memory. Balatro, comforting

tressed by this accident and Nomentanus tries to comfort him with platitudes on the cruelty of fortune. At least one of the guests is highly amused by this fuss over such a trifle, and Balatro ironically seconds Nomentanus' efforts by exaggerating Nasidienus' efforts to please, which may be so easily ruined by a mishap. Petronius makes more farcical use of Trimalchio's accident and develops it in his own way, but the reflections on Fortune in Horace's satire are paralleled by a similar conversation among Trimalchio's guests (55.1) and by an insipid epigram on the power of Fortune produced by Trimalchio (55.3).

Nasidienus has been childishly relieved by Balatro's mocking comfort and leaves the room, while the guests gossip in whispers behind his back and Vibidius demands more wine (75 ff.). This is very like Trimalchio's exit at 41.9; again, the guests gossip, although not about their host, and Dama asks for more (or stronger) drink (41.10). Nasidienus returns, determined to repair his misfortune by his skill as a host. But the elaborateness of the rest of the delicacies is spoilt for the guests by Nasidienus' tedious comments on their quality and preparation (85 ff.). Trimalchio's return (47.1) is succeeded by an even more tasteless set of comments on his digestive system.

Horace has not lavished many of his artistic resources on this unambitious, although successful, piece, which may have gained some extrinsic interest because it was supposedly based on a real person.[1] This of course would not make it an unworthy model for imitation and expansion by an admirer of Horace. In fact, the outline above does not exhaust the resemblances between the two *Cenae*: one might point also to the remarks on the service

his host, enumerates some of the mishaps that may befall a dinner party: *adde hos praeterea casus, aulaea ruant si / ut modo; si patinam pede lapsus frangat agaso* (71–2), with which cf. *puer . . . delapsus est* (54.1). The suggestion that there is an allusion in the Petronius passage to a similar accident to Nero (Suet. *Ner.* 12) is not incompatible with this.

[1] Lambinus tells us that it was Salvidienus Rufus, advanced to equestrian rank by Octavian *ex infima fortuna* (Suet. *Aug.* 66), and later executed for conspiracy against his interests. The scholiast comments: '*Nasidienus eques Romanus in aliis elegans, in enumeratione autem lauticiarum putidus.*' We should not, however, follow G. Bagnani in taking Trimalchio as a real person also: see *Phoenix* 8 (1954), 77 ff.

(cf. 52.4 with 70–72); the guests demanding larger cups (cf. 41.10 with 33.5); and the final motif of flight from the scene (cf. 78.8 with 93, where both authors have the word *fugimus*).

The main target in each satire is the tasteless and pretentious host with his habit of lecturing the guests on the fare he offers them, much as some modern connoisseurs of wine do. In Horace's case however a brief, though adequate, gesture is made towards the presentation of this trait (43–53) with little of the continuous exemplification that is to be found in Petronius:

> 'suaves res, si non causas narraret earum et
> naturas dominus . . .'
>
> (92–3)

> 'Delightful stuff, if only the host didn't tell us where
> they came from and what they were . . .'

Horace of course rams the point home; Petronius lets the criticism emerge dramatically, for Encolpius is not a trustworthy guide on all matters aesthetic. Another target which the two satirists share is the excessive desire of the hosts to impress their guests, although they have different ways of doing this, Nasidienus being the worried and fussy sort of boaster, Trimalchio an apparently more self-confident and ignorant braggart. They are both *lautus*, but neither is *urbanus*, and against both the standard invoked is good taste.

Horace's piece however is clearly satire, a fact marked by the frequency of the moral comment (cf. 18, 79–80, 94–5 etc), either from the poet himself or from the guests. Petronius however adds to the satiric sketch of Trimalchio a great variety of further traits from life and literature, until he becomes a great comic creation, and the initial satiric impulse is lost in creative empathy and an artistic interest in the character-drawing. Such almost autonomous blossomings of a character beyond the original intention are not uncommon in literature–one thinks of Don Quixote, who was originally a mere satiric butt, Joseph Andrews, and Pickwick, whose genesis was merely in the text for Seymour's sporting sketches.

Although the thesis has been disputed, it would seem that a further important source for the portrait of Trimalchio himself is one of Seneca's latest philosophical works, the *Epistulae Morales ad Lucilium*, which were probably written and published by A.D. 63–4, and some books possibly a little earlier. The whole question of Petronius' intentions in drawing on these letters may be deferred for the moment: here we are primarily interested in the use made of certain anecdotes and descriptions to add to the characterization of the central figure of the *Cena*.[1]

The use of two particular passages has often been commented on and they deserve quotation here as they illustrate Petronius' rehandling of the original. The first is the well-known description of Calvisius Sabinus:

Calvisius Sabinus memoria nostra fuit dives; et patrimonium habebat libertini et ingenium; numquam vidi hominem beatum indecentius. Huic memoria tam mala erat, ut illi nomen modo Ulixis excideret, modo Achillis, modo Priami, quos tam bene quam paedagogos nostros novimus. Nemo vetulus nomenclator, qui nomina non reddit sed imponit, tam perperam tribus quam ille Troianos et Achivos persalutabat. Nihilominus eruditus volebat videri. Hanc itaque compendiariam excogitavit: magna summa emit servos, unum qui Homerum teneret, alterum qui Hesiodum; novem praeterea lyricis singulos adsignavit. Magno emisse illum non est quod mireris: non invenerat, faciendos locavit. Postquam haec familia illi comparata est, coepit convivas suos inquietare. Habebat ad pedes hos, a quibus subinde cum peteret versus quos referret, saepe in medio verbo excidebat. Suasit illi Satellius Quadratus, stultorum divitum adrosor et, quod sequitur, adrisor, et, quod duobus his adiunctum est, derisor, ut grammaticos haberet analectas. Cum dixisset Sabinus centenis millibus sibi constare singulos servos,

[1] For further discussion, see below, pp. 193 ff. On the date of the composition of the *Epistulae Morales*, see e.g. H. Hilgenfeld, *Fleckeisen Supp.* 17 (1890), 601 ff.; O. Binder, *Die Abfassungszeit von Senecas Briefen* (Tübingen, 1905), and the examination of this by Schultess in *PhW* 26 (1906), 324 ff.; K. Münscher, *Senecas Werke, Untersuchungen zur Abfassungszeit und Echtheit, Philologus Supplbd.* 16 (1922), 76 ff.

'minoris' inquit, 'totidem scrinia emisses'. Ille tamen in ea opinione erat ut putaret se scire quod quisquam in domo sua sciret. Idem Satellius illum hortari coepit ut luctaretur, hominem aegrum, pallidum, gracilem. Cum Sabinus respondisset, 'et quomodo possum? Vix vivo,' 'Noli, obsecro te' inquit 'istuc dicere: non vides quam multos servos valentissimos habeas?' Bona mens nec commodatur nec emitur; et puto, si venalis esset, non haberet emptorem: at mala cotidie emitur.

(*Ep.* 27.5–8)

We still remember Calvisius Sabinus the millionaire. He had the fortune of a freedman–and the brains: I never saw such tasteless wealth. His memory was so bad that he'd forget Ulysses' name one minute, Achilles' the next, and Priam's the next, men we know as well as our tutors. No aged receptionist, inventing names instead of announcing them, confused his master's clients as badly as he confused the Trojan and Greek heroes. None the less he wanted to appear cultured. So he thought up the following easy method: he paid high prices for slaves, one who knew Homer by heart, another Hesiod, and he assigned a special slave to each of the nine lyric poets. The high prices are not surprising; if he didn't find them, he had them trained to order. After building up this domestic service, he began to torment his guests. He would have these fellows at the foot of his couch, and ask them from time to time for verses for him to quote, but then frequently break down in the middle of a word. Satellius Quadratus, who practically lived with silly millionaires and consequently laughed with them, and, what goes along with both of these, laughed at them, advised him to get grammarians to pick up the pieces. When Sabinus told him that each slave cost him a hundred thousand sesterces, he said, 'You could have bought as many bookcases for less.' Sabinus however held to his idea that what anyone in his household knew, he knew also. So this same Satellius began urging him to take up wrestling–although Sabinus was a sickly, pale, thin sort of man. When Sabinus replied, 'And how can I? I'm barely breathing,' he said, 'Now don't say that, please. Can't you see how many perfectly healthy slaves you have?' A fine mind can't be borrowed or bought. And I think that if it could be sold, it would have no takers. There are daily sales of the other.

The second is the anecdote about the strange behaviour of Pacuvius:

> Pacuvius, qui Syriam usu suam fecit, cum vino et illis funebribus epulis sibi parentaverat, sic in cubiculum ferebatur a cena, ut inter plausus exoletorum hoc ad symphoniam caneretur: 'βεβίωται, βεβίωται.' Nullo non se die extulit.
>
> (*Ep.* 12.8)

Pacuvius, who practically owned Syria he was there so long, used to hold a regular burial service over himself with wine and a funeral feast, and then he would be carried from the dining-room to his bedroom, while his boy playmates would clap, and the Greek for 'It's all over, it's all over!' would be sung with a musical accompaniment. He had himself carried to his last rest every day.[1]

Petronius' borrowings from these passages are highly selective. Trimalchio, like Calvisius, is a very rich freedman, of whom it could just as easily be said, *et patrimonium habebat libertini et ingenium*, and there is no reason to think that Petronius did not share Seneca's prejudice against this very unpopular class of citizens, whose rapid advance to political and financial power–with its

---

[1] With this last should be compared the following passage from the *De brevitate vitae* (20.3):

S. Turannius fuit exactae diligentiae senex, qui post annum nonagesimum, cum vacationem procurationis ab C. Caesare ultro accepisset, componi se in lecto et velut exanimem a circumstante familia plangi iussit. Lugebat domus otium domini senis nec finivit ante tristitiam quam labor illi suus restitutus est.

Sextus Turannius was an old man of long-tested conscientiousness. When, after his ninetieth year, he had been retired from the duties of his office by Gaius Caesar, he had himself laid out on his bed and mourned by the assembled household as though he were dead. The house wept over its old master's retirement and did not shed its sorrow until his work was restored to him.

This work has been convincingly dated to A.D. 55 by M. T. Griffin, *JRS* 52 (1962), 104 ff.

consequent arrogance–is a notable feature of the early principate.[1]
Calvisius' inability to remember mythology or poetry and his
constant confusion of ancient heroes is paralleled by similar characteristics in Trimalchio (48.7–9, 50.4–6, 52.1–2, 59.3–5), although
Petronius' treatment is both freer and more specific. Both of them
have specially trained troupes of artistic slaves (cf. *comoedos* 53.13,
Homeristae, 59.3), although Trimalchio's point up his bad taste
more effectively. The unfounded erudition which both wish to
display is central to their characters. In the case of Pacuvius, the
bizarre custom of a mock-funeral, which seems almost too strange
not to be true, was prompted by a bad conscience, as Seneca goes
on to tell us, whereas Petronius uses the idea rather as a humorous
and dramatic close to the tasteless dinner, a close that would be in
keeping with Trimalchio's obsession with death (34.7–10, 55.3,
71.5 ff., 77.2), and his insistence on a philosophy of *carpe diem*
(55.3). It is of course no coincidence that Seneca's *Letters* are also
preoccupied with death and the proper way to face it.

The possibility cannot be entirely excluded that both Petronius
and Seneca are drawing on common gossip or a common source
for such anecdotes. A decision would depend on whether the
many coincidences can be plausibly shown to be just that. But it
may be agreed that the use of the stories of Calvisius and Pacuvius
seems neutral enough. They are used for literary rather than parodic purposes, whereas the next example seems to have a double
function.

It has often been observed that Seneca's views on the proper
treatment and regard for slaves in *Ep.* 47 are echoed by Trimalchio in the *Cena* (71.1), where he speaks in the tones of a Stoic
humanitarian:

> diffusus hac contentione Trimalchio 'amici' inquit 'et servi
> homines sunt et aeque unum lactem biberunt, etiam si illos
> malus fatus oppresserit. tamen me salvo cito aquam liberam
> gustabunt.'

Trimalchio became expansive after this argument. 'My dear

[1] The evidence is collected in Duff, *Freedmen in the Early Roman Empire* (Cambridge, 1958), pp. 73 ff., 130 ff.

people,' he said, 'slaves are human beings too. They drink the same milk as anybody else, even though luck's been agin them. Still, if nothing happens to me, they'll have their taste of freedom soon.'

This brief remark is merely to draw our attention to Trimalchio's previous and subsequent behaviour towards his slaves, behaviour that would no doubt strike the average upper class Roman as tasteless, and perhaps senseless. (It might be remembered that Tacitus' account of Petronius in his last hours, meting out rewards and punishments to his household, hardly points to any belief in the brotherhood of man, but rather to an unsentimental –and Epicurean–acceptance and preservation of the social hierarchy.) It looks as though Trimalchio's behaviour in this respect all through the *Cena* is meant to reflect cynically on all of Seneca's recommendations to Lucilius in the letter, as the following passages should make clear:

Libenter ex iis qui a te veniunt cognovi familiariter te cum servis tuis vivere: hoc prudentiam tuam, hoc eruditionem tuam decet. 'Servi sunt.' Immo homines. 'Servi sunt.' Immo contubernales. 'Servi sunt.' Immo humiles amici. 'Servi sunt.' Immo conservi, si cogitaveris tantumdem in utrosque licere fortunae. Itaque rideo istos qui turpe existimant cum servo suo cenare: quare, nisi quia superbissima consuetudo cenanti domino stantium servorum turbam circumdedit? . . . Cum ad cenandum discubuimus, alius sputa deterget . . . alius pretiosas aves scindit; per pectus et clunes certis ductibus circumferens eruditam manum frustra excutit, infelix, qui huic uni rei vivit, ut altilia decenter secet . . . Vis tu cogitare istum quem servum tuum vocas ex isdem seminibus ortum eodem frui caelo, aeque spirare, aeque vivere, aeque mori! . . . sic cum inferiore vivas quemadmodum tecum superiorem velis vivere . . . Vive cum servo clementer, comiter quoque, et in sermonem illum admitte et in consilium et in convictum. Hoc loco adclamabit mihi tota manus delicatorum 'nihil hac re humilius, nihil turpius'. Hos ego eosdem deprehendam alienorum servorum osculantes

manum... 'Quid ergo? omnes servos admovebo mensae meae?'
Non magis quam omnes liberos ... Quare non est quod fastidiosi isti te deterreant quominus servis tuis hilarem te praestes et
non superbe superiorem: colant potius te quam timeant. Dicet
aliquis nunc me vocare ad pilleum servos et dominos de fastigio
suo deicere.

(*Ep.* 47 *passim*)

I was happy to learn from those who come from you that you
live on familiar terms with your slaves. This suits your good
sense and your education. 'They're *slaves.*' Say rather, men.
'They're *slaves.*' Say rather, comrades-in-arms. 'They're *slaves.*'
Say rather, lower class friends. 'They're *slaves.* 'Say rather,
fellow slaves, if you consider that Fortune has as much power
over both of you. So I'm highly amused by those people who
think it disgraceful to have dinner with their slaves. What
reason is there except that a very arrogant custom surrounds a
master at dinner with a crowd of slaves standing there? . . .
When we take our places to dine, one wipes round our
mouths . . . another carves expensive game, and, running his
skilled hand round the breast and backside with sure strokes,
he cuts off the slices – poor man, whose only reason for existence
is that he can carve fowl decently . . . Are you ready to consider
that the man you call your slave sprang from the same seed,
lives under the same sky, breathes like you, is alive like you,
and dies like you! . . . you should live with your inferiors as
you would wish your superiors to live with you . . . Live with a
slave in mercy, in comradeship too, and admit him to your
conversation, to your counsels, and to your daily life. At this
point the whole gang of gracious livers will howl: 'There is
nothing more degrading or more disgraceful than such a thing.'
Yet I'll catch these very men kissing the hands of other people's
slaves . . . 'Well then, am I to invite all my slaves to my table?'
No more than you invite all free men . . . So there is no reason
why that snobbish set should deter you from being affable to
your slaves without any arrogant superiority: let them court
you rather than fear you. Someone will now say that I am

inviting slaves to put on the cap of freedom and that I am pulling their masters down from their pedestal.

It seems plausible that Petronius in his description of Trimalchio's way of life is making obvious allusions to this letter, and finally caps them with Trimalchio's enunciation of the letter's main thesis. Trimalchio has an enormous number of slaves waiting at table (74.7); they perform menial tasks for him (27.5-6); he has skilful carvers (36.7, 59.7); and although his treatment of them is alternately harsh and permissive, it is clear that his behaviour would not appeal to those members of Roman society that Seneca describes as *delicati* and *fastidiosi*. The chaos and the exhibition of bad taste that follow the seating of the slaves at the dinner table (70.10 ff.) naturally reflect on the unsoundness of Seneca's advice, and what to Petronius would be the absurdity of his Stoic views on slavery. And such views, whether Seneca's alone or all the Stoics', seem more the object of Petronius' hits than the already 'placed' character of Trimalchio.

If this passage seems too much of a Stoic commonplace and the similarities between Trimalchio's behaviour and Seneca's prescriptions are taken as purely coincidental, we may turn to the final major contribution from the *Epistulae Morales* that may be suggested for the characterization of Trimalchio. The portrait of Maecenas that Seneca offers us in *Ep.* 114, although intended to illustrate that character and style are intimately connected, has so much in common with Trimalchio that it is difficult to continue to believe in the theory of pure coincidence, particularly when we remember that Trimalchio intends to have carved on his tomb the usurped *agnomen* 'Maecenatianus' (71.12), which, failing other explanations, may be taken as a direct hint from Petronius. The relevant passages are worth laying out in full:

Non statim . . . hoc tibi occurret . . . hunc esse qui ⟨in⟩ tribunali, in rostris, in omni publico coetu sic apparuerit ut pallio velaretur caput exclusis utrimque auribus, non aliter quam in mimo fugitivi divitis solent; hunc esse cui . . . comitatus hic fuerit in publico, spadones duo, magis tamen viri quam ipse . . . Ubi

luxuriam late felicitas fudit, cultus primum corporum esse dili-
gentior incipit; deinde suppellectili laboratur; deinde in ipsas
domos inpenditur cura ut in laxitatem ruris excurrant, ut pari-
etes advectis trans maria marmoribus fulgeant, ut tecta varientur
auro, ut lacunaribus pavimentorum respondeat nitor; deinde ad
cenas lautitia transfertur et illic commendatio ex novitate et soliti
ordinis commutatione captatur, ut ea quae includere solent
cenam primam ponantur, ut quae advenientibus dabantur exeun-
tibus dentur . . . Aspice culinas nostras et concursantis inter tot
ignes cocos: unum videri putas ventrem cui tanto tumultu comparatur cibus? Aspice veteraria nostra et plena multorum saecu-
lorum vindemiis horrea: unum putas videri ventrem cui tot
consulum regionumque vina cluduntur? Aspice quot locis terra
vertatur, quot millia colonorum arent, fodiant: unum videri
putas ventrem cui et in Sicilia et in Africa seritur? . . . Nihil
tamen aeque tibi profuerit ad temperantiam omnium rerum
quam frequens cogitatio brevis aevi et huius incerti: quidquid
facies, respice ad mortem.

(*Ep.* 114.6,9,26 f.)

It will not immediately . . . occur to you that . . . this is the
man who on the bench, on the platform, at every public function, appeared in public with his head covered in a wrap and
with his ears sticking out on each side, exactly like the rich man's
runaway slaves in the farce; that this is the man whose entourage
in public consisted of two eunuchs, who were however more
masculine than their master . . . When prosperity releases the
floodgates of luxury, first of all bodily adornment begins to get
more attention; then work goes into furnishings; then care is
lavished on the houses themselves so that they take on the
physical ease of a country estate; the walls gleam with imported
marble; the roofs are tricked out with gold; and the brightness
of the floors answers the coffered ceilings; then elegance is
cultivated in dining and there praise is courted by means of
novelty and the departure from normal practice, so that what
usually concludes a dinner is served first, and what used to
be given to guests on their arrival is given them on their

departure . . . Look at our kitchens and the cooks running round among all those burners. Do you think it seems like one stomach for which food is prepared with all that excitement? Look at our old barns full of the vintages of many decades. Do you think it seems like one stomach for which the wines of so many different years and different regions are laid down? Look at the cultivation of so many places, at the thousands of sharecroppers ploughing and digging them. Do you think it seems like one stomach for which seed is sown in both Sicily and Africa? . . . Nothing however will help you towards temperance in all things as much as frequent consideration of the brevity–and uncertainty–of our mortal span. Whatever you do, have an eye for death.

Whereas Trimalchio's ignorance and pretensions are based on Calvisius, his physical circumstances are reminiscent of the description of Maecenas himself, and Seneca's general criticisms of modern luxury. He has two eunuchs waiting on him (27.3); his clothes are pretentiously different from the usual, a red tunic (27.1) and elaborate scarlet wrap (*pallio coccineo*, 32.2); the extravagance of his house and the novelty of his dining arrangements need no illustration–he even departs from the normal seating practice (*novo more*, 31.8); he has a plethora of cooks (47.12); he is planning to add Sicily to his demesne so that he can sail to Africa through his own territory (48.3); he is proud of his vintage wines (34.7); he has lavish holdings in grain (53.2) and other things (37.8 ff.); and, finally, he often thinks about life's uncertainty and death (34.7 ff., 39.14, 55.2–4, 71.4 ff., 77.2, 77.7 ff.). Of course, his anxiety about the uncertainty of life and the prospect of death has none of the effect on his behaviour that Seneca confidently predicts in Lucilius' case.

It is hard to believe that the four letters of Seneca (12, 27, 47, 114) brought forward here are not put under direct contribution for the depiction of Trimalchio, particularly when we bear in mind the many other echoes from other letters. Petronius is discriminating and selective in the use he makes of them–I would argue that his *main* interest is in the creation of Trimalchio–but it is reasonable to suppose that he intended the source of some of Trimalchio's traits and behaviour to be recognized, and that one secondary purpose of the *Cena* was satirical parody at Seneca's expense, a motive which seems to be at work elsewhere in the *Satyricon* (see below, pp. 193 ff.).

Other sources are drawn upon for rounding out Trimalchio's character as so far established by Petronius. It has been suggested, not too convincingly, that he made use of certain Epicurean and Peripatetic works on morality and character in general, in particular, Philodemus' *Peri kakiōn*, of which fragments of Book X survive, and Theophrastus' *Characters*. There are indeed similarities between some of Trimalchio's traits and the vices and lapses described by these authors: the wealthy contempt for philosophy, the alternating harshness and familiarity with slaves, the discourteous treatment of guests, pretensions to knowledge, complimenting one's own wife, the taste for commonplaces, the interest in what people have eaten, playing with the house dog, singing in the bath, a fondness for unseemly dances, superstitiousness, and, not least, the vulgar habit of talking about one's digestive functions at table. Less specific resemblances have been suggested between the portraits of Trimalchio and some of his guests and such general descriptions in Theophrastus as those of the babbler, the chatterbox, the malicious gossip, the flatterer, the boor, the shameless man, and the imperious man.[1] The difficulty is that few, if any, of these parallels are really exact, and the additional postulate that Petronius may have known of Theophrastus' work, say, through excerpts or other authors of diatribe literature does not carry a great deal of conviction. Moreover, such moral topics, as well as being commonplaces of the diatribe, were also no doubt the precise faults to which the less good-mannered members of ancient society continued to be prone–otherwise the *Cena Trimalchionis* would be an unreal exercise in archaic reconstruction from moral handbooks. And this would be contrary to Petronius' inclinations and principles. He deploys *literary* models, not manuals. It must be concluded therefore that for the lighter strokes of character-

---

[1] For the details and the Greek references, see Raith, *Petronius ein Epikureer* (Nuremberg, 1963), pp. 26 ff.

ization we are unable to decide exactly how far Petronius is relying
on personal observation and common knowledge, and how far
he is working into the *Cena* recherché reminiscences of such
philosophical authors as Theophrastus and Philodemus. But the
latter is to some degree unlikely, and the possibility of minor
coincidences and unconscious allusions, which are common in all
highly literate writers, is not to be excluded.

It is debatable whether we should here include mime, which is
drawn upon heavily for the incidents and accidents of the *Cena*,
under the heading of literary or non-literary sources. The artistic
mimes of Sophron, Theocritus, and Herodas, and even the doubtlessly more stageable mimes of Laberius and Publilius Syrus might
present a case for the one, as the character of the mimes sometimes
put on for the Roman public and frequently castigated by the
satirists and Christian apologists might argue for the other. But
as mime is used largely for the incidents and does not contribute
that much to the *satirical* motifs of the *Cena*, except in so far as
Trimalchio's fondness for home-made mimes is itself a target, this
question may be conveniently left for later discussion (see below,
pp. 219 ff.).

v. *Trimalchio: the non-literary Sources*

It seems fairly clear that Petronius, apart from his literary models,
drew upon his general knowledge and his own observations. This
last is evident from the flair Petronius has for the careful, but
nonetheless realistic, dialogue which he gives Trimalchio and his
guests, and from his acute observation of physical details, lower-
class interests, and contemporary social and economic life.
Whether the same *nostalgie de la boue* that drove Nero to slumming
in Rome led Petronius to an intimate acquaintance with Puteoli
and its mercantile inhabitants is a matter of speculation, even
though he had a villa at nearby Cumae; but his presentation, as
far as we can check it from contemporary evidence and the ex-
cavations at Pompeii and Herculaneum, is accurate and thorough.[1]

---

[1] See e.g. A. Maiuri, *La Cena di Trimalchione di Petronio Arbitro* (Naples, 1945),
passim; G. Bagnani, *Phoenix* 8 (1954), 77 ff.; and P. Veyne, *Annales Economies
Sociétés Civilisations* 16 (1961), 213 ff.

The speech of Trimalchio and his friends is a careful literary representation of the *sermo plebeius*, whose authenticity may be checked by the *graffiti* of Pompeii and Herculaneum and by certain later documents of 'vulgar' Latin.[1] A large number of the vulgarisms, solecisms, Grecisms, instances of bad grammar, and so on, may be paralleled in these sources, and perhaps more would be, were our knowledge of how the lower classes talked in the mid-first century A.D. less defective. More interestingly, Petronius seems to have caught the tone as well as the style of the *populus minutus* of his day. Some examples will bring this out better than any schematic analysis. The monologue of Seleucus catches nicely the personal triviality, the free association of ideas, of lower class conversation, and in particular, the interest in death and rather malicious gossip:

> excepit Seleucus fabulae partem et 'ego' inquit 'non cotidie lavor; †baliscus† enim fullo est, aqua dentes habet, et cor nostrum cotidie liquescit. sed cum mulsi pultarium obduxi, frigori laecasin dico. nec sane lavare potui; fui enim hodie in funus. homo bellus, tam bonus Chrysanthus animam ebulliit. modo modo me appellavit. videor mihi cum illo loqui. heu, eheu. utres inflati ambulamus. minoris quam muscae sumus, tamen aliquam virtutem habent, nos non pluris sumus quam bullae. et quid si non abstinax fuisset! quinque dies aquam in os suum non coniecit, non micam panis. tamen abiit ad plures. medici illum perdiderunt, immo magis malus fatus; medicus enim nihil aliud est quam animi consolatio. tamen bene elatus est, vitali lecto, stragulis bonis. planctus est optime – manu misit

---

[1] Cf. A. von Guericke, *De linguae vulgaris reliquiis apud Petronium et in inscriptionibus parietariis Pompeianis* (Gumbinnen, 1875); H. L. W. Nelson, *Petronius en zijn 'vulgair' Latijn* (Utrecht, 1947); W. Heraeus, *Die Sprache des Petronius und die Glossen* (Leipzig, 1899); E. Löfstedt, *Syntactica* I and II (Lund, 1956), *passim*. Even Trimalchio's disquisition on the Zodiac dish (39.4 ff.) has some claims to be a knowledgeable and humorous amalgam of popular astrological beliefs and associations, see J. G. W. M. de Vreese, *Petron 39 und die Astrologie* (Amsterdam, 1927): Petronius as an Epicurean would have nothing but a literary or sociological interest in unsophisticated – or sophisticated – astrological beliefs.

aliquot–etiam si maligne illum ploravit uxor. quid si non illam optime accepisset! sed mulier quae mulier milvinum genus. neminem nihil boni facere oportet; aeque est enim ac si in puteum conicias. sed antiquus amor cancer est.'

(42)

♪ This started Seleucus off. 'Me now,' he said, 'I don't have a bath every day. It's like gettin' rubbed with fuller's earth, havin' a bath. The water bites into you, and your heart turns to water. But when I've knocked back a hot glass of wine and honey, kiss-my-arse I say to the cold weather. Mind you, I couldn't have a bath–I was at a funeral today. Poor old Chrysanthus has just given up the ghost–nice man he was! It was only the other day he stopped me in the street. I still seem to hear his voice. Dear, dear! We're just so many walking bags of wind. We're worse than flies–at least they have got some strength in them, but we're no more than empty bubbles.

'And what would he have been like if he hadn't been on a diet? For five days he didn't take a drop of water or a crumb of bread into his mouth. But he's gone to join the majority. The doctors finished him–well, hard luck, more like. After all, a doctor is just to put your mind at rest. Still, he got a good send-off–he had a bier and all, beautifully draped. His mourners –several of his slaves were left their freedom–did him proud, even though his widow was a bit mean with her tears. Suppose now he hadn't been so good to her! But women as a sex are real vultures. It's no good doing them a favour, you might as well throw it down a well. An old passion is just like an ulcer.'

The next speaker, Phileros, continues in the same gossiping vein, equally malicious and showing more clearly the usual slightly disapproving interest in other people's sexual activities and their financial status. Seleucus is boring because he confines himself to his own doings and talks in mere generalities; his clichés and popular turns of phrase do not give the interesting information the audience expects; Phileros' talk is just as colloquially textured, but the familiar turns of phrase and the vivid popular catch-phrases are directed at a target:

141

molestus fuit, Philerosque proclamavit: 'vivorum meminerimus. ille habet, quod sibi debebatur: honeste vixit, honeste obiit. quid habet quod queratur? ab asse crevit et paratus fuit quandrantem de stercore mordicus tollere. itaque crevit, quicquid tetigit, tamquam favus. puto mehercules illum reliquisse solida centum, et omnia in nummis habuit. de re tamen ego verum dicam, qui linguam caninam comedi: durae buccae fuit, linguosus, discordia, non homo . . . et quot putas illum annos secum tulisse? septuaginta et supra. sed corneolus fuit, aetatem bene ferebat, niger tamquam corvus. noveram hominem olim oliorum et adhuc salax erat. non mehercules illum puto in domo canem reliquisse. immo etiam puellaris* erat, omnis minervae homo. nec improbo, hoc solum enim secum tulit.'

(43.1–3,7–8)

* puellaris *Mentel* puellarius *H*

He was being a bore, and Phileros said loudly: 'Let's think of the living. He's got what he deserved. He lived an honest life and he died an honest death. What has he got to complain about? He started out in life with just a penny, and he was ready to pick up less than that from a manure-heap if he had to use his teeth. He went up in the world. And so whatever he touched got bigger, like a honeycomb. I honestly think he left a solid hundred thousand and he had the lot in hard cash. But I'll be honest about it–seeing I'm a bit of a cynic–he had a foul mouth and too much lip. He wasn't a man, he was just murder . . .

'And how old do you think he was? Seventy or more! But he was hard as nails and carried his age well. His hair was black as a raven's wing. I knew the man for ages, and he was still an old lecher. I honestly don't think he left the dog alone. What's more, he was a bit of a queer–he could turn his hand to anything. Well, I don't blame him–after all, he couldn't take anything else with him.'

The next speaker, Ganymedes, turns from one age-old obsession to another: the high cost of living, corrupt local government, and the general decadence of the times, particularly in everyday attitudes to religion and money:

'narratis quod nec ad caelum nec ad terram pertinet, cum interim nemo curat, quid annona mordet. non mehercules hodie buccam panis invenire potui. et quomodo siccitas perseverat. iam annum esur⟨it⟩io fuit. aediles-male eveniat, qui cum pistoribus colludunt-'serva me, servabo te'. itaque populus minutus laborat; nam isti maiores maxillae semper Saturnalia agunt. o si haberemus illos leones, quos ego hic inveni, cum primum ex Asia veni. illud erat vivere. si milium, si alica inferior esset,* larvas sic istos percolopabant, ut illis Iuppiter iratus esset . . . heu heu, quotidie peius. haec colonia retroversus crescit tamquam coda vituli. sed quare habemus aedilem non trium cauniarum, qui sibi mavult assem quam vitam nostram? itaque domi gaudet, plus in die nummorum accipit, quam alter patrimonium habet. iam scio unde acceperit denarios mille aureos. sed si nos coleos haberemus, non tantum sibi placeret. nunc populus est domi leones, foras vulpes. quod ad me attinet, iam pannos meos comedi, et si perseverat haec annona, casulas meas vendam. quid enim futurum est, si nec dii nec homines huius coloniae miserentur? ita meos fruniscar, ut ego puto omnia illa a diibus fieri. nemo enim caelum caelum putat, nemo ieiunium servat, nemo Iovem pili facit, sed omnes opertis oculis bona sua computant. antea stolatae ibant nudis pedibus in clivum, passis capillis, mentibus puris, et Iovem aquam exorabant. itaque statim urceatim plovebat: aut tunc aut numquam, et omnes redibant udi tamquam mures. itaque dii pedes lanatos habent, quia nos religiosi non sumus. agri iacent-'

(44.1-5,12-18)

* si milium . . . esset *Bagnani* similia sicilia interiores *H*

'You're all talking about things that don't concern heaven or earth. Meanwhile, no one gives a damn the way we're hit by the corn situation. Honest to God, I couldn't get hold of a mouthful of bread today. And look how there's still no rain. It's been absolute starvation for a whole year now. To hell with the food officers! They're in with the bakers-"you be nice to me and I'll be nice to you". So the little man suffers, while those grinders of the poor never stop celebrating. Oh, if only we still had the sort of men I found here when I first arrived from Asia. Like lions they were. That was the life! If the millet or the corn wasn't up to scratch, they used to box the ears of those bogey-men till they thought God Almighty was on their tails . . .

'Ah me! It's getting worse every day. This place is going down like a calf's tail. But why do we have a third-rate food officer who wouldn't lose a penny to save our lives? He sits at home laughing and rakes in more money a day than anyone else's whole fortune. I happen to know he's just made a thousand in gold. But if we had any balls at all, he wouldn't be feeling so pleased with himself. People today are lions at home and foxes outside.

'Nobody believes in heaven, see, nobody fasts, nobody gives a damn for the Almighty. No, people only bow their heads to count their money. In the old days, high-class ladies used to climb up the hill barefoot, their hair loose, and their hearts pure, and ask God for rain. And he'd send it down in bucketfuls right away–it was then or never–and everyone went home like drowned rats. Since we've given up religion the gods nowadays keep their feet well wrapped up. The fields just lie . . .'

Echion, who breaks in at this point, is a rather different type: more of an optimist, but also much tougher in his attitude to life. There is a coarse heartiness about him, but the initial appeal of this quickly vanishes as his general insensitivity, which is different from the ultimately more charitable, even idealistic, judgments of Seleucus and Phileros, makes itself felt:

'oro te' inquit Echion centonarius 'melius loquere. "modo sic, modo sic" inquit rusticus: varium porcum perdiderat. quod hodie non est, cras erit: sic vita truditur. non mehercules patria melior dici potest, si homines haberet. sed laborat hoc tempore, nec haec sola. non debemus delicati esse; ubique medius caelus est. tu si aliubi fueris, dices hic porcos coctos ambulare. et ecce habituri sumus munus excellente in triduo die festa; familia non lanisticia, sed plurimi liberti. et Titus noster magnum animum habet, et est caldicerebrius: aut hoc aut illud, erit quid utique. nam illi domesticus sum, non est mixcix. ferrum optimum

daturus est, sine fuga, carnarium in medio, ut amphitheater
videat. et habet unde: relictum est illi sestertium trecenties,
decessit illius pater male. ut quadringenta impendat, non sentiet
patrimonium illius, et sempiterno nominabitur. iam Manios
aliquot habet et mulierem essedariam et dispensatorem Gly-
conis, qui deprehensus est, cum dominam suam delectaretur.
videbis populi rixam inter zelotypos et amasiunculos. Glyco
autem, sestertiarius homo, dispensatorem ad bestias dedit. hoc
est se ipsum traducere. quid servus peccavit, qui coactus est
facere? magis illa matella digna fuit quam taurus iactaret. sed
qui asinum non potest, stratum caedit. quid autem Glyco
putabat Hermogenis filicem umquam bonum exitum facturam?
ille milvo volanti poterat ungues resecare; colubra restem non
parit. Glyco, Glyco dedit suas; itaque quamdiu vixerit, habebit
stigmam, nec illam nisi Orcus delebit. sed sibi quisque peccat...'

(45.1-9)

'Please, please,' broke in Echion the rag merchant, 'be a bit
more cheerful. "First it's one thing, then another," as the yokel
said when he lost his spotted pig. What we haven't got today,
we'll have tomorrow. That's the way life goes. Believe me,
you couldn't name a better country, if it had the people. As
things are, I admit, it's having a hard time, but it isn't the only
place. We mustn't be soft. The sky don't get no nearer wherever
you are. If you were somewhere else, you'd be talking about
the pigs walking round ready roasted back here.

'And another thing, we'll be having a holiday with a three-
day show that's the best ever–and not just a hack troupe of
gladiators, but freedmen for the most part. My old friend Titus
has a big heart and a hot head. Maybe this, maybe that, but
something at all events. I'm a close friend of his and he does
nothing by halves. He'll give us cold steel, no quarter, and the
slaughterhouse right in the middle where all the stands can see
it. And he's got the wherewithal–he was left thirty million
when his father died–poor old boy! Even if he spent four
hundred thousand, his pocket won't feel it, and he'll go down
in history. He's got some big brutes already, and a woman who

fights in a chariot, and Glyco's steward, who was caught having fun with his mistress. You'll see quite a quarrel in the crowd between jealous husbands and romantic lovers. But that half-pint Glyco threw his steward to the lions, which is just giving himself away. How is it the servant's fault when he's forced into it? It's that old pisspot who really deserves to be tossed by a bull. But if you can't beat the ass, you beat the saddle. But how did Glyco imagine that poisonous daughter of Hermogenes would ever turn out well? The old man could cut the claws off a flying kite, and a snake don't hatch old rope. Glyco–well, Glyco's got his. He's branded for as long as he lives, and only the grave will get rid of it. But everyone pays for his mistakes . . .'

• Naturally, for a careful stylist, it would be easy enough to insert into the conversation the obvious colloquialisms (*coleos habere*; *pannos meos comedi*; *sic vita truditur*; *habet unde*); the solecisms (*malus fatus, ita meos fruniscar*; *ubique medius caelus est*; *munus excellente in triduo*); the vivid popular phrases and proverbs (*discordia, non homo*; *manus manum lavat*; *frigori laecasin dico*; *dices hic porcos coctos ambulare*); and the vulgar coinages (*burdubasta, mixcix*). But to see how well Petronius has captured the inconsequential tone and the materialistic, gossiping attitudes of popular speech, we should compare, perhaps unorthodoxly, a similar modern passage. If allowances are made for greater prosperity, sobriety, and feminine delicacy, Mrs. Bolton's conversation on village life with Sir Clifford in D. H. Lawrence's *Lady Chatterley's Lover*, another once-banned classic, presents a useful parallel:[1]

'I suppose you heard as Miss Allsopp was married last week! Would you ever! Miss Allsopp, old James' daughter, the boot-

---

[1] Penguin edn. (Harmondsworth, 1960), pp. 104 ff. Lawrence's introductory remarks in the novel have some bearing on the critical question of the spirit in which Petronius represents Trimalchio's circle, and are worth quoting:

. . . one may hear the most private affairs of other people, but only in a spirit of respect for the struggling, battered thing which any human soul is, and in a spirit of fine, discriminative sympathy. For even satire is a form of sympathy. It is the way our sympathy flows and recoils that really determines our lives . . .

and-shoe Allsopp. You know they built a house up at Pye Croft. The old man died last year from a fall; eighty-three, he was, an' nimble as a lad. An' then he slipped on Bestwood Hill, on a slide as the lads 'ad made last winter, and broke his thigh, and that finished him, poor old man, it did seem a shame. Well, he left all his money to Tattie: didn't leave the boys a penny. An' Tattie, I know, is five years—yes she's fifty-three last autumn. And you know they were such Chapel people, my word! She taught Sunday school for thirty years, till her father died. And then she started carrying on with a fellow from Kinbrook, I don't know if you know him, an oldish fellow with a red nose, rather dandified, Willcock, as works in Harrison's woodyard. Well, he's sixty-five, if he's a day, yet you'd have thought they were a pair of young turtle-doves, to see them, arm in arm, and kissing at the gate; yes, an' she sitting on his knee right in the bay window on Pye Croft Road, for anybody to see. And he's got sons over forty, only lost his wife two years ago. If old James Allsopp hasn't risen from his grave, it's because there is no rising: for he kept her that strict! Now they're married and gone to live down at Kinbrook, and they say she goes round in a dressing-gown from morning to night, a veritable sight. I'm sure it's awful the way the old ones go on! Why they're a lot worse than the young, and a sight more disgusting . . .'

Mrs. Bolton shows the same interest in money and, muted though the tone is, in sex, that is to be found in the conversation of Trimalchio's guests. Equally striking is the next passage where she also talks about 'the good old days' and the growing moral decadence:

But there you are, grown-ups are worse than the children: and the

But the novel, like gossip, can also excite spurious sympathies and recoils, mechanical and deadening to the psyche. The novel can glorify the most corrupt feelings, so long as they are conventionally 'pure'. Then the novel, like gossip, becomes at last vicious, and, like gossip, all the more vicious because it is always ostensibly on the side of the angels . . .

For this reason the gossip was humiliating. And for the same reason, most novels, especially the popular ones, are humiliating too. The public responds now only to an appeal to its vices.

old ones beat the band. Talk about morality! Nobody cares a thing. Folks does as they like, and much better off they are for it, I must say. But they're having to draw their horns in nowadays, now th' pits are working so bad, and they haven't got the money. And the grumbling they do, it's awful, especially the women. The men are so good and patient! What can they do, poor chaps! But the women, oh, they do carry on! . . . And boys the same. The lads spend every penny on themselves, clothes, smoking, drinking in the Miners' Welfare, jaunting off to Sheffield two or three times a week. Why, it's another world. And they fear nothing, and they respect nothing, the young don't. The older men are that patient and good, really they let the women take everything. And this is what it leads to. The women are positive demons. But the lads aren't like their dads. They're sacrificing nothing, they aren't: they're all for self. If you tell them they ought to be putting a bit by, for a home, they say: That'll keep, that will, I'm goin' t' enjoy mysen while I can. Owt else'll keep! Oh, they're rough an' selfish, if you like. Everything falls on the older men, an' it's a bad outlook all round.

The painstaking care with which Petronius has set Trimalchio in his social setting is paralleled by the meticulous detail of his depiction of Trimalchio's physical ambience. It is not to any critical purpose to document Petronius' concern to present a convincing set of appointments for Trimalchio's house and a plausible career for the man himself, but it may be interesting to look briefly at the lighter strokes Petronius added to the broad literary outline that was to end in the creation of Trimalchio. When all qualifications are made, the ultimate standard invoked is, as we might expect from an arbiter of elegance, *taste*, and this becomes the guiding principle in the selection of appropriate traits for the rich freedman.

The words *lautus* and *lautitiae* are constantly and ironically emphasized as the *Cena* proceeds.[1] Sometimes the objects, customs,

---

[1] *Lautus*: 26.9; 31.8; 65.10; *lautitiae*: 27.4; 32.1; 34.8; 47.8; 57.2; 70.7; 73.5. For such near-synonyms as *elegans*, *strophae* etc, see J. Segebade and E. Lommatzsch, *Lexicon Petronianum* (Leipzig, 1898).

or delicacies so described are subtly wrong in their context, sometimes they lack taste in themselves, although often to understand
these strokes we are forced to rely on historical and antiquarian
evidence. Moreover, where what is described obviously lacks taste
in itself, as opposed to Trimalchio's getting it wrong or overdoing
it, the possibility cannot be excluded that Petronius is attributing
it to Trimalchio in order to satirize that particular thing, not
Trimalchio. Just as he is willing to criticize certain contemporary
literary tendencies, so Petronius might be ready to play in literature the dangerous game Plutarch tells us he played in real life,
and criticize certain innovations in Roman high society, or even
at Nero's court. This looks the case at 70.8 where the guests' feet
are anointed and perfumed, a thing Encolpius mildly castigates as
unheard of: we discover from Pliny (*H.N.* 13.22) that this Eastern
custom was introduced to Nero's court by Otho, the future emperor, who was exiled in A.D. 58.

Now although this, and one or two other examples, may be
accepted, they must not be taken as evidence for the old theory
that the *Cena* is a direct satire on Nero, or indeed on any other
emperor.[1] Petronius was not sailing as close to the wind as all that.
In any case, the vast majority of the satiric points racked up against
Trimalchio simply will not fit the luxurious and literate Nero.
Petronius, as often, is opportunistic in a highly original way. In
fact, he is even willing to use against Trimalchio certain characteristics of earlier emperors as well as such innovations in contemporary high society as he disapproved of. Claudius' notorious
Edictum de flatu (Suet. *Claud.* 32) seems hinted at in Trimalchio's
vulgar table-talk about his and Fortunata's bodily functions and
in his advice about the dangers of wind (47.2–6). Augustus' fondness for the rebus game (Suet. *Aug.* 75) is shared by Trimalchio,
and Ascyltos gets into a quarrel for sneering at the frigid puns
involved (56.8–57.2).

In effect, to display both Trimalchio's bad taste and ignorant

---

[1] The theory was first put forward by J. A. Gonzales de Salas (Burman II,
p. 126). For the allusions, real or illusory, see R. H. Crum, *CW* 45 (1952),
161 ff., 197 ff.; R. B. Steele, *CJ* 15 (1920), 283 ff.; and for critical comment,
Rose, *Arion* 5 (1966), 280 ff.

pretensions, Petronius draws on contemporary or recent social fashions:[1] those of which he disapproves are given to Trimalchio straight; those he approves of, or is neutral about, Trimalchio must get subtly or badly wrong. The latter cases are interesting. Trimalchio gets literature and mythology wildly wrong, because it is more amusing that way. Some of the fashions that he tries to imitate are only dimly seen by us to be in bad taste, although this fits the subtlety of Petronius' portrait. His tomb is big, but there were tombs of great Republican worthies which dwarf its dimensions: the 'Tomb of Cicero', for instance, along the via Appia near Formiae has three times the extension.[2] His fortune is considerable – 30,000,000 sesterces – but it is small by comparison with the great fortunes of the freedmen of Claudius: Narcissus had 400,000,000 and Pallas 300,000,000. His house is old-fashioned and has been converted and enlarged (73.2, 77.4), rather than newly built on a Texan scale.[3] He is happy to be lord of his own little circle, and although he intends to add the *agnomen* 'Maecenatianus' to his tomb, when he is safely dead, he drops no big names as he might be expected to do – the Scaurus he mentions (77.5), who prefers Trimalchio's house to his father's seaside villa, must be the rich Pompeian manufacturer of *garum* whom we know from inscriptions rather than one of the aristocratic house of the Scauri, who were extinct by A.D. 34.[4]

The examples could be multiplied. But there is always a danger in deciding how far Petronius is subtle or crude in his characterization of Trimalchio, because we can but laboriously and imperfectly reconstruct the nuances of Roman taste and good manners, and it is easy to become hypersubtle. It is reasonable to see the cruelty of one hundred lashes for slaves leaving the house without permission in the inscription of 28.7, for this contrasts with Trimalchio's later mawkish and tasteless humanitarianism

[1] For the topicality of some of Petronius' humour, cf. P. Grimal, *RPh* 16 (1942), 161 ff., although his general conclusions are not acceptable.

[2] See Maiuri's edition, p. 210, and L. Pepe, *Studi Petroniani* (Naples, 1957), pp. 45 ff.

[3] See G. Bagnani, 'The House of Trimalchio', *AJP* 75 (1954), 16 ff.

[4] See L. Friedländer, *Petronii Cena Trimalchionis*[2] (Leipzig, 1906), *ad loc.*

towards them, but are we to make much of the pleonasm in *foras exierit?*[1] What is important is that by humorous exaggeration, subtle points of usage, mild satire on current fashions or philosophy, and the use of contrast of character and rapid dramatic change of mood and atmosphere, Petronius has managed to present a satiric portrait that is motivated neither by the deep moral indignation of the true satirist, nor the indifferent superiority of the man of taste simply, but by the more disinterested and humane sympathy of the literary artist, whose care is not the castigation of vice or even of bad taste–although that impulse may have been there initially–but the presentation of a very human and alive creation. Petronius succeeded.

vi. *Trimalchio as a Comic Figure*

We have seen the sources upon which Petronius drew for his inspiration and treatment; it remains to consider how something which began presumably as a conventional sketch of a typical satiric target grew into a great comic figure, a figure that invites comparison with such creations as Falstaff and Mr. Micawber, and which has added another character to the literary pantheon.[2] We are of course familiar with literary works where the creation takes on life of its own, as it were, and transcends what was clearly the author's original intention, often radically altering the final shape and impact of the whole work. Milton's Satan is an obvious example, and it would not be too bold to suggest that something similar happened with Dido in the fourth book of the *Aeneid*.

[1] See P. Tremoli, *Le iscrizioni di Trimalchione* (Trieste, 1960), p. 5.
[2] F. Scott Fitzgerald describes Gatsby as a modern Trimalchio (*The Great Gatsby*, ch. 7 *ad init.*); see P. L. MacKendrick, *CJ* 45 (1950), 307 ff. It has been suggested that the Malchio Martial refers to, glancingly, in one of his epigrams against Zoilus (*Malchionis . . . improbi*, 3.82) may hark back to Trimalchio (cf. J. Dousa, *Praecidanea* I, xiv *ap.* Burman), as some of the incidents criticized by Martial are reminiscent of parts of the *Cena*, and the truncated form of the name might be due to a defective memory or a reliance on literary hearsay. It is just as likely however that the name chosen in its different forms by Petronius and Martial had an established connotation which suited their purposes. The main root (malekh) is semitic and Trimalchio's name might come over to a Roman ear as something like 'Mr. Trelord'.

Petronius is not a great satirist, which is not to say that he is not a talented artist, and the early invocation of a standard of mere taste, which is anyway undercut by throwing doubts on the standards of the narrator, and by having Hermeros quite rightly take Ascyltos and Giton to task for their bad manners and assumed superiority (57-8), provides no more than a guide to the qualities which Petronius decided to give Trimalchio. Thereafter, as the full elaboration of his ambience, his guests, and his material appurtenances shows, the satiric or parodic impulse is transcended in a literary sympathy and interest which is much more akin to the full presentation of personality and setting that we are accustomed to in fiction. Trimalchio is not pinned down like a moth: he is allowed to fly. The result is a realism that operates for its own sake rather than the sketchy realism which is all the satirist requires. The smiling distaste that the satirist would aim for is lost in the interest, the sympathetic interest, that the modern reader feels. If it be objected that this is due to historical distance, to our lack of snobbery, or the absence of freedmen around us, it may be retorted that Petronius gives us adequate guidance for at least an attempt to place Trimalchio, and we have equivalent paradigms, as T. S. Eliot's line, 'As like a silk hat on a Bradford millionaire' indicates. But Trimalchio survives even the monotonous description of the courses of the dinner, which appealed to Roman tastes more than to ours.

The impulse then that eventually predominates in Petronius' presentation of Trimalchio is sympathetic rather than satirical. The target could be an easy one, and Martial and Juvenal hit similar targets with economy and ease. But Petronius lavishes a great deal of care on his portrait of the vulgar freedman. We are given first, from a distance, his eccentricity, his mannered and lazy luxury, his physical appearance (27.1 ff.). Next his house and its appointments (28.6 ff.) become the focus of our attention; then the ostentatious setting for the dinner that follows (31.3 ff.); finally, Trimalchio enters (32.1). From here onwards the careful portrayal of the host is interwoven with the depiction of his social milieu and the bizarre events of the dinner, counterpointed by the frequent critical remarks of the narrator, who is then himself 'placed' by his inconsistency and impressionable naïvety. The satiric criteria become weaker and more irrelevant. If Trimalchio is trying to appear cruel to his slaves to impress his guests (witness the notice at 28.7 and the outburst at 52.4) or to provide an occasion for a joke (49.5ff.) or for parody, his cruelty is mitigated by his humanitarian sentiments (71.1-3) and his actual behaviour (70.10 etc); Encolpius is a poor and inconsistent contrast, for his initial humaneness is cancelled by some of his later sentiments. He is willing to plead for the steward's attendant (30.9) and for the clumsy slave boy (52.6), but he is intolerably fierce about the chef's pretended forgetfulness in the matter of the ungutted pig (49.7). Meanwhile the incidents of the feast and Trimalchio's reaction to them, or his stage-managing of them, combine with the chatter of his guests to illuminate different aspects of his mutable character, the key to which is Encolpius' remark at 52.11:

nihil autem tam inaequale erat; nam modo Fortunatam ⟨verebatur⟩, modo ad naturam suam revertebatur.

But you never saw anything so inconsistent – one minute he would be frightened of Fortunata and the next minute he would be back in character again.

The final touches are left to Trimalchio himself: his pretentiousness, his knowingness, his superstitions, and his obsessions, all of which had been foreshadowed earlier, are now presented in their true colours in Trimalchio's speech to his guests:

'vos rogo, amici, ut vobis suaviter sit. nam ego quoque tam fui quam vos estis, sed virtute mea ad hoc perveni. corcillum est quod homines facit, cetera quisquilia omnis. "bene emo, bene vendo"; alius alia vobis dicet. felicitate dissilio . . . ad hanc me fortunam frugalitas mea perduxit. tam magnus ex Asia veni quam hic candelabrus est. ad summam, quotidie me solebam ad illum metiri, et ut celerius rostrum barbatum haberem, labra de lucerna ungebam. tamen ad delicias ipsimi annos quattuordecim fui. nec turpe est quod dominus iubet. ego tamen et ipsimae satis faciebam. scitis quid dicam: taceo, quia non sum de gloriosis. ceterum, quemadmodum di volunt, dominus in domo factus sum, et ecce cepi ipsimi cerebellum. quid multa? coheredem me Caesari fecit, et accepi patrimonium laticlavium. nemini tamen nihil satis est. concupivi negotiari. ne multis vobis morer, quinque naves aedificavi, oneravi vinum—et tunc erat contra aurum—misi Romam. putares me hoc iussisse: omnes naves naufragarunt, factum, non fabula. uno die Neptunus trecenties sestertium devoravit. putatis me defecisse? non mehercules mi haec iactura gusti fuit, tamquam nihil facti. alteras feci maiores et meliores et feliciores, ut nemo non me virum fortem diceret. sc⟨it⟩is, magna navis magnam fortitudinem habet. oneravi rursus vinum, lardum, fabam, seplasium, mancipia. hoc loco Fortunata rem piam fecit; omne enim aurum suum, omnia vestimenta vendidit et mi centum aureos in manu posuit. hoc fuit peculii mei fermentum. cito fit quod di volunt. uno cursu centies sestertium corrotundavi. statim redemi fundos omnes, qui patroni mei fuerant. aedifico domum, venalicia coemo, iumenta; quicquid tangebam, crescebat tamquam favus. postquam coepi plus habere quam tota patria mea habet, manum de tabula: sustuli me de negotiatione et coepi ⟨per⟩ libertos faenerare. et sane nolentem me negotium meum agere exhortavit mathematicus, qui venerat forte in coloniam nostram, Graeculio, Serapa nomine, consiliator deorum. hic mihi dixit etiam ea quae oblitus eram; ab acia et acu mi omnia exposuit; intestinas meas noverat; tantum quod mihi non dixerat quid pridie cenaveram. putasses illum semper mecum habitasse. rogo, Habinna—puto, interfuisti—"tu dominam tuam de rebus illis fecisti. tu parum felix in amicos es. nemo umquam tibi parem gratiam refert. tu latifundia possides. tu viperam sub ala nutricas" et, quod vobis non dixerim, etiam nunc mihi restare vitae annos triginta et menses quattuor et dies duos. praeterea cito accipiam hereditatem. hoc mihi dicit fatus meus. quod si contigerit fundos Apuliae iungere, satis vivus pervenero. interim dum Mercurius vigilat, aedificavi hanc domum. ut scitis, casula* erat; nunc templum est. habet quattuor cenationes, cubicula viginti, porticus marmoratos duos, susum cellationem, cubiculum in quo ipse dormio, viperae huius sessorium, ostiarii cellam perbonam; hospitium hospites ⟨C⟩ capit. ad summam, Scaurus cum huc

venit, nusquam mavoluit hospitari, et habet ad mare paternum
hospitium. et multa alia sunt, quae statim vobis ostendam.
credite mihi: assem habeas, assem valeas; habes, habeberis. sic
amicus vester, qui fuit rana, nunc est rex. interim, Stiche, profer
vitalia, in quibus volo me efferri. profer et unguentum et ex illa
amphora gustum, ex qua iubeo lavari ossa mea.'

(75.8–77)

* casula *Heinsius* cusuc H

'I want you to enjoy yourselves, my dear people. After all, I
was once like you are, but being the right sort, I got where
I am. It's the old headpiece that makes the man, the rest is all
rubbish. "Buy right–sell right!"–that's me! Different people
will give you a different line. I'm way ahead of the game . . .
It was my shrewd way with money that got me to my present
position. I came from Asia as big as this candlestick. In fact,
every day I used to measure myself against it, and to get some
whiskers around my beak quicker, I used to oil my lips from
the lamp. Still, for fourteen years I was the old boy's fancy.
And there's nothing wrong if the boss wants it. But I did all
right by the old girl too. You know what I mean–I don't say
anything because I'm not the boasting sort.

'Well, as heaven will have it, I became boss in the house, and
the old boy, you see, couldn't think of anything but me. That's
about it–he made me co-heir with the emperor and I got a
senator's fortune. But nobody gets enough, never. I wanted to
go into business. Not to make a long story of it, I built five
ships, I loaded them with wine–it was absolute gold at the
time–and I sent them to Rome. You'd have thought I ordered
it–every single ship was wrecked. That's fact not fable! In one
single day Neptune swallowed up thirty million. Do you think
I gave up? This loss honestly wasn't more than a flea-bite to
me–it was as if nothing had happened. I built more boats,
bigger and better and luckier, so nobody could say I wasn't a
man of courage. You know, the greater the ship, the greater
the confidence. I loaded them again–with wine, bacon, beans,
perfumes, and slaves. At this point Fortunata did the decent

thing, because she sold off all her gold trinkets, all her clothes, and put ten thousand in gold pieces into my hand. This was the yeast my fortune needed to rise. What heaven wants soon happens. In one voyage I carved out a round ten million. I immediately bought back all my old master's estates. I built a house, I invested in slaves, horses. Whatever I touched grew like a honeycomb. Once I had more than the whole country, then down tools! I retired from business and began advancing loans through freedmen.

'Actually I was tired of trading on my own account, but it was an astrologer who convinced me. He happened to come to our colony, a little Greek, Serapa by name, and he could have told heaven itself what to do. He even told me things I'd forgotten. He went through everything for me from A to Z. He knew me inside out–the only thing he didn't tell me was what I ate for dinner the day before. You'd have thought he'd never left my side.

'Wasn't there that thing, Habinnas?–I think you were there: "You got your lady wife out of those *certain circumstances*. You are not lucky in your friends. Nobody thanks you enough for your trouble. You have large estates. You are nursing a viper in your bosom." And he said–though I shouldn't tell you– I have thirty years, four months, and two days to live. What's more, I shall soon receive a legacy. My horoscope tells me this. If I'm allowed to join my estates to Apulia, I'll have lived enough.

'Meantime, under the protection of Mercury, I built this house. As you know, it was just a shack, now it's a shrine. It has four dining-rooms, twenty bedrooms, two marble colonnades, a row of box-rooms up above, a bedroom where I sleep myself, a nest for this viper, and a really good lodge for the porter. The guest apartment takes a hundred guests. In fact, when Scaurus came here, he didn't want to stay anywhere else, even though he's got his father's guest house down by the sea. And there are a lot of other things I'll show you in a second.

'Believe me: have a penny and you're worth a penny. You

got something, you'll be thought something. Like your old friend—first a frog, now a king.

'Meantime, Stichus, bring out the shroud and the things I want to be buried in. Bring some cosmetic cream too, and a sample from that jar of wine I want my bones washed in.'

CHAPTER V

Criticism and Parody in the *Satyricon*

i. *The Vehicles of Criticism*

One of the difficulties felt by commentators on the literary, as opposed to the moral, criticism in the *Satyricon* is that the apparently straightforward attacks on contemporary rhetoric and epic are put in the mouths of highly disreputable characters, and consequently the critiques may not be serious, or must have a purely dramatic or parodic function.[1] This reasonable doubt about the sincerity of the views expounded, which is reinforced by certain local problems, may be dispelled by a number of considerations. Even if Petronius wished to express his critical views in considered and artistic form, he had himself deliberately restricted the means open to him. He had chosen as his main plot the sexual escapades and misadventures of Encolpius and his acquaintances: the literary criticism is, structurally at least, digression. Eumolpus, whose function in the *plot* is largely to arouse Encolpius' jealousy and to be the architect of the Crotonian imposture, is made a poet, not only to satirize pretentious poets and untimely reciters, but also to provide plausible occasions for Petronius' longer verse pieces, which might be out of character for Encolpius. Petronius is not exclusively concerned with verisimilitude, as is indicated by the blatant intrusion into the reader's world of the *apologia* for the work itself (132.15), but even Encolpius' criticism of Agamem-

---

[1] See e.g. A. D. Nock, *CR* 46 (1932), 173 and, most recently, the doubts of P. A. George, 'Style and Character in the *Satyricon*', *Arion* 5 (1966), 336 ff., who points out that the style of 1–5 smells strongly of parody, and that the views offered on style are parodied by the language in which they are expressed.

non's teaching is in a way unexpected: the true parasite, as even Agamemnon knows (3.3), says what is most gratifying to the listener, not what is highly critical of his way of life.

Petronius of course would not want himself to be identified with his narrator, even when he is talking sense: he makes that very clear in the *Cena* by showing us Encolpius as absurdly impressed by Trimalchio's *lautitiae*, and then giving us a very detailed and objective description of Trimalchio's bad taste. In this instance, separating the views of the author and of the narrator is easy, and a reasonable rule of thumb for this procedure is to assume that when Encolpius is not directly involved in the action or when he is not reporting dialogue, parody or his emotional states, the narrative medium is pretty much governed by Petronius' own stylistic preferences: one might point to such objective passages as the description of Trimalchio's ambience (26.10 ff.), and some of the scenes on shipboard (100 ff.).

But the criticism is put into the mouths of different characters, and I think we must accept that Petronius was prepared, for his local purposes, to allow his judgments on art to emerge from what are at first sight unexpected sources, even at the risk of their being weakened by their disreputable provenance. It may be added that the method offers excellent opportunities for irony and preserves the general distancing, indeed insouciance, about everything, taste, sex, morality, or emotion, that is one of the more striking characteristics of the *Satyricon*. The objectivity is achieved by firmly *placing*, often by stylistic parody, the emotionality and rhetoric of the characters and the narrator.

The most compelling reason to take the literary criticism seriously, is surely the character of the criticism itself. Petronius' own objective style, for instance, exemplifies some of the principles propounded in the criticism of rhetoric and epic. The oratorical style was regarded by the Romans simply as the paradigm of prose and not as something different from other literary prose, as we tend to think in an age where the printed word is more familiar. How could an author who offered criticisms of contemporary rhetorical style, criticisms echoed by the greatest of his contemporaries or near-contemporaries, write in a style which is consonant with his critical principles, and then not hold them? For if Petronius did not hold them and was merely parodying them, what possible principles could he have held? If he did hold them, what is the point of the alleged parody? Similarly his art criticism (83) reflects the typical mimetic principles of the ancient art critic.

This is not to say however that the use of disreputable *personae* does not have an effect on Petronius' manner of voicing these criticisms. Indeed the criticism, while perfectly coherent internally, is brief, glancing, and ironic, performing as it does a critical and a dramatic function at the same time. We do not find the carefully worked-out arguments and comparisons that are to be seen in the elder Seneca, Tacitus' *Dialogus*, and Quintilian. Encolpius' attack on rhetoric is a fairly stock attack in an inflated style itself, and his examples are chosen from the past, and the Greek past at that– Plato, Demosthenes, Thucydides, and Hyperides. He claims that the Asiatic style came to Athens *lately* (*nuper*) and he is not even as up to date as Agamemnon, who at least mentions Cicero, still the darling of the traditionalists in Quintilian's time, although probably under something of a cloud during Neronian times. Now Petronius, even more than Seneca in the *Epistulae Morales*, avoids any reference to important contemporaries: the problem of his dating would otherwise have hardly existed. He wishes to preserve the fictional context where possible, hence he omits Lucan's name in a critique which can only have been directed at him, although there may have been additional non-literary reasons for the omission. Too topical a realism may jar in fiction, as when some contemporary famous figure occurs in the pages of a modern novel concerning mainly imaginary characters; too little may jar also. So here, how should Eumolpus have heard of Lucan's *Pharsalia*? It is better therefore to omit his name altogether. Again, how should Encolpius be familiar with the more prominent orators who were Petronius' contemporaries? His criticism is correspondingly non-specific and fairly traditional, but it seems to reflect Petronius' own views as seen from his practice.

ii. *The Criticism of Contemporary Rhetoric*

The criticism of 1–5 is important, not so much for its perceptiveness, as for the light it throws on Petronius' own work. I do not wish to discuss the rights and wrongs of the education attacked by Encolpius or that laid out by Agamemnon,[1] but to examine the elements in the dialogue which illustrate Petronius' style, subject matter, and his whole idea of literature.

Encolpius has heard a declamation on some theme and has been invited no doubt to give his opinion; he then launches a vigorous attack on the whole drift of Roman higher education. He–or Agamemnon–has made some elaborate comparison, as our text opens with its other term:

'num alio genere furiarum declamatores inquietantur, qui clamant: "haec vulnera pro libertate publica excepi, hunc oculum pro vobis impendi: date mihi ducem qui me ducat ad liberos meos, nam succisi poplites membra non sustinent"? haec ipsa tolerabilia essent, si ad eloquentiam ituris viam facerent. nunc et rerum tumore et sententiarum vanissimo strepitu hoc tantum proficiunt ut, cum in forum venerint, putent se in alium orbem terrarum delatos. et ideo ego adulescentulos existimo in scholis stultissimos fieri, quia nihil ex his quae in usu habemus aut audiunt aut vident, sed piratas cum catenis in litore stantes, sed tyrannos edicta scribentes quibus imperent filiis ut patrum suorum capita praecidant, sed responsa in pestilentiam data, ut virgines tres aut plures immolentur, sed mellitos verborum globulos et omnia dicta factaque quasi papavere et sesamo sparsa. qui inter haec nutriuntur non magis sapere possunt quam bene olere qui in culina habitant. pace vestra liceat dixisse, primi omnium eloquentiam perdidistis. levibus enim atque inanibus sonis ludibria quaedam excitando effecistis ut corpus orationis enervaretur et caderet. nondum iuvenes declamationibus continebantur, cum Sophocles aut Euripides invenerunt verba quibus deberet loqui. nondum umbraticus doctor ingenia deleverat, cum Pindarus novemque lyrici Homericis versibus canere

[1] See H.L.W. Nelson, *Ein Unterrichtsprogramm aus neronischer Zeit* (Amsterdam, 1956), pp. 3 ff.

timuerunt. et ne poetas [quidem] ad testimonium citem, certe neque Platona neque Demosthenen ad hoc genus exercitationis accessisse video. grandis et, ut ita dicam, pudica oratio non est maculosa nec turgida, sed naturali pulchritudine exsurgit. nuper ventosa istaec et enormis loquacitas Athenas ex Asia commigravit animosque iuvenum ad magna surgentes veluti pestilenti quodam sidere adflavit, semelque corrupta regula eloquentia stetit et obmutuit. quis postea ad summam Thucydidis, quis Hyperidis ad famam processit? ac ne carmen quidem sani coloris enituit, sed omnia quasi eodem cibo pasta non potuerunt usque ad senectutem canescere. pictura quoque non alium exitum fecit, postquam Aegyptiorum audacia tam magnae artis compendiariam invenit.'

'Our professors of rhetoric are hag-ridden in the same way, surely, when they shout "I got these wounds fighting for your freedom! This eye I lost for you. Give me a leader to lead me to my children. I am hamstrung, my legs can't support me." We could put up with even this stuff if it were a royal road to eloquence. But the only result of these pompous subjects and this empty thunder of platitudes, is that when young speakers first enter public life they think they have been landed on another planet. I'm sure the reason such young nitwits are produced in our schools is because they have no contact with anything of any use in everyday life. All they get is pirates standing on the beach, dangling chains, tyrants writing orders for sons to cut off their fathers' heads, oracles advising the sacrifice of three or more virgins during a plague–a mass of sickly sentiments: every word, every move just so much poppycock.

'People fed on this kind of thing can no more learn sense than kitchen hands can smell sweet. If you'll pardon my saying so, you professors of rhetoric are mainly responsible. You have ruined good speaking. Your smooth and empty sound effects provided a few sniggers, and as a result you took the guts out of real oratory, and that was the end of it. Young men were not tied down to rhetorical exercises when

Sophocles and Euripides managed to write the way one should speak. Academic pedants had not addled their wits when Pindar and the nine lyric poets grew nervous of the Homeric style. And apart from the poets I can cite, I certainly cannot see Plato or Demosthenes going in for this sort of training. The elevated, what one might call the pure style, is not full of purple patches and bombast: it is lifted up by its intrinsic beauty. It is not so long since that long-winded spouting of yours travelled from Asia to Athens and its foul pestilential breath infected every youthful ambition. Once its standards dropped, eloquence lost vigour and voice. Who since then has attained the reputation of Thucydides or of Hyperides? Why, not even poetry has shown a spark of life. All forms of literature have been faced with the same diet and lost their chance of a ripe old age. Even the great art of painting has met the same fate since the unscrupulous Egyptians came up with their painting-made-easy methods.'

Encolpius is making several criticisms at once: he is complaining of the unreal subjects of the *controversiae* and *suasoriae* in Roman oratorical training, which was still of course directed towards the law courts and the Senate, even though the real power once exercised by the great politicians and orators had been greatly attenuated by the principate. The topics were simply occasions for the exercise of ingenuity in style and argument, and were of little moment, even if the choice of more cogent themes might not in fact be politically dangerous. Encolpius is also complaining of the style encouraged in these declamatory exercises (cf. *controversiam sententiolis vibrantibus pictam*, 118.2): the unreal and exaggerated sentiments expressed in epigrams, alliteration, assonance, and various rhetorical tropes, which do not ultimately help their practitioners in the real life of politics and the law. Similar criticisms may be found in both Senecas, in Tacitus, and in Quintilian.[1]

---

[1] For these parallel criticisms see: Tac. *Dial.* 35; Sen. *Ep.* 106.12; 114; Sen. *Contr.* 3 *praef.* (13); Pers. 1; 3.44 ff. [Longinus] *De Sublim.* 44; Juv. 7.150; Quint. *Inst.* 2.10.3–5; 2.10.7–9; 2.20.4; 8.3.22–3,76; 12.10.16; 9.2.72–92 etc. In general, see S. F. Bonner, *Roman Declamation under the Empire* (Liverpool, 1948), ch. 4.

The pejorative remark about the spread of Asianism into Athens may indicate that Petronius himself leaned rather to Atticism,[1] but his conception of that oratorical range is not a narrow one, to judge from the examples he quotes of the great Greek writers and the fact that Agamemnon later offers Cicero as a model, for Cicero had himself been accused in his time of Asianism.[2] Indeed his point of view seems that expressed by Cicero in the *Orator* and in the *De optimo genere oratorum*, which cuts across the Asianic-Attic controversy and prefers the theory of the plain, the grand, and the intermediate style, each being appropriate to different types of subject matter or for producing different effects. This seems indicated by Petronius' remark about the truly elevated style (*grandis . . . et pudica oratio*), where of course Asianism would be the greatest temptation: this style is *not* 'full of purple patches and bombast' (*maculosa, turgida*). As we might expect from such a position, Petronius himself has several distinguishable styles. There is the elaborate style, exemplified in the passage quoted above, which is used for literary criticism, parody, and various rhetorical purposes, such as Encolpius' complaints and moralizings (cf. e.g. 81.3-6; 83.1-7; 107.1-6; 115.12-19; 118; 126.14-18); there is the plain but careful and rhythmical style which is the chief narrative medium, a kind of artistic *sermo urbanus*, capable of its own variations between leisurely elaboration, as in the story of the Widow of Ephesus (111 ff.), and rapid descriptions of action; and there is also the vulgar style (*sermo plebeius*), equally artificial in a way, but intended to imitate the nuances and speech characteristics of Trimalchio and his circle. In each case, Petronius would see a particular style as suitable to a particular subject matter and this would be part of his and the Roman idea of literary *decorum*.[3]

The other critical and cultural implications of the first five

---

[1] See A. Desmouliez, *REL* 30 (1952), 168 ff; U. von Wilamowitz-Moellendorf, *H* 35 (1900), 1 ff.; and E. T. Sage, *TAPA* 46 (1915), 47 ff.

[2] Quintilian (*Inst.* 12.10.12–14) tells us that some of Cicero's contemporaries accused him of being *tumidiorem et Asianum et redundantem*.

[3] See W. Süss, 'Petronii imitatio sermonis plebeii qua necessitate coniungatur cum grammatica illius aetatis doctrina', *Acta et Comm. Univ. Tartuensis* 13 (1927), 103 ff.

chapters need merely a brief glance. Agamemnon, recognizing the truth of Encolpius' criticisms, pleads in his defence that pupils and their parents have to be humoured. The fault lies in the parents' overeager ambitions for their children. What is needed is discipline, diligence, and time in their studies, careful attention to the lessons and models of the past, and stern self-criticism. The sketch of an ideal education, or at least a reading course, that he offers in his verses (5) consists, roughly, of Homer, Socratic dialogues, and Demosthenes; then for Latin literature, history, possibly including such things as Ennius' *Annales*,[1] followed by Cicero. This would provide, it is assumed, a decent literary background for the hopeful young orator, as opposed no doubt to the study of rhetoric only. The poem is meant as a mere sketch and, while it was probably rather different from current educational practice, it is by no means a revolutionary scheme. It is clear both from Encolpius' speech and from Agamemnon's verses that Petronius is a traditionalist, which, of course, is not necessarily incompatible with a high degree of sophistication. The latter is seen perhaps in the expressive perfunctoriness of the educational views propounded (*surtout pas de zèle*) and his ironic awareness of his fictional vehicles.

iii. *The Criticism of Contemporary Historical Epic*

These two characteristics of Petronius' criticism – propriety and classicism – recur in 118, where Eumolpus on the road to Croton discusses contemporary verse practice and, specifically, the difficulties of writing an historical epic on the Civil War. He puts his finger on what all later critics of Roman literature have noted as a main characteristic of Silver Latin literature, the influence of rhetoric on poetry. (The earlier and continuing influence of poetry on rhetoric has always impressed critics less, and the training proposed by Agamemnon for the budding orator makes much, as does Quintilian, of an education in poetry as well as prose, but this does not concern us here.)

[1] Cf. Nelson, *op. cit.* The text and interpretation are doubtful at this point, but it is not impossible that Ennius and poets like him may be meant: Petronius shows a typical, but non-partisan, interest in archaic writings as is shown by his imitations of Lucilius and Lucretius (5, Fgt. XXX).

It has been well said that the unit of criticism is the paragraph and Petronius' insights in this passage, short as it is, deserve some scrutiny, for they are at the service of a coherent, if debatable, thesis. The passage, for which I have adopted a number of emendations, runs:

'Multos iuvenes carmen decepit. nam ut quisque versum pedibus instruxit sensumque teretiore verborum ambitu intexuit, putavit se continuo in Heliconem venisse. sic forensibus ministeriis exercitati frequenter ad carminis tranquillitatem tamquam ad portum feliciorem refugerunt, credentes facilius poema extrui posse, quam controversiam sententiolis vibrantibus pictam. ceterum neque generosior spiritus sanitatem amat, neque concipere aut edere partum mens potest nisi ingenti flumine litterarum inundata. refugiendum est ab omni verborum, ut ita dicam, vilitate et sumendae voces a plebe summotae, ut fiat "odi profanum vulgus et arceo". praeterea curandum est, ne sententiae emineant extra corpus orationis expressae, sed intexto vestibus colore niteant. Homerus testis et lyrici, Romanusque Vergilius et Horatii curiosa felicitas. ceteri enim aut non viderunt viam qua iretur ad carmen, aut visam timuerunt calcare. ecce belli civilis ingens opus quisquis attigerit nisi plenus litteris, sub onere labetur. non enim res gestae versibus comprehendendae sunt, quod longe melius historici faciunt, sed per ambages deorumque ministeria et fabulosum sententiarum †tormentum† praecipitandus est liber spiritus, ut potius furentis animi vaticinatio appareat quam religiosae orationis sub testibus fides.'

'Poetry has deceived many a young man. As soon as each of them has made his lines scan and wrapped up his ideas in elegant periphrases, he thinks he's gone straight up Helicon. Tired by their practice at the bar they often fly to the calm waters of poetry, as though it were a port in a storm, believing it must be easier to construct an epic poem than a speech that glows with scintillating epigrams. But a noble genius does not cling to what is merely sane and a mind cannot conceive or bear fruit unless it is soaked in a mighty flood of literature. One must avoid all vulgarity of language and one must select expressions not in common use. We need a sort of "I hate the profane herd and I keep it out!" Besides this, one must be careful that witty lines are not made to stand out from the body of the narrative, but add their colour and brilliance to the texture of the poem. Witness Homer and the lyric poets, Roman Vergil, and Horace's careful felicity. Other poets either have not seen the way to approach poetry, or, if they have seen it, have been frightened to take it. Above all, whoever attempts the great theme of the Civil War without being full of the great writers, will fail under the task. For it is not historical fact that has to be handled in the poem—historians do this far better. No, the unfettered inspiration must be sent soaring through riddles and divine interventions and strange stories (?), so that it gives the impression of prophetic ravings rather than the accuracy of a solemn speech before witnesses.'

The ideas are no more strikingly original than were the criticisms of contemporary rhetoric and they may be paralleled in various earlier writers. Poetry is more than a matter of versification and language.[1] Because one can produce a *controversia* glittering with neat and specious points (*sententiolis*), it does not follow that one can even more easily write a poem. True poetry needs a rich awareness of literary tradition and an avoidance of what is bizarre or unsound. Petronius is obviously thinking of epic (*carmen*, not *nugae* or *lusus*), because he insists that lofty, non-vulgar language is the appropriate style. The great rhetorical vice of unassimilated *sententiae* that stand out from the texture of the poem must be avoided. The examples Petronius cites are the conventional great writers of the epic and lyric traditions: Homer and the Greek lyric poets, Vergil, and Horace, whose combination of natural talent and artistic labour he characterizes by the happy and memorable phrase—*Horatii curiosa felicitas*.

His general criticism, stressing the great tradition and literary *decorum*, and showing an aversion to the dominating Silver style so influenced by rhetoric and point, is now applied to a subgenre

[1] Cf. Hor. *Sat.* 1.4.62: *disiecti membra poetae.*

of epic, namely historical epic on the delicate political subject of the Civil War. Such a subject, says Petronius, not only requires a poet steeped in the epic tradition, but one who will adhere to what is proper to the epic genre, as seen in the great exemplars: not an accurate versified account of events–for accuracy is the historian's virtue–but rather an inspired narrative which makes use of the traditional machinery of the gods, as used by Homer and Vergil, and the stories, not necessarily verifiable, which grow up around great events–in effect, the divine and the fabulous. It is clear how conventionally Petronius, for all his own originality in a different genre and despite his Epicurean philosophy which would deny any divine influence on human affairs, has defined what was proper to epic. He is rejecting Lucan's experiment in the *Pharsalia* of jettisoning the divine machinery in favour of the more Stoic and, in a way, more realistic motifs of divination and omens, which indicate the involvement of the unseen and the divine in human affairs, but do not represent this involvement so anthropomorphically. Lucan is also open to Petronius' general criticism of the rhetorical style, for it must be admitted that occasionally his epigrams *are* strained and stand out from the narrative in a way the more closely woven Vergilian periods do not allow.

Now it has been argued, notably by Collignon (pp. 185 ff.), that the critique is not directed at Lucan, who was well-read and too young to have been in political or forensic life for very long, but rather at those Neronian poets who deserved such animadversions. It is true that the critique is academic and moderate in tone, and may indeed apply to other poets than Lucan, but Petronius' invidious reference to lawyers turned poets is reminiscent of the standard criticisms of Lucan from Quintilian and Servius;[1] the evidence of the *Bellum Civile* itself, and the applicability of the last part of the critique to the characteristics of the *Pharsalia*, are decisive in favour of Lucan's being the main target.

---

[1] Cf. Quint. *Inst.* 10.1.90: *sententiis clarissimus, et . . . magis oratoribus quam poetis imitandus*; Mart. 14.194; Serv. *ad Aen.* 1.382: *Lucanus ideo in numero poetarum non meruit quia videtur historiam composuisse non poema*; Schol. *ad Phars.* 1.1; and Isid. *Orig.* 8.7.10.

What Petronius' motives were here–whether a mild wish to please Nero who was jealous of Lucan's abilities, along with an unwillingness to offend Lucan or his court friends directly, or an honest distaste for Lucan's innovations and excesses with a reluctance to add to his fame–we cannot know. It will be observed that Petronius contrasts a poem with a *controversia*, not an *oratio*, and we know that Lucan was a highly admired declaimer–*declamavit et Graece et Latine cum magna admiratione audientiae*, as the Life attributed to Vacca puts it. As for the *forensia ministeria*, the declamations were supposed to be training for these, and Lucan in any case had an early taste of public life, holding through Nero's favour both the quaestorship (before the legal age) and a priesthood. Admittedly Lucan was well trained and his work shows great familiarity with earlier poets, including Petronius' admired Vergil, but Petronius may have felt this was not what he meant by *mens ingenti flumine litterarum inundata* or *plenus litteris*: such an education might be a mere beginning. This possibility is supported by Agamemnon's words in another but similar context (4.2 ff.), where he talks of the dangers of raw and youthful enthusiasm in the forum and the need for severe literary training (*severa lectione*), long attention to what one wishes to imitate, and the worthlessness of youthful taste. Lucan's youth and precociousness are among the best known features of his life.

As for the objection that Petronius too has *sententiae* in his poem unconnected properly with the narrative, and is therefore not following his own advice (118.5), surely he is not against *sententiae*, and presumably he believed that his own were woven into the texture of the poem. Many of Lucan's *sententiae* are a line or more long;[1] Petronius' usually less than a line. He may have thought that this secured their closer connection with the narrative. And it is true that many of Lucan's epigrams, which are not infrequently trite and commonplace, do seem removable excrescences on the narrative (e.g. 1.81, 5.260, and 9.211). I believe that Petronius' charges of colloquialisms and vulgar usages might be substantiated,

---

[1] See Heitland's list in *M. Annaei Lucani Pharsalia*, Ed. C. E. Haskins, with an Introduction by W. E. Heitland (Cambridge, 1887), pp. lxvi–vii; Gaselee, Excursus V, p. 118.

although these may have been due to hasty composition and unrevised work: one may point to certain substantives in -*tor*; *felix* as a neuter accusative (*Phars.* 4.520); such oddities as *assuescis* for *assuefacis* (5.776), otherwise found in literature only in Horace's *Satires*; *aestimat* in the sense of 'gauges' (10.474); clumsy relative clauses freely used; lax and sloppy use of participles. It may be objected that Petronius' criticism here is unjust, or at best carping, and that it is rather Lucan's obscurity and strain that we notice, but there is the other possibility that until we have for Lucan such stylistic studies as B. Axelson's *Unpoetische Wörter*, we cannot know how occasionally flat and prosaic in his diction Lucan might appear to the sensitive eye. All the same, the obvious reasons for assuming that Lucan is the object of Petronius' critique are because his epic poem exhibits the characteristics criticized, and because the apparently unfinished poem of some 290 lines that Eumolpus proceeds to recite is a reworking of material from the *Pharsalia* into a more conventional epic structure.

iv. The Intentions of the Bellum Civile

The poem on the Civil War–*carmen de bello civili*–has attracted a good deal of critical discussion.[1] The main questions are the relationship between the poem and Lucan's *Pharsalia*; Petronius' intentions and principles, the merits of the critique, if such it is, and of the poem itself; and finally, its setting in the *Satyricon*.

Oddly enough, the last question has to be tackled first. Whatever the poem's merits and intentions, it is after all given to Eumolpus, whose morals and abilities have already been satirized. His recitation of his *Troiae Halosis* was received by a shower of

---

[1] The question is discussed by J. G. Mössler, *Commentatio de Petronii poemate* '*De bello civili*' (Breslau, 1842) and *Quaestonium Petroniarum specimen quo poema* '*De bello civili*' *cum* '*Pharsalia*' *Lucani comparatur* (Hirschberg, 1857); W. E. Heitland *ap.* Haskins (*op. cit.* above), pp. xxxvi f.; M. Westerburg, *RhM* 38 (1883), 92 ff.; E. Trampe, *De Lucani arte metrica* (Berlin, 1884); B. Kindt, *Philologus* 51 (1892), 355 ff.; Collignon, pp. 149 ff.; F. T. Baldwin, *The Bellum Civile of Petronius* (New York, 1911); H. Stubbe, *Die Verseinlagen im Petron*, *Philologus Suppltbd.* 25 (1933), 50 ff.; A. F. Sochatoff, *TAPA* 93 (1962), 449 ff., and *Arion* 5 (1966), 359 ff.; and Rose, pp. 167 ff. In this section these discussions will be referred to simply by their author's names.

stones (90.1) and Encolpius tries more than once to damp his *furor poeticus* (90.3, 93.3, 113.12). This might indicate that any claim to seriousness the poem has is again invalidated by its provenance. But, as was pointed out earlier, Petronius has *no* admirable characters in his work; Encolpius, who does at times voice the author's serious views (e.g. at 1 ff. and 132.15), is even one of the most disreputable. Nor is it uncommon in Roman literature to use lowly, or even low, speakers to express what purports to be serious matter–Horace, for instance, uses Davus to put forward Stoic philosophy, and Juvenal uses the pathic Naevolus to satirize homosexuality. The disreputable old hag who tells the story of Cupid and Psyche in Apuleius' *Metamorphoses* is another familiar instance. The uses of such characters may not be quite straightforward, of course; the *personae* may be in turn satirized. In the case of Eumolpus, the critique and the poem have their serious intentions, but the apologetic, if conventional, remark:

'tamquam, si placet, hic impetus, etiam si nondum recepit ultimam manum'

'as an example, see if you like this hurried attempt, even though it has not received the final touches',

perhaps indicates that Petronius would make no great critical claims for its poetic merits or, if he would, his sophistication and ironic pose will not allow him to do so overtly. Defensive he may be, but the critique and the poem are both elaborate productions despite their brevity, and the brevity is partly to be accounted for by the exigencies of the plot and the structural balance.

Before we discuss the intentions of the work, it would be well to see its indisputable relation to Lucan's *Pharsalia*. Petronius' poem begins with a description of Rome's affluence, decadence, and greed, to which the outbreak of the war is attributed. Greed has infected the army, the people, and the senate alike (1–44). Cato, the symbol of Rome's better self and the morality which was the source of her power, is defeated at the polls through corruption. This purely mercenary attitude produces misery among the lower classes and war represents a way out (45–60). The three leaders are introduced: Crassus, Pompey, and Julius Caesar, and their deaths described (61–6). The poem now moves on to the mythological plane, and there is a conversation between Dis, lord of the underworld, and Fortune, who is addressed as the supreme arbiter of human and divine affairs; the greed and luxury of Rome and the radical discontent they have given rise to are represented both as a threat to the realm of Dis, and as an opportunity for Fortune to display her fickleness and for Dis to gratify his thirst for blood. He pleads with her to embroil Rome in war (67–99). Fortune agrees to his proposal; professes an equal anger and blood lust, and sketches briefly some of the main battles and campaigns which will consummate their aims (100–21). The conversation is interrupted by thunderbolts from Jupiter, which, despite the temporary alarm they cause Dis, are clearly signs of Jupiter's approval, for a list follows of the omens foretelling the horrors coming to mankind (122–40). The significance of the omens is quickly made clear. Caesar brooks no more delay and the Gallic War is succeeded by the Civil War. A careful description is given of a spot in the Maritime Alps, which is represented as the barrier Caesar crosses as his first overt act of hostilities. Here Caesar addresses Jupiter and Italy, and claims, piously, that the war is forced upon him by the vengeful ingratitude of the alien populace who are blocking his further victories. He therefore encourages his troops to save him and themselves (141–76). The omens favouring his enterprise are described, and the difficult crossing of the Alps is depicted in great physical detail (177–209). The exaggerations of Rumour put the people of Rome in a quandary–whether to fight or escape by land or sea. The sad and painful abandoning of the city by the people reaches its climax in Pompey's desertion of Rome (210–44). The poem moves again to the mythological plane. A list of the gods who abandon earth is given and a description of the powers of the underworld who come raging hot from hell. The enumeration of the gods on each side or neither culminates in a description of Discord and her exhortation to the peoples of the earth and the main actors in the coming struggle to continue on their course towards Civil War (244–94). The poem concludes with a line, which Heinsius proposed to delete, saying that all Discord commanded came to pass.

It would of course be tedious to set out in detail the distortions of fact, motive, and event that make up the short narrative. It was the Rubicon and not the Alps which Caesar crossed illegally; the gibe against the populace is singularly odd–or cynical–in Caesar's mouth, himself a *popularis*; Pompey did not get as far in his conquests as the River Hydaspes, and so on. But this is exactly the poetic licence that Petronius had insisted upon in his remarks prefacing the poem. More important for our purposes are the similarity and differences between it and the *Pharsalia*.

Lucan of course presents us with the luxury and corruption of Rome and the general causes of the conflict (1.158–82), but he has nothing corresponding to Petronius' divine machinery. He has, more expectedly, a description of the omens of the Civil War (1.522–83). Corresponding to Petronius' single speech for Caesar, Lucan offers us three: a brief speech before the passage of the Rubicon (1.195–203); an even briefer one after (1.225–7); and finally a speech at Ariminum after the arrival of Curio (1.299–351). Against this, he has merely one line to describe what Petronius presented in detail: Caesar's crossing of the Alps is represented simply by

Iam gelidas Caesar cursu superaverat Alpes (1.183).

He does describe at some length the panic at Rome and Pompey's flight (1.466–522), and arguably Lucan's description of people consulting the Etruscan deities is a reasonable equivalent of Petronius' mythological scenes and the harangues of Discordia and Fortuna, granted his anti-Vergilian premises.

The differences however bring us directly to the problem of Petronius' intentions. The theories offered are varied and frequently qualified, but they may be divided into a few classes: (a) that Petronius is parodying and criticizing Lucan; (b) that he is imitating and defending him; (c) that he is reworking Lucanic matter into a more acceptable epic form; (d) that he has a different primary object to which his use of Lucan is strictly secondary: he is really satirizing the vices of the age that led to Civil War; or he is defending Caesar from Lucan's Republican bias; or he is criticizing the decay of oratory and poetry that resulted in a Lucan.[1]

The most acceptable theory is that he is offering in a brief and eclectic sketch some of Lucan's material, which is reworked in a Vergilian manner and has the proper Vergilian mythological machinery. The poem invites comparison with Lucan, and indeed forcibly reminds us of this by constant reminiscences of the *Pharsalia*. It may be simpler to lay out the arguments for this theory before disposing of the other possibilities or incorporating into it their partial insights. The question is not a simple one.

Petronius seems to have known the whole *Pharsalia* in one way or another. The first three books however supply him with as many reminiscences as the last seven. It would be tedious to list the parallels, as they are available elsewhere,[2] and an example or two should suffice to show how Petronius invites the comparison even in small ways: compare

> praeterea gemino deprensam gurgite plebem
> faenoris inluvies ususque exederat aeris (*BC* 51–2)

with

> hinc usura vorax, avidumque in tempora faenus
>
> (*Phars.* 1.181);

> Orbem iam totum victor Romanus habebat,
> qua mare, qua terrae, qua sidus currit utrumque (*BC* 1–2)

with

> haud multum terrae spatium restabat Eoae,
> ut tibi nox, tibi tota dies, tibi curreret aether,
> omniaque errantes stellae Romana viderent . . .
> te geminum Titan procedere vidit in axem . . .
> quae mare, quae terras, quae totum possidet orbem
>
> (*Phars.* 7.423–5.422; 1.110);

---

[1] See Sochatoff, *art. cit.* and *Arion* 5 (1966), 359 ff.
[2] See Baldwin, pp. 71 ff. and Rose, pp. 276 ff.

fames premit advena classes (*BC* 16)

with

    quas premit aspera classes
    Leucas.   (*Phars.* 1.42–3);

iam Phasidos unda (*BC* 36)

with

    ad Phasidos undas

and

    peteret cum Phasidos undas (*Phars.* 2.585,715);

et quasi non posset tellus tot ferre sepulcra
divisit cineres.   (*BC* 65–6)

with

Europam, miseri, Libyamque Asiamque timete:
distribuit tumulos vestris Fortuna triumphis
                    (*Phars.* 6.816–17)

and in particular

    '. . . vix navita Porthmeus
sufficiet simulacra virum traducere cumba;
classe opus est.   (*BC* 117–19)

with

praeparat innumeras puppes Acherontis adusti
portitor   (*Phars.* 3.16–17)

It is evident that Petronius draws on Lucan for ideas, conceits, phrasing, and even rhythms, quite apart from the larger themes which he adapts from Books 1 and 7. These two books, incidentally, are put under the largest contribution, not because Petronius knew them best, but because they deal with the opening of the Civil War and the *Pharsalia*'s climax, the events leading up to and including the Battle of Pharsalia, particularly Caesar's address to his soldiers. Petronius, working within a smaller compass, offers his challenge to this last set-piece in Caesar's address to his soldiers before he breaks the law and begins the Civil War by going beyond his province.

It is just as easy to see that Petronius is superimposing Vergilian modes on Lucan's material and language. There is, first of all, the reintroduction of the divine machinery from which Lucan had tried to break away, no doubt seeing rightly that this is the least successful part of Vergil's epic, but rejecting the apparently humorous or lightly ironic treatment of the gods that is to be found in Homer and is even more evident in Apollonius Rhodius. This presumably offended the now narrower canons of epic *decorum* that Vergil and even Lucan subscribed to: epic subjects were to be inspiringly noble or tragic. Petronius has a dialogue between Fortune and Dis (67–125); the usual array of signs and omens (124–41, 177–82), a feature which of course he shares with Lucan; the Homeric division of the gods, including personified abstractions such as *Fides*, into two camps; and a horrifying description of Discord and her warmongering speech (271–94). The attempt to make Lucan more like Vergil goes still further than this. There are echoes of Vergilian phrasing, rhythms, and metrical practice.[1] Compare the language of

'rerum humanarum divinarumque potestas' (79)

with

'o pater, o hominum rerumque aeterna potestas'

(*Aen.* 10.18);

extulit in lucem nutritas sanguine fruges (99)

with

nec fuit indignum superis bis sanguine nostro
Emathiam et latos Haemi pinguescere campos

(*Georg.* 1.491–2);

Actiacosque sinus et Apollinis arma timentes (115)

with

Actius haec cernens arcum intendebat Apollo

(*Aen.* 8.704);

---

[1] See Collignon, pp. 165–9.

armorum strepitu caelum furit (134)

with

armorum sonitum toto Germania caelo
audiit   (Georg. 1.474–5);

intentans cum voce manus ad sidera dixit (155)

with

et duplices cum voce manus ad sidera tendit (*Aen.* 10.667);

perque duas scinduntur territa causas (217)

with

scinditur incertum studia in contraria vulgus (*Aen.* 2.39);

and

maerens lacera Concordia palla (253)
ac scisso Discordia crine (271)

with

et scissa gaudens vadit Discordia palla (*Aen.* 8.702).

Such similar phrases as *alpibus aeriis* and *aerias Alpes* (144, *Georg.*
3.474); *hunc nive dura claudit hiems* and *rura gelu tum claudit hiems*
(146–7, *Georg.* 2.317); *Saturnia tellus* (156, *Georg.* 2.173); *nec rupti
turbine venti* and *rupto ceu quondam turbine venti* (197, *Aen.* 2.416);
magnam nixus in hastam and *ingentem nixus in hastam* (203, *Aen.*
12.398); *Fama volat* (211, *Aen.* 3.121); *facibusque armata Megaera* and
flammisque armata Chimaera (256, *Aen.* 6.288); *lurida Mortis imago*
and *plurima mortis imago* (257, *Aen.* 2.369); *Cyllenia proles* (269,
Aen. 4.258); *scabra rubigine dentes* and *scabra robigine pila* (274,
Georg. 1.495) may be cited as possible allusions of a more or less
conscious sort. Sometimes the reminiscences are of effective
Vergilian line endings, such as:

dextrae coniungere dextram (100, *Aen.* 8.164)

or

flamma medullas (106, *Aen.* 4.66)

or

rupta corusco (122, *Aen.* 8.391)

or

miserabile visu! (222, *Aen.* 1.111).

177

This of course is not to deny Lucan's own use of Vergil: even for an innovator in epic Vergil at this time was impossible to shake off as a poetic influence.[1]

Just as striking is the less verbal aspect of Petronius' 'Vergilianization'. Petronius is almost as lavish as Vergil, if not as skilful, in his use and blending of initial, medial, and final alliteration of both vowels and consonants; Lucan's use of this poetic device, generally initial alliteration, is of course noticeable, but one must agree with Heitland's verdict that he 'uses it timidly and seldom well: it generally has a hard and unnatural effect: sometimes none at all, so far as I can see' (*op. cit.*, p. xcix). A few examples of Petronius' use will suffice, although there are few lines in which it is not visible to some extent. These lines are typical:

tres tulerat Fortuna duces, quos obruit omnes	(61)
qui furit effusus, funesto spargitur aestu	(70)
aedificant auro sedesque ad sidera mittunt	(87)
vulneribus confossa cruenta casside velat	(260).

Although naturally his use of this technique is not as subtle as Vergil's,[2] there seems a clear attempt on Petronius' part, taking care rather than pains, to outdo Lucan in this respect. Again, his use of elision is more Vergilian, there being 23 instances per hundred lines, compared to 9 in the rest of his hexameters, 18 in the *Pharsalia*, and 28 in the *Eclogues*. Moreover the position of elisions in the line tends to correspond to the practice of Vergil.[3] Even the much criticized repetition of words at the end of his lines (e.g. *arvum, potestas, os, iaceo, relinquo*, four times each; *orbis, arma*, five times each) are generally words which Vergil uses also as line-endings in the *Aeneid*.[4] Although, like Lucan, Petronius often uses strong penthemimeral and hepthemimeral caesuras, he

[1] For echoes of Vergil in Lucan, see Heitland's list, Haskins pp. cx–cxxvi, and Collignon, pp. 155 ff.

[2] See A. Cordier, *L'allitération latine. Le procédé dans l'"Énéide' de Virgile* (Paris, 1939); G. Michenaud, *LEC* 21 (1953), 343 ff.

[3] See the statistics in E. H. Sturtevant and R. G. Kent, *TAPA* 46 (1915), 148 ff. For a fuller analysis of Petronius' metrical practice, see Stubbe, pp. 95 ff.

[4] Stubbe, p. 92.

is more Vergilian in his use of the pause after the bucolic diaeresis, e.g.

> verticibus lapsis montis iuga, nec vaga passim (132)

or

> 'thesaurosque rapis? nescis tu, Magne, tueri' (292).

This occurs in nearly seven per cent of the lines. His use of spondaic words to begin his lines (30 examples in some 290 lines) is consonant with Vergilian rules (e.g. with proper names or for meaningful effect). His proportion of dactyls to spondees keeps a middle course, although, because of his subject perhaps, there is a slight tendency towards a slower movement.

More details of this sort could be piled up, but one finally finds oneself in agreement with Stubbe and Trampe that Petronius lines up with Silius, Statius, and Valerius Flaccus in turning his back on Lucan's epic innovations and endeavouring to give, without, be it said, fully succeeding, a classical and Vergilian impression. No doubt he would have wished to go further than he did, but of course in a work of the scope of the *Satyricon*, where Petronius is offering a mere sketch of the proper epic and metrical practice (to which incidentally his other hexameters do not fully conform, e.g. in the proportion of elisions), he had no time for the poetic *labor limae* that is partly the secret of Vergil's technical success. No doubt the apology offered by Eumolpus at 118.6 reflects his consciousness of this–and perhaps of greater than merely technical inadequacy.

If the above considerations are accepted, then it is easy enough to dispose of the alternative theories of the poem's intention. The theory of Mössler and Westerburg that the poem is a *parody* of Lucan may be dismissed on the ground that it simply does not parody any of the obvious faults of Lucan, even though some of the great faults in the *Pharsalia* were surely fair game for parody, e.g. the excessive detail of some of the incidents, such as Cato's remarriage of Marcia (2.350–71); such catalogues as the Gallic places and tribes from which Caesar withdrew his army (1.396–465); the hyperbole and conceits that throng the work, with corpses choking the Tiber until the stream of blood flushes it

(2.211–20), or the storm in which all the winds blow at once and the consequent equilibrium alone prevents the sea from being blown away (5.610–53). Petronius also has rhetorical, and sometimes forced, points, but they seem to be too mild for parody and may be in fact his own concessions to Neronian taste.

The theory that he is imitating and defending Lucan against the strictures of contemporary traditionalists is dependent on the assumption that Eumolpus, being himself a disreputable and not very good poet, must be undercutting his own criticisms, and that his words therefore cannot be taken seriously. But as we have seen, Petronius *has* to use disreputable figures even for his serious discussions or comments. And toning down Lucan's faults and making the metre more Vergilian seems an odd way of producing a sympathetic imitation. From the opposite point of view, the theory that he is attacking most contemporary Neronian poets in the preface and the parody, and not, or not specifically, Lucan, is best answered by Collignon (p. 178): '*parodier tout le monde, c'est en réalité ne parodier personne.*'

Kindt's theory that the poem is a partisan defence, perhaps to please Nero, of Julius Caesar against Lucan's Republican bias, is even less convincing. Lucan *is* unfair to Caesar, but hardly so unjust as to invite such a riposte, and Petronius deals just as fairly with the Republican side.

The subtler theory that the primary concern–or at least a main object–of Petronius was an attack on the vices of the age that led to the Civil War, and perhaps also the general literary and moral decadence of the post-war era, requires closer examination. Medieval *florilegia*, for instance, generally took the work as a straight satire on the vices of Rome, although given the medieval tendency to look for moralizing even in unexpected places, too much reliance should not be placed on this insight–consider what happened to Vergil! It is true that about one-fifth of the poem is taken up with an attack on the corruption of the era of the Civil War, and that this proportion far exceeds that of Lucan's similar criticisms; it is true that Petronius is a literary conservative, particularly in poetry, and that this often has conservative moral corollaries; and it is true that elsewhere in the work Petronius delivers himself of attacks, which he may have meant at least half-seriously, on current vices and decadence. Nevertheless, the contention that this is a primary object of the work cannot stand. The poem's intentions are above all literary. Any such epic poem had to present an early discussion of the origins of the immediate action – Homer and Vergil plunge into their respective causes immediately; Statius discusses what is the best cause to begin with; and Silius begins the *Punica* with Vergilian directness. From both a philosophical and a literary standpoint Petronius would wish to have little truck with the Stoic theories advanced by Lucan (*Phars.* 1.70 ff.). He develops instead the more Epicurean idea of Fortune (cf. Epicur. *Ep.* 3.133 and Fgt. 77) and her disillusionment with the Romans, to whom she has been so beneficent (cf. *Phars.* 1.84). She and Dis are introduced as supernatural machinery (67 ff.), but to give some sort of reason for the divine anger against Rome, Petronius develops, quite naturally, the *publica belli semina* of Lucan (*Phars.* 1.158–82), omitting the more immediate causes, the fortunes and characters of the three leaders which Lucan regarded as causal factors to be dealt with before the general conditions that allowed them to set to work. Petronius may or may not have taken his criticisms here seriously – greed, extravagant luxury, the consequent political corruption and economic misery. Perhaps he did as a sophisticated Epicurean, but they were standard explanations of the Civil War, as is evident from Lucan and other sources, and Petronius does not have to be novel in his beliefs or literary practices. What he had to offer however was a human *and* a divine ground of the war and this he does – had he been outlining a *Punica* we would no doubt have had Rome and Carthage and the wrath of Juno again, which is more or less the mixture in Silius, with a cursory bow to Fortune (*Punica* 1.8).

Indeed, as further evidence that Petronius intended a sketch of how Lucan should do it, it may be noticed that he incorporates into his narrative incidents drawn from other literary sources. This was presumably to get away from a rehandling of only Lucan's material, which might indicate a poverty of resources, or leave him open to the charge that he could only treat what Lucan had already tackled. The obvious case of this is Caesar's crossing of the Alps (184-203), which seems based on Livy's description of Hannibal's crossing of the Alps (21.35 ff.).[1]

Finally, one may wonder, as does Collignon (p. 194), why there is no praise of Nero, no opening invocation of the Muses, nor even an apostrophe on the Civil War such as we find in Lucan. Praise of Nero, however, would remove us from the fantasy world in which Encolpius and his friends move, a world realistic enough in its plebeian and sexual detail, but essentially removed from the *haut monde* of Rome. As for the other possibilities, Petronius plunges *in medias res* in accordance with the best classical precept and practice, but he cannot outline the extent of his subject as Vergil and Lucan do, because the *Bellum Civile* is merely a sketch of the opening of an epic, which is hastily, almost arbitrarily, brought to a close with a line which, if it is not spurious, leaves the poem's future continuation possible, at least in the fictional context. In epic invocations of the Muses or Apollo, poets were more or less bound to sketch their selected material: Petronius presumably wanted his poem to be both self-sufficient and apparently part of a longer effort.

v. *How Valid is Petronius' Critique of Lucan?*

The *Bellum Civile* is not as bizarre and obscure as many have found it, particularly those who were trying to read it as a parody of the *Pharsalia*. But it has to be stated that Petronius' vocabulary, although Vergilian, is jejune and imitative, while his verse effects are frequently mechanical, unsubtle, and monotonous. His excessive repetition of words and endings, even though he may not have thought this too unvergilian (despite the unfinished state of the *Aeneid*),[2] is not always effective, although our modern ears may be more sensitive to this aspect of his poetry than were the ancients'.

The strongest criticism, however, has to be levelled at his strategy and talent. The re-introduction of epic divine machinery was more of a mistake than Vergil's quite unhomeric use of it; whatever one thinks of the *Pharsalia* as a whole, one cannot but

---

[1] For the comparison in detail, see Collignon, pp. 173 ff.

[2] See J. Sparrow, *Half-Lines and Repetitions in Virgil* (Oxford, 1931), pp. 55 ff.

applaud Lucan's attempt to break away from this aspect of Vergil's epic and develop some sort of substitute along the lines adumbrated in the sixth book of the *Aeneid*, where the mysterious, the numinous, and the supernatural come more into their own than in the scenes in heaven, as Dante clearly saw. And the fact is that for all Lucan's defects of taste and the bad signs in the *Pharsalia* of the influence of rhetoric, Lucan is more like a real poet, despite ancient and modern criticism, and Petronius is not.

The question is a complicated one. It is not so much a question of divine machinery being inevitably out of place in secondary epic, but rather of the way it contributes to the whole, whether by its conviction or seriousness, as in Dante and Milton, or by its humorousness and contrast, as in Homer and Apollonius of Rhodes. Alexander Pope's remarks are apposite here:

> The *marvellous fable* includes whatever is supernatural, and especially the machines of the Gods. If Homer was not the first who introduced the deities (as Herodotus imagines) into the religion of Greece, he seems the first who brought them into a system of machinery for poetry, and such a one as makes its greatest importance and dignity. For we find those authors who have been offended at the literal notion of the Gods, constantly laying their accusation against Homer as the undoubted inventor of it. But whatever cause there might be to blame his *Machines* in a philosophical or religious view, they are so perfect in the poetic, that mankind have ever since been contented to follow them: none have been able to enlarge the sphere of poetry beyond the limits he has set: every attempt of this nature has proved unsuccessful; and after all the various changes of times and religions, his Gods continue to this day the Gods of poetry.[1]

Vergil's scenes in heaven are not really convincing: he takes the gods more seriously than Homer but, in poetic terms, not seriously enough. This defect was, one imagines, clear to Lucan, and a seriously conceived Stoic supernaturalism was his answer. Petronius' return to Vergilian practice with perhaps the addition of

[1] From the Preface to the *Iliad*, *Complete Poetical Works of Alexander Pope* (Boston, 1903), p. 253.

more abstract deities such as Pietas, Fides, and so on, a growing Silver age tendency, seems a purely conservative reaction; there is no new spirit or deeper treatment than Vergil offered. What symbolic use could be made of the traditional machinery by a near-contemporary is best seen in Statius' unfairly neglected *Thebaid*, where the theme of power and the corruption of power is almost as fully and roundly presented on the divine as on the human plane.[1] Petronius' handling of mythological deities, like Silius' in his *Punica*, is largely inert, even when, as in the scene in Phlegraean Fields (*BC* 67 ff.), he is trying to be impressive and curdle the readers' blood. Epic machinery, largely through Vergil's influence, one suspects, was due for a long history, but in order to keep the Homeric deities viable, fresh poetic ichor had to be poured into the conventional bottles: allegory and symbolism, foreshadowed in Statius, were to play their parts in the Renaissance epic of Tasso and Camoens; other writers such as Ariosto with his lost Christian angels were to revive the humorous or mocking treatment of supernatural figures that was so characteristic of the Homeric poems; and sophisticated literary allusions to the traditional pagan gods could make more interesting poetic effects possible, as Milton was to show in the earlier books of *Paradise Lost* by his glancing parodies of Homer and Vergil.[2] But these criticisms are perhaps superficial. What has to be stated is that secondary epic is a difficult genre and its successes are rarer than it is customary to admit. Even these are sometimes *tours de force* or badly flawed in some respects—one thinks of Milton's God. There is only one truly great epic, the *Iliad*, and its nearest competitor is the *Odyssey*. Callimachus and his Alexandrian and Roman followers displayed a sound insight in their critical theories about the unwisdom of writing epic outside such societies as produced the Homeric poems. Unfortunately achievement inspires imitation, and Vergil made a profound choice for the future of literature when he decided, or was pressed, to start work on the *Aeneid*,

[1] See F. M. Ahl, *Kings, Men and Gods in the Thebaid of Statius*. Univ. of Texas Diss. (Austin, 1966), pp. 102 ff.

[2] I am grateful to my colleague, D. S. Carne-Ross, for several helpful suggestions about the development of post-classical epic.

which was a direct contradiction of his earlier Alexandrian principles and practice. Unfortunately, because Vergil was a great poet, the *Aeneid* was left to posterity as perhaps the most impressive failure in literary history, although English literature has a number of contenders for that title. Thereafter any great talent – or any small one with delusions of adequacy – might be tempted into competition. Accordingly, in Latin literature alone, a long line of unsuccessful, mediocre, or boring epic poets followed: Cornelius Severus, Albinovanus Pedo, Saleius Bassus, Valerius Flaccus, Silius Italicus, Claudian, Sidonius Apollinaris, Cresconius Corippus, and many others. None of them, so far as we know, was able to rejuvenate the tradition, and the fault in the extant authors just cited was mainly their slavish hewing to the established conventions as laid down by Vergil. Vergil had at least made important changes in the tradition, even if in some ways they were not radical enough with regard to the supernatural plane of the epic story. What was needed was a fresh vision and the proper critical perceptions, the sort of vision and perceptions Dante displayed when he saw that the sixth book of the *Aeneid* brought out Vergil's genius at its best and added specifically Latin qualities to the eleventh book of the *Odyssey*: indeed, the tradition of the *Nekuia* achieves its finest culmination in *The Divine Comedy*.

Among the ruck of Latin writers of epic, Lucan and Statius are surely the foremost. Lucan's instincts were good, witness his admiration for Persius, but the sheer imposing *fact* of the epic tradition, and Vergil's *éclat*, were too much for his talent and versatility, particularly when they were abetted by the then current tendencies of Latin verse. But at least he felt disturbed enough by the Vergilian achievement and imagined, not without reason, that some of the dimly perceived faults of Vergil could be avoided by changing the epic structure, by abolishing much of the divine machinery, and searching for a different but equally effective way of imitating, on a larger scale, one of Vergil's greatest poetic triumphs, the presentation of the numinous and the mysterious. Statius showed what could be done with the traditional machinery, if a new and unifying idea took them into service; in his case, the transference of contemporary realities and problems into a mythological setting. Here the human and the divine planes both have symbolic ties and are properly complementary: contemporary life and history are there and not there, as in the *Aeneid*. Lucan had chosen historical epic and saw that the supernatural plane, treated as Vergil had treated it, would produce the lamentable results the modern reader sees in Silius, and he chose a radical solution. Petronius' firm insistence on the reinstatement of the *deorum ministeria* overlooks the general problems of epic machinery for each new literary generation, and the particular problems it gives rise to in historical epic.

vi. *The Troiae Halosis*

The purpose of Eumolpus' poem on the Fall of Troy is rather more difficult to discern, lacking as we do any critical introduction.[1] We cannot assume that its specific purpose is similar to that of the *Bellum Civile*, although, like the latter, it serves to display Petronius' versatility in poetic metres. The context of the poem adds to our difficulties. Encolpius, abandoned by his friends, meets Eumolpus in a picture-gallery. After introducing himself as a poet and lamenting 'what ills the scholar's life assail', he tells the disreputable if amusing anecdote of the Pergamene boy. The story, although presumably to comfort Encolpius for his loss of Giton, contrasts oddly–and deliberately–with the high-flown morality of his opening remarks (83.8–84.3). It is idle to speculate on the exact nature of the painting of the capture of Troy which prompts him to break into verse, as such subjects were common enough in paintings. Dramatically, however, the poem is used to fill out Eumolpus' character not only as a rather hypocritical old lecher, but also as an incontinent versifier. The latter trait is emphasized both by the shower of stones from people strolling in the colonnades, and by Encolpius' own scoldings at 90.1 and 103.3. All this acts as an ironic disclaimer of any great merits in the poem itself, even if we do not take it as a clear hint that it is intended as a parody of Senecan tragedy.

Its dramatic function apart, the *Troiae Halosis* consists of 65

[1] For the theories about its purpose, see Stubbe, p. 24, and add Gaselee, Excursus IV, who states that the poem is a parody of Senecan tragedy in general.

iambic trimeters or *senarii Graecanici*, of the type Seneca used in his tragedies. The poem describes the building of the Wooden Horse; the credulity and excitement of the Trojans when the Greek fleet departs; Laocoön's vain attempt to unmask the threat; the slaying of himself and his two sons by two sea-serpents; and the sack of the city by the warriors hidden in the Horse. In effect, it is a retelling, with different emphases, details, and various omissions, of the first part of Aeneas' narrative in the second book of the *Aeneid* (13–265). There is a considerable number of allusions to Vergil's images and languages: compare, e.g., *ecce alia monstra* . . . (lines 29–52) with *ecce autem gemini* . . . (*Aen.* 2.203 ff.). The resemblance between such phrases as *iam morte pasti* (line 50) and *miseros morsu depascitur artus* (*Aen.* 2.215) or *sepultos Priamidas nocte et mero* (line 56) and *urbem somno vinoque sepultam* (*Aen.* 2.265) seems unmistakable.[1]

Equally unmistakable is Petronius' familiarity with the technique of the Senecan trimeter.[2] He obeys its rules with very few exceptions. Metrical parody, however, is a subtle thing and, although not unknown in Latin literature, may be here safely ruled out. There is, on the other hand, one noticeable feature of Petronius' poem, observable also in the *Bellum Civile*: the high proportion of words which are repeated in one form or another at the ends of lines, sometimes quite close to each other. Examples are: *metus/metu* (1,3 cf. 26, 47); *manus/manum* (21,23 cf. 44); *mare/mare* (29,33 and cf. Tollius' emendation of †*minori* † to *mari* at 31; *mero/mero* (62,56); *iubae/iubas* (38,60); *iubar/iubar* (39,54). These and other lessstriking repetitions are partly due to the poverty of Latin vocabulary or certain metrical needs, and it must be repeated that the Romans were more tolerant of verbal repetitions than we are.[3] Nevertheless the device seems so deliberate that it is probably intentional and points directly to Seneca's tragedies. And indeed an analysis of a typical piece of Senecan *senarii* on a roughly similar

---

[1] For fuller details, see Collignon, pp. 136 ff., and Stubbe's commentary, pp. 40 ff.

[2] See the analysis in Stubbe, pp. 93 ff.

[3] Cf. e.g. A. Poutsma, 'De repetitionis genere quodam' *Mnem.* 4 (1913), 397 ff.

subject confirms this. *Agamemnon* 406–578 consists mainly of Eury-bates' description of the destruction of the fleet of Agamemnon on the way home from Troy; the repetitions there, granted its greater length, are even more obvious. In some form or other, *ratis* occurs eight times; *fretum* seven, *malus* or *malum* six times; and, most strikingly, *mare* twelve times, three occurrences being in 540–6. It would be tedious to offer further examples from either of these pieces.

When we add to this the many echoes of Senecan tragedy to be found in the *Troiae Halosis*, the conclusion is hard to resist that the poem is a general imitation and parody of Seneca's tragic style. The fall of Troy and Vergil's version of the Laocoön story pro-vided subject matter which recalls vaguely such Senecan plays as the *Agamemnon* and the *Troades*; Petronius simply exercises his poetic versatility by imitating Seneca's technique and offering a pastiche of his language. Again, it would serve little purpose to enumerate in detail the echoes and reminiscences, as this has been done by others, notably Gaselee.[1] One may just point to the close resemblance between the passage of the *Agamemnon* cited and the *Troiae Halosis*: compare, e.g., *ecce alia clades* (*Agam.* 528) and *ecce alia monstra* (line 29) or *nitidum cadentis inquinat Phoebi iubar* (*Agam.* 463) and *iam plena Phoebe candidum extulerat iubar* (line 54), as well as the repetitions and the very similar marine descriptions. Seneca's very rhetorical style is not difficult to see in such lines as:

> peritura Troia perdidit primum deos   (53)

or

> ibat iuventus capta, dum Troiam capit   (27)

or

> contraque Troas invocat Troiae sacra   (65).

Seneca's gory melodrama, so popular with the Elizabethan play-wrights, and which is best seen in his elaborate description of the death of Hippolytus in the *Phaedra*, is briefly but, I think, clearly satirized in the detailed vignette of the death of the sons of Laocoön (35 ff.), although Petronius was doubtless unwilling to

---

[1] See Gaselee, Excursus IV.

overload the already lengthy scene in the picture-gallery with too much Senecan effusiveness.

If the above theory is correct, as I believe, then there is little need to linger over the alternative possibilities. It is unlikely that the *Troiae Halosis* is a parody of either Lucan's *Iliacon* (Stat. *Silv.* 2.7), which would be a hexametric redaction of Homeric themes, or of Nero's notorious poem on the same subject, which he is said to have recited during the fire of Rome (Suet. *Ner.* 38). Teuffel's hypothesis about a relationship between Nero's and Eumolpus' poems will not hold because there is no substantial description in Petronius of the firing of Troy, which alone would have made Nero's recital appropriately heartless, and there is an *a priori* unlikelihood that Petronius would seriously satirize Nero's poetic gifts, however frank he may have pretended to be in his criticisms of Nero's way with money.

vii. *Other Allusions and Imitations*

Having seen the slightly different purposes–and, incidentally, Petronius' great technical versatility–in the two main verse insertions in the *Satyricon*, we may turn to the other poems that appear in the work. Some of these need not detain us long. In accordance with the laws of Menippean form Petronius offers us, more or less as he thinks fit, verse comments on the action or general reflections on the theme of the action, written in a fairly standard way. Such would be, for example, 14.2, 137.9 (on the power of money); 79.8, 126.18 (on amorous topics); 128.6 and Fgt. XXX (on dreams). The style is generally undistinguished, a slight prevalence of alliteration and anaphora being their most notable technical characteristics. There seems to be an occasional imitation of Ovid, particularly in the amatory scenes in Croton.[1] Sometimes these are verbal echoes: compare e.g.

> florida tellus
> cum volo, siccatis arescit languida sucis,
> cum volo, fundit opes . . .   (134.12 lines 1–3)

---

[1] See Collignon, p. 260 ff.

with

> cum voluit, toto glomerantur nubila caelo:
> cum voluit, puro fulget in orbe dies   (*Am.* 1.8.9–10);

and

> lunae descendit imago
> carminibus deducta meis, trepidusque furentes
> flectere Phoebus equos revoluto cogitur orbe
>
> (134.12 lines 8–10)

with

> carmina sanguineae deducunt cornua lunae
> et revocant niveos Solis euntis equos   (*Am.* 2.1.23–4).

There is moreover a fairly extended imitation of the same author in the description of Oenothea's home (135.8), which recalls the famous Baucis and Philemon episode in the *Metamorphoses* (8.611 ff.).[1] In the prose description of Encolpius' impotence (128 ff.) it is of course obvious that the Ovidian motif to be found in the *Amores* (3.7) is good-humouredly parodied.[2]

Some reminiscences of Tibullus and Propertius have been traced but these seem more likely to be accidental similarities.[3] The same may be said of such apparent *rapprochements* as *morientia ripis/ morientia ripas* in Manilius' *Astronomicon* 4.627 and *BC* 133. Horace of course was largely drawn upon for the *Cena Trimalchionis* and Petronius' admiration for him is clearly expressed at 118.5. A number of his phrases, ideas, and colourings may be found in the prose: compare e.g.

> quod quisque ⟨puer⟩ perperam di dicit, in senectute confiteri
> non vult (4.4)

with

> turpe putant quae
> imberbes didicere, senes perdenda fateri   (*Ep.* 2.1.84–5),

---

[1] See I. M. Garrido, *CR* 44 (1930), 10.
[2] There is another possible allusion to this poem at 82.5 (cf. *Am.* 3.7.50–3), but the image is such a commonplace that the Ovidian passage is of little help for reconstructing the lost Petronian context.
[3] See Collignon, p. 268.

and there are several natural resemblances between the episode with the legacy hunters 161–17, (124.2–125.4, 140–1) and Horace's satire on the same subject (2.5). But we find no obvious imitation of his poetry.

Two of the poems in the *Satyricon* that present real problems need some brief consideration: the *schedium Lucilianae humilitatis* (5) and the poem attributed to Publilius Syrus by Trimalchio (55.6). In the first it is clear that, whether or not Encolpius has earlier quoted Lucilius, this is Agamemnon's *ad hoc* composition retailing some sound, if not revolutionary, ideas on education. Although we may take the content of the poem as serious enough, the use of verse here merely conforms to the Menippean character of the work; on the other hand, the Lucilian practice of mixing metres, here hexameters and choliambics, is a further display of Petronius' poetic versatility. In this Petronius is following the example of the Roman founder of Menippean satire, Varro, who also produced pastiche of earlier poetry and imitated other writers such as Pacuvius.[1] In this passage we probably have what was meant to be a real imitation of Lucilius. For Agamemnon's description of his poem as a *schedium* recalls Lucilius' use of that word to describe his work when it was simply trifling or unfinished.[2] Petronius is very tolerant of repetitions elsewhere, as we have seen, but it may be that in these lines the inartistic repetitions are meant to give an effect of improvisation, e.g. *mentem, mentis* (lines 2, 7); *plenus* (lines 13, 22); *det, dent* (lines 17, 19); *trucem, truci* (lines 4, 19);. *verba* (lines 20, 22); *sono, sonet* (lines 16, 18); *pectore* (lines 12, 22) The same explanation may hold of the banal phrases (*armigerae . . . Tritonidis*, etc) and the confused metaphors in lines 15 ff., where

[1] See G. Boissier, *Étude sur M. T. Varron* (Paris, 1861), pp. 66 ff., 78 ff. One may compare Persius' prologue for a contemporary use of choliambics as a preface to diatribes in hexameters.

[2] See Festus with Paul Diac. (p. 450, Lindsay); *qui schedium fa⟨cio⟩*, and App. *de deo Socr.: in isto, ut ait Lucilius, schedio ⟨rudi⟩ et incondito.* Petronius' idea of imitation is here of course fairly broad. There is no real evidence that Lucilius ever juxtaposed choliambics and hexameters, although his admirer, Persius, did, and the language of Agamemnon's poem does not strike one as closely resembling the texture of Lucilius as we know him from the extant fragments: his verse principles rather than his practice in any particular work justify the allusion.

admittedly the text is often corrupt, but it is quite likely that this, in Petronius' view, was the mark of Lucilius' style, an impression made more plausible by Horace's criticism of him (*Sat.* 1.4.9–10; 1.10.1–2). A number of the ideas and words may also have been taken from Lucilius.[1]

The other interesting poem, if we exclude the deliberately bad and unmetrical three lines recited by Trimalchio (55.3) and composed *non diu cogitatione distorta*, is the piece on luxury which Trimalchio attributes to Publilius Syrus. This has been taken by some (Ribbeck, Mössler and Wehle) as really his, although the extant mime fragments offer no proof. Almost certainly it is an imitation by Petronius. To begin with, if it were really by Publilius, then Trimalchio's quoting of it would be quite an educated feat for the ignorant freedman, particularly as he has just been making an idiotic comparison between him and Cicero, whereas the author himself would gain credit for no more than a good memory or an extensive library. It is therefore much more likely that Petronius allows him to step out of character in order to introduce another example of his poetic expertise. This stepping out of character, after all, happens in other cases. Encolpius is used as the vehicle of literary criticism and the author's *apologia* (1–2, 132.15) and Eumolpus has his serious moments (118 ff.). The piece has a dramatic motive also: here is an attack on decadent luxury in the middle of a most ostentatious and bizarre dinner party by a host who does not see the disparity between the quotation and his own behaviour, although I suspect that the dramatic justification is subordinate to the less central literary intention. There are other, internal, reasons for believing the piece to be an imitation. The theme is traditional enough: Rome is decaying through luxury. No expense, trouble, or virtue is spared in the pursuit of exotic food and adornment. The style however gives it away. The heavy alliteration of

luxuriae rictu Martis marcent moenia.
tuo palato clausus Pavo pascitur

[1] See Collignon, pp. 233 ff.

In luxury's maw Mars' walls will wilt:
Your palate pens peacocks in plumage of gilt . . .

and archaizing vocabulary (*pietaticultrix, gracilipes, crotalistria*) might be more acceptable, but there are certain signs of a later age and style, e.g. the woven breeze (*ventus textilis*) and such precious turns of phrase as *titulus tepidi temporis*. There are also echoes of Horace, not to mention commonplace ideas used elsewhere in the *Satyricon*.[1]

Petronius then is quite happy to display his imitative facility by using worn and familiar themes. The fictional personages take he discredit for any banality and Petronius the credit for the imitations, although the actual merits of the pieces vary a great deal. As is clear, the list of authors he imitates or uses is fairly long and includes Lucilius, Syrus, Ovid, Horace and Vergil, Lucretius (in Fgt. XXX–although he does not hit off the powerful ruggedness of that author), and Catullus (compare 133 with *Carm.* 19). There were doubtless others in the lost portions of the work. No more than a line or two of the anacreontics, for instance, which Terentianus Maurus tells us cropped up frequently in Petronius (cf. Fgts. XIX and XX), have survived.

viii. *Morality in the Satyricon and Seneca's Prose*

I am not proposing here to discuss whether any larger moral or artistic vision pervades the *Satyricon*. That question may be deferred to the final chapter. My present object is more limited; it is to examine the brief scraps and longer pieces of moralizing, philosophizing, and social reflection that are given various characters throughout the work. Sometimes their function seems purely dramatic, as when Eumolpus puts forward Epicurus' sceptical theory of dreams to discredit the supposedly veridical visions of Lichas and Tryphaena, which had revealed that the runaways were aboard the ship (104.3). Perhaps Petronius held some such theory himself, but his purpose here, surely, is not to voice his

---

[1] For transparent garments, cf. e.g. Hor. *Sat.* 1.2.101; Sen. *Ben.* 7.9.5; for the Horatian and Petronian echoes, cf. Hor. *Sat.* 2.2.22–8, 2.5.49–50; *BC* 33 ff. and 93.2, where a less archaic treatment of the theme is offered by Eumolpus.

own views or enlighten the reader, but to delay the *dénouement* through Eumolpus' ingenuity and heighten the suspense of the narrative. Similarly, Eumolpus' brisk attack on the fickleness and unreliability of women (110.6–8), although ostensibly prompted by Tryphaena's *louche* behaviour, is largely to provide a plausible introduction for the story of the Widow of Ephesus. Again, certain general remarks of Encolpius are suggested by the specific context, witness his complaints at 82.6 that men's schemes often go awry, because Fortune has a way of her own.[1]

Nevertheless it has been assumed by those who take the *Satyricon* as a serious indictment of contemporary Roman civilization that some of these moralizing passages may be used as contributing evidence for their theory.[2] We must therefore examine some of the more important passages of this type in some detail.

At 100.1 Encolpius, realizing that Eumolpus is attracted to Giton, tries to console himself with these words:

'molestum est quod puer hospiti placet. quid autem non commune est quod natura optimum fecit? sol omnibus lucet. luna etiam feras ducit ad pabulum. quid aquis dici formosius potest? in publico tamen manant. solus ergo amor furtum potius quam praemium erit? immo vero nolo habere bona nisi quibus populus inviderit.'

'It's annoying that our new acquaintance likes the boy. But aren't the best things in life free to all? The sun shines on everyone. The moon leads even the beasts to pasture. What can you think of lovelier than water? But it flows for the whole world. Is love alone then to be something furtive rather than something to be gloried in? Exactly, that's just it–I don't want any of the good things of life unless people are envious of them.'

The platitudinous moralizing has not even convinced Encolpius himself and one is tempted to look for further explanation of the passage. And the best explanation that suggests itself is the fre-

---

[1] Other possible examples of this sort are: 18.6, 71.1, 83.4, 84.1–4, 88, 94.1, 99–100.2, 106.3, 107.11, 111.3, 111.6, 112.1, 115.8–18, 140.14–15.

[2] See e.g. W. Arrowsmith, *Arion* 5 (1966), 304 ff.

quently mooted theory of a direct parody of Seneca's moral writings.[1] Here is the relevant passage:

Nisi forte tam iniquum putas esse sapientem ut nihil viritim se debere pro communibus bonis iudicet. Soli lunaeque plurimum debeo, et non uni mihi oriuntur; anno temperantique annum deo privatim obligatus sum, quamvis nihil in meum honorem ⟨annua⟩* discripta sint. Stulta avaritia mortalium possessionem proprietatemque discernit nec quicquam suum credit esse quod publicum est; at ille sapiens nihil magis suum iudicat quam cuius illi cum humano genere consortium est. Nec enim essent ista communia, nisi pars illorum pertinet ad singulos; socium efficit etiam quod ex minima portione commune est. Adice nunc quod magna et vera bona non sic dividuntur ut exiguum in singulos: ad unumquemque tota perveniunt.[2]

(73.6–8)

*annua scripsi exempli gratia: tempora Hense: ista Castiglioni

Unless perhaps you think that the wise man is so unjust as to consider that he as an individual owes nothing for benefits shared by all. I am highly indebted to the sun and the moon, and they do not rise for me alone. I am personally obligated to the year and the deity that keeps it under control, although its annual changes are in no way fixed in my honour. The foolish avarice of mankind distinguishes between possession and

---

[1] On the whole question, see G. Studer, *RhM* 2 (1843), 89 ff.; J. Gottschlich, 'De parodiis Senecae apud Petronium' in *Misc. Philol. lib. zu Frid. Haase Jubiläum* (Breslau, 1863) and the sceptical examination of the thesis in Collignon, pp. 291 ff.; P. Thomas, *L'âge et l'auteur du Satyricon* (Ghent, 1905), pp. 11 ff., 17; Gaselee, pp. 36 ff.; P. Faider, *Études sur Sénèque* (Ghent, 1921), pp. 15 ff.; Paratore I, p. 124 n. 3; H. C. Schnur, *The Age of Petronius Arbiter* (Ann Arbor microfilm, 1957), pp. 123 ff.; Rose, pp. 205 ff. These list most of the parallels, convincing or unconvincing, although the authors vary in their critical evaluation of them. The conclusions that follow are based on a re-examination of the evidence and in particular a close re-reading of the *Epistulae Morales* in L. D. Reynolds' excellent new text, *L. Annaei Senecae ad Lucilium Epistulae Morales* (Oxford, 1965).

[2] Cf. also *Ep.* 88.12: hoc quod tenes, quod tuum dicis, publicum est et quidem generis humani.

ownership and believes that nothing is one's own that is in the public domain. The wise man on the other hand regards nothing as more his than that in which he has a partnership with the human race. For those things would not be common to all, did not a part of them belong to individuals. Even what is to the smallest extent a public holding produces a partner. Add to this now the fact that great and true blessings are not so divided that only a little goes to individuals: each and every one gets the whole of them.

The setting of Encolpius' remarks, which are prompted by his jealousy and followed by some dirty-minded reflections on what would happen if Eumolpus made successful advances to Giton, make the moralizing absurd and the parodic intent clear.

An even more obvious and extended example of such parody is to be found in Encolpius' speech on discovering Lichas' body washed up by the sea. The style is extremely rhetorical and generally reminiscent of the high-pitched tone of much Senecan prose, particularly in the *Letters*. Here is the Petronius passage:

substiti ergo tristis coepique umentibus oculis maris fidem inspicere et 'hunc forsitan' proclamo 'in aliqua parte terrarum secura expectat uxor, forsitan ignarus tempestatis filius, aut pater; utique reliquit aliquem, cui proficiscens osculum dedit. haec sunt consilia mortalium, haec vota. en homo quemadmodum natat.' . . . 'ubi nunc est' inquam 'iracundia tua, ubi impotentia tua? nempe piscibus beluisque expositus es, et qui paulo ante iactabas vires imperii tui, de tam magna nave ne tabulam quidem naufragus habes. ite nunc mortales, et magnis cogitationibus pectora implete. ite cauti, et opes fraude captas per mille annos disponite. nempe hic proxima luce patrimonii sui rationes inspexit, nempe diem etiam, quo venturus esset in patriam, animo suo finxit. dii deaeque, quam longe a destinatione sua iacet. sed non sola mortalibus maria hanc fidem praestant. illum bellantem arma decipiunt, illum diis vota reddentem penatium suorum ruina sepelit. ille vehiculo lapsus properantem spiritum excussit, cibus avidum strangulavit, abstinentem frugalitas. si bene calculum ponas, ubique naufragium est. at enim

fluctibus obruto non contingit sepultura. tamquam intersit,
periturum corpus quae ratio consumat, ignis an fluctus an mora.
quicquid feceris, omnia haec eodem ventura sunt. ferae tamen
corpus lacerabunt. tamquam melius ignis accipiat; immo hanc
poenam gravissimam credimus, ubi servis irascimur. quae ergo
dementia est, omnia facere, ne quid de nobis relinquat sepultura?'

(115.8-10, 12-19)

I stopped sadly and began gazing at this example of the sea's
treachery with moist eyes. 'Perhaps somewhere,' I cried out, 'a
carefree wife waits for him, perhaps a son, not knowing about
the storm, or a father. At the very least he left someone he kissed
when he set out. So much for mortal schemes and mortal
desires. Look at him now–how the man floats!' . . . 'Where
now,' I said, 'are your bad tempers and your ungovernable
rages? You have been at the mercy of fishes and other horrible
creatures. A brief while ago you boasted of your power and
your position, but you haven't even a plank left from the wreck
of your great ship. Go now, mortals, and fill your hearts with
great schemes. Go and carefully invest your ill-gotten gains for
a thousand years. Yesterday he must have looked at the accounts
of his investments, he must have fixed the day he would reach
his home town. O heavens, how far away he lies from his
destination! Yet it is not only the seas that serve mortals like
this. Weapons play a man false in wartime; the collapse of his
family shrine buries a man giving thanks to heaven; a man falls
from his carriage and hastily gasps his last. Food chokes the
gluttonous, abstinence the abstemious. If you reckon it up right,
there is shipwreck everywhere. Mind you, a man drowned at
sea does not get buried–as though it matters what destroys a
corpse that is doomed to perish anyway–water, fire, or time!
Whatever you do, it all comes to the same thing. But of course,
wild beasts will mangle the carcass. As though it were better
that fire should have it–and yet we consider this the severest
possible punishment when we are angry with our slaves. So
what is the point of this craze to make sure that no part of us
escapes burial?'

So many Senecan passages can be cited to parallel the various ideas in this speech and there are so many verbal and stylistic similarities between it and parts of the Senecan corpus that it reads like a free pastiche of the philosopher: it reads as parody because of the out-burst–Lichas was no friend of Encolpius'–and because of what we know of the speaker's character. The elaboration of the set-piece makes it less likely that it was the humorous use of stock moral commonplaces: only a specific literary target would merit such careful treatment for the audience Petronius had in mind, and, as we shall see, this view provides a more plausible motive than the desire to aim at stock butts. A comparison of the putative sources reveals how the Senecan *topoi* are carefully woven together by Petronius, and although it would be tedious to belabour the point, the most obvious resemblances ought to be adduced both to prove the general theory, which is, I think, important and which has been sometimes disputed (by Collignon, for instance), and to shed further light on Petronius' method of composition.

The theme of the sea's uncertainty seems based on such phrases of Seneca's as:

> fortunam maris ... incertam fidem ruris, incertiorem fori ...
>
> (QN 4 praef. 8)

or remarks of this sort:

> pendemus et fluctuamur ... et aliquando naufragium facimus. In hoc tam procelloso et ad omnes tempestates exposito mari navigantibus nullus portus nisi mortis est.
>
> (Cons. Polyb. 9.6–7)

> We hang suspended and go with the waves ... and one day we shipwreck. In this stormy sea that is exposed to every blast, there is no haven for its sailors save death.

The folly of making money and long-range plans is criticized in such passages as:

> ille qui et mari et terra pecuniam agitavit, qui ad publica quoque nullum relinquens inexpertum genus quaestus accesserat, in ipso

actu bene cedentium rerum, in ipso procurrentis pecuniae impetu raptus est . . . quam stultum est aetatem disponere ne crastini quidem dominum! o quanta dementia est spes longas inchoantium . . . navigationes longas et pererratis litoribus alienis seros in patriam reditus proponimus . . . cum interim ad latus mors est . . .

(*Ep.* 101.4,6);

The man who chased money over land and sea, who had gone into tax-farming also, leaving no way of acquiring wealth untried, at the very climax of success, in the very onslaught on increasing profits, was snatched away . . . What folly it is to organize for an age, when a man is not even master of tomorrow! What madness they show who conceive distant hopes . . . We propose long voyages and deferred arrivals home from touring foreign shores . . . when meanwhile death is at our side . . .;

hoc quod vivimus proximum nihil est; et tamen, o dementiam nostram, late disponitur

(*Ep.* 99.31);

The fact that we are alive next day counts for nothing; and yet, such is our madness, our plans range far and wide;

and

interim dum rapiuntur [sc. homines] et rapiunt, dum alter alterius quietem rumpit, dum mutuo miseri sunt . . . nemo in conspicuo mortem habet, nemo non procul spes intendit. quidam vero disponunt etiam illa quae ultra vitam sunt . . .

(*Brev. Vit.* 20.5)

Meantime while men are victims and aggressors, while one man disturbs another's peace, while they are reciprocally unhappy . . . no one keeps death before his eyes, no one hesitates to build high hopes. Indeed some people make arrangements even for things beyond their lifetime.

The point Encolpius makes about the myriad possibilities of

sudden death from seemingly harmless causes is also made by
Seneca, as witness:

> Quid est homo? quodlibet quassum vas et quolibet fragile
> iactatu. non tempestate magna, ut dissiperis, opus est. ubicum-
> que arietaveris, solveris. quid est homo? imbecillum corpus et
> fragile, nudum, suapte natura inerme, alienae opis indigens, ad
> omnis fortunae contumelias proiectum, cum bene lacertos exer-
> cuit, cuiuslibet ferae pabulum, cuiuslibet victima, ex infirmis
> fluidisque contextum et lineamentis exterioribus nitidum,
> frigoris, aestus, laboris impatiens, ipso rursus situ et otio iturum
> in tabem, alimenta metuens sua, quorum modum ⟨in copia
> excedens vel⟩ in inopia rumpitur, anxiae sollicitaeque tutelae,
> precarii spiritus et male haerentis . . . soli semper sibi nutri-
> mentum vitiosum et inutile. miramur in hoc mortem, quae
> unius singultus opus est? numquid enim ut concidat, magni res
> molimenti est? odor illi saporque et lassitudo et vigilia et humor
> et cibus et sine quibus vivere non potest, mortifera sunt. quo-
> cumque se movit statim infirmitatis suae conscium, non omne
> caelum ferens, aquarum novitatibus flatuque non familiaris
> aurae et tenuissimis causis atque offensionibus morbidum, putre,
> causarium . . . cum interim quantos tumultus hoc tam contemp-
> tum animal movet? in quantas cogitationes oblitum condicionis
> suae venit? immortalia, aeterna volutat animo et in nepotes
> pronepotesque disponit, cum interim longa conantem eum mors
> opprimit . . .
>
> (Cons. Marc. 11.3–5);

What is man? A sort of cracked jar that could be broken by a
push. No great storm is needed for you to crack up. Wherever
you are rammed, you come apart. What is man? A weak and
frail body, naked, and of his own nature weaponless, needing
outside help, exposed to every insult of fortune; when he has
trained his muscles, a meal for any animal, anybody's victim;
put together of weak and watery materials and, if sleek as far
as his outside features go, unable to bear cold, heat, or work,
prone to go to seed through inactivity and rest; afraid of his
food, by which he is ruined if he goes beyond the limit of excess

or deficiency; requiring an anxious and troubled watchfulness and relying on a precarious and untenacious breath ... He alone constantly ingests bad and useless nourishment. With this are we surprised at death, when only one sigh is needed? Is it a matter of any great effort to drop dead? Smell, taste, tiredness, wakefulness, liquid, food, and the things he cannot live without, are deadly to him. Wherever he goes, he is immediately conscious of his weakness, unable to stand every weather, his delicate and poor health ruined by the unfamiliarity of the water, the blast of a strange wind, and the most insignificant circumstances and shocks ... and meanwhile how big is the rumpus this contemptible creature kicks up? What great thoughts does he entertain in obliviousness of his condition? He is turning over matters of immortal and eternal moment in his mind and is arranging things for his grandsons and great-grandsons, when meanwhile death comes upon him in the middle of his far-ranging endeavours.

Perhaps more significantly, there is a similar passage in the *Letters*:

omnis eadem condicio devinxit: cui nasci contigit mori restat. intervallis distinguimur, exitu aequamur. hoc quod inter primum diem et ultimum iacet varium incertumque est: si molestias aestimes, etiam puero longum, si velocitatem, etiam seni angustum. nihil non lubricum et fallax et omni tempestate mobilius; iactantur cuncta et in contrarium transeunt iubente fortuna, et in tanta volutatione rerum humanarum nihil cuiquam nisi mors certum est ...

(*Ep.* 99.8–9)

All are bound by the same condition: he who chances to be born has death waiting. We differ in the time intervening, but we are all the same in our departure. What lies between our first and last day is various and uncertain; if you count the troubles, it is too long for even a child; if you count the speed, it is too short for even an old man. There is nothing that is not slippery, deceptive, and more fickle than any tempest; everything is thrown this way and that and moves into its opposite at the behest of fortune; in all this flux of human affairs there is nothing certain for anyone except death . . .

Of course Seneca's attitude to these facts is different from Encolpius', who accepts them apparently as part of life, criticizes men's folly in overlooking them, but finds no comfort or redeeming feature or rational plan in them, as a Stoic might and as Seneca does in this passage:

> omnia quae ad mortem ducunt contempta sunt, sive illa bella sunt seu naufragia seu morsus ferarum seu ruinarum subito lapsu procidentium pondera. numquid amplius facere possunt quam ut corpus ab animo resolvatur?

(QN 2.59.3-4)

Every road to death is to be regarded with contempt, whether it be war, shipwreck, the bite of a wild beast, or the weight of a building that suddenly collapses. What more can these do but separate the body from the soul?

The most striking resemblances, however, to Encolpius' soliloquy may be found in his various discussions of the unimportance of the way a man is buried. Encolpius' thoughts on this are hardly to be taken too seriously in the fictional context, as the three do in fact bury Lichas properly before moving on to Croton. Of the several Senecan passages that might be quoted the following are the most convincing:

> ille divinus animus egressurus hominem, quo receptaculum suum conferatur, ignis illud exurat an terra contegat an ferae distrahant, non . . . ad se iudicat pertinere . . . utrum proiectum aves differant an consumatur 'canibus data praeda marinis', quid ad illum qui nullus ⟨est⟩? . . . neminem de supremo officio rogo, nulli reliquias meas commendo. ne quis insepultus esset rerum natura prospexit: quem saevitia proiecerit dies condet.

(Ep. 92.34-5)

That divine soul, when it is about to leave a man, does not consider it matters to it where its integument is bestowed, whether fire burns it or earth covers it or wild beasts mangle it . . . Whether it is abandoned and birds scatter it or whether it is consumed 'prey to the dogs of the sea', what boots it to someone who no longer exists? . . . I charge no one with my last rites, I entrust my remains to no one. Nature has ensured that no man remains unburied: if barbarity exposes him, time will hide him.

Again:

'Insepultus iacebis.' Quid interest ignis me an fera consumat an tempus, ultima omnium sepultura? . . . 'Non sepelieris.' Quid in re tutissima trepidas? ultra poenarum omnium terminum iste locus est . . . alios terra obruit, alios flamma consumpsit, alios lapis ad ossa redacturus inclusit . . . 'Insepultus abiciar.' alitibus invides an feris an piscibus?

(Rem. Fort. 5.2,4,5)

'You will lie there unburied.' What does it matter whether fire consumes me, a wild beast, or time, the final grave of all? . . . 'You will not be buried.' What are you frightened of where the safest thing in the world is concerned? That place you speak of lies beyond the limit of any punishment . . . some have been weighted down by earth, some have been consumed by fire, others have been enclosed in stone that will reduce them to bones . . . 'I shall be flung out unburied?' Is it the birds or the beasts or the fishes that you begrudge?

And finally:

[sc. Fortuna] alios per incerta nudos maria iactabit et luctatos cum fluctibus ne in arenam quidem aut litus explodet, sed in alicuius immensae ventrem beluae decondet.

(Cons. Marc. 10.6)

[Fortune] will toss some naked through uncertain seas and, after their struggle with the waves, will not even throw them out on the sand or the shore, but she will hide them in the belly of some vast monster.[1]

[1] Cf. also Ben. 5.20.4.

These resemblances, which I find difficult to ascribe to co-incidence, may be supported by a comparison of the style of the Petronian passage with Seneca's style in his more elevated and high-pitched apostrophes to the recipients of his works. To take but one example, Encolpius' rhetorical formulas *ite nunc mortales et . . .* and *ite cauti et* (115.14) are reminiscent of similar phrases in Seneca, *i nunc et, eat aliquis et,* and so on.[1]

Now if there is parody in *these* Petronian passages, where little is at stake except the reader's amusement, then we may turn with this possibility in mind to those more general moralizing passages which have been claimed as reflecting, to some extent at least, Petronius' own serious criticism of the age's decadence. The most important case is the elaborate attack on modern corruption in the arts put into the mouth of the disreputable Eumolpus:

'pecuniae' inquit 'cupiditas haec tropica instituit. priscis enim temporibus, cum adhuc nuda virtus placeret, vigebant artes ingenuae summumque certamen inter homines erat, ne quid profuturum saeculis diu lateret. itaque herbarum omnium sucos Democritus expressit, et ne lapidum virgultorumque vis lateret, aetatem inter experimenta consumpsit. Eudoxus in cacumine excelsissimi montis consenuit, ut astrorum caelique motus de-prehenderet, et Chrysippus, ut ad inventionem sufficeret, ter elleboro animum detersit. verum ut ad plastas convertar, Lysippum statuae unius lineamentis inhaerentem inopia ex-tinxit, et Myron, qui paene animas hominum ferarumque aere comprehendit, non invenit heredem. at nos vino scortisque demersi ne paratas quidem artes audemus cognoscere, sed ac-cusatores antiquitatis vitia tantum docemus et discimus. ubi est dialectica? ubi astronomia? ubi sapientiae occultissima (?) via? quis umquam venit in templum et votum fecit, si ad eloquentiam pervenisset? quis, si philosophiae fontem attigisset? ac ne bonam quidem mentem aut bonam valetudinem petunt, sed statim antequam limen tangant, alius donum promittit, si propinquum divitem extulerit, alius, si thesaurum effoderit, alius, si ad tre-

---

[1] *i nunc et* is found in *Brev. Vit.* 12.8; *QN* 1.16.3; *Ep.* 88.37; *eat (nunc) aliquis et* in *Cons. Polyb.* 1.2; *Ben.* 6.35.5.

centies sestertium salvus pervenerit. ipse senatus, recti bonique praeceptor, mille pondo auri Capitolio promittere solet, et ne quis dubitet pecuniam concupiscere, Iovem quoque peculio exorat. noli ergo mirari, si pictura defecit, cum omnibus diis hominibusque formosior videatur massa auri quam quicquid Apelles Phidiasque, Graeculi delirantes, fecerunt.'

(88)

'Financial greed,' he replied, 'has caused this revolution. In former days when mere merit was still sufficient, the liberal arts flourished and there was great competition to bring to light anything of benefit to posterity. Democritus, for instance, distilled all forms of vegetable life and spent his days in scientific experiments to discover the properties of minerals and plants. Eudoxus grew old on the top of one of the highest mountains to further his knowledge of astronomy, and Chrysippus purged his brain three times with hellebore to allow himself to continue his investigations.

'To turn to the plastic arts, Lysippus was so preoccupied with the lines of one statue that he died of starvation, and Myron, who almost captured the souls of men and animals in his bronzes, left no heir. But we, besotted with drink and whoring, daren't study even arts with a tradition. Attacking the past instead, we acquire and pass on only vices. What has happened to dialectic? Astronomy? Or the hidden (?) road of wisdom? Who has ever gone into a temple and prayed to become eloquent—to approach the fountain head of philosophy? People do not even ask for a sound mind or body, but before they touch the threshold one man immediately promises an offering if he can arrange the funeral of a rich relation, another if he can dig up some treasure, another if he can come into a safe thirty million. Even the senate, the standard of rectitude and goodness, habitually promises the Capitol a thousand pounds of gold, and to remove anyone's doubts about financial greed, tries to influence even Jove with money. So don't be surprised that painting is on the decline, when a lump of gold seems more beautiful to everybody, gods and men, than anything those crazy little Greeks, Apelles and Phidias, ever made.

Now as it happens there is an obvious parallel to this in a passage in the *Letters to Lucilius*:

Haec ipsa res quae tot magistratus, tot iudices detinet, quae et magistratus et iudices facit, pecunia, ex quo in honore esse coepit, verus rerum honor cecidit, mercatoresque et venales in vicem facti quaerimus non quale sit quidque sed quanti; ad mercedem pii sumus, ad mercedem impii, et honesta quamdiu aliqua illis spes inest sequimur, in contrarium transituri si plus scelera promittent. Admirationem nobis parentes auri argentique fecerunt, et teneris infusa cupiditas altius sedit crevitque nobiscum. Deinde totus populus in alia discors in hoc convenit: hoc suspiciunt, hoc suis optant, hoc dis velut rerum humanarum maximum, cum grati videri volunt, consecrant. Denique eo mores redacti sunt ut paupertas maledicto probroque sit, contempta divitibus, invisa pauperibus. Accedunt deinde carmina poetarum, quae adfectibus nostris facem subdant, quibus divitiae velut unicum vitae decus ornamentumque laudantur. Nihil illis melius nec dare videntur di immortales posse nec habere.

(Ep. 115.10–12)

Ever since this very thing, money, that has all those officials and judges in its grip, that in fact creates officials and judges, began to command respect, true respect has vanished. Selling and sold by turns, we ask not *what* anything is, but how much. We are respectable for a price: we are disreputable for a price. We are honest as long as we hope there is something in it for us, but we are ready to change sides if crime offers more. Our parents instil in us a high opinion of gold and silver and the greed, implanted in our tender years, takes deep root and grows up with us. Then the whole population, despite its different views on other matters, is of one mind on this: this they look up to, this they yearn for for their families, this they consecrate to the gods, when they wish to appear grateful, as though it were the greatest of human advantages. Finally our morals have been so degraded that poverty is a curse and a reproach, despised by the rich and hated by the poor. And then there is the case of poetry, which puts a torch to our passions: in our poems riches are praised as the sole glory and adornment of life. There is nothing that the immortal gods seem able to bestow or possess better than these.

For the lists Eumolpus offers to prove the degeneracy of modern times, there is a parallel in an earlier work of Seneca's, the *Naturales Quaestiones*: the same point is at issue, but Petronius, to suit the fictional setting in the art-gallery, has concentrated more on the high-mindedness of painters and sculptors than of philosophers, as Seneca does. Here is the Senecan passage in abbreviated form:

adhuc in processu vitia sunt: invenit luxuria aliquid novi in quod insaniat; invenit impudicitia novam contumeliam sibi; invenit deliciarum dissolutio et tabes aliquid adhuc tenerius molliusque quo pereat . . . adhuc quicquid est boni moris, exstinguimus laevitate et politura corporum . . . miraris si nondum sapientia omne opus suum implevit? nondum tota se nequitia protulit. adhuc nascitur et huic omnes operam damus: huic oculi nostri, huic manus serviunt: ad sapientiam quis accedit? quis dignam iudicat, nisi quam in transitu noverit? quis philosophiam aut ullum liberale respicit studium . . .? Itaque tot familiae philosophorum sine successore deficiunt: Academici et veteres et minores nullum antistitem reliquerunt. quis est qui tradat praecepta Pyrrhonis? Pythagorica illa invidiosa turbae schola praeceptorem non invenit. Sextiorum nova et Romani roboris secta inter initia sua, cum magno impetu coepisset, exstincta est. At quanta cura laboratur ne cuius pantomimi nomen intercidat! . . . mares inter se uxoresque contendunt, uter det latus illis . . . philosophiae nulla cura est. Itaque adeo nihil invenitur ex his quae parum investigata antiqui reliquerunt, ut multa quae inventa erant, oblitterentur . . .

(QN 7.31.1 ff.)

Our vices still continue their progress. Luxury finds some novelty to go crazy over; loose living finds itself some new outrage; the dissoluteness and degeneracy of our soft socialites finds something even more delicate and decadent with which to destroy itself . . . whatever good moral fibre remains, we wipe out by making our bodies smooth and gleaming . . . Are you surprised that scientific knowledge has not yet completed all of its work? Wickedness has not yet entirely dominated the scene. It is still emerging from the womb and we are all devoting our attention to this: our eyes and our hands are at *its* disposal. Who goes in for scientific knowledge? Who considers it worthy of attention, except for a passing acquaintance? Who respects philosophy or any of the liberal arts . . .? As a result many philosophical schools founder without a successor: the Old and the New Academies left not a single arch-priest behind. Who is there who expounds the teachings of Pyrrho? The great Pythagorean school that shunned the mass of mankind has not found a professor. The recent philosophical movement started by the followers of Quintus Sextius, a sect that has a character-istically Roman toughness, lost its fire at its very beginning, although it started off with great *élan*. But what pains people take to ensure that the names of ballet dancers are not forgotten! Males fight with their wives to see which shall grant them their sexual favours . . . for philosophy there is no concern. Indeed so far from any further discovery being made in the areas which the ancients left inadequately investigated that many past dis-coveries are being obliterated . . .

If we take all this as a commonplace, or perhaps a view to which both Seneca and Petronius independently subscribe, our credulity is likely to be strained by the resemblance between

'dii deaeque, quam male est extra legem viventibus: quicquid meruerunt, semper expectant.'

(125.4)

'Heavens above, how awful it is to live outside the law–one is always expecting what one rightly deserves.'

and Seneca's remarks, again in the *Letters*, on the same subject:

Securitatis magna portio est nihil inique facere: confusam vitam et perturbatam inpotentes agunt; tantum metuunt quantum nocent, nec ullo tempore vacant. Trepidant enim cum fecerunt, haerent; conscientia aliud agere non patitur ac subinde respondere ad se cogit. *Dat poenas quisquis expectat; quisquis autem meruit expectat.* Tutum aliqua res in mala conscientia praestat, nulla securum; putat enim se, etiam si non deprehenditur, posse deprendi, et inter somnos movetur et, quotiens alicuius scelus loquitur, de suo cogitat; non satis illi oblitteratum videtur, non satis tectum. Nocens habuit aliquando latendi fortunam, numquam fiduciam.

(*Ep.* 105.7–8)

A large element in inner tranquillity is doing nothing wrong. Those who cannot control themselves lead a confused and chaotic existence. They are as frightened as they are guilty, and they are at no time free from this. They tremble when the act has been committed; they hesitate. Their conscience does not allow them to do anything else, and then it forces them to render their accounts. *Whoever is waiting for punishment is suffering it, yet whoever has deserved it, is waiting for it.* Some things offer security despite a bad conscience, but nothing offers tranquillity. For a man thinks he *can* be caught, even if he is not caught; he sleeps uneasily and whenever he speaks of someone's crime, he is thinking of his own; it does not seem to him sufficiently blotted out or sufficiently protected. A guilty man has sometimes had the good fortune, but never the confidence, of getting away with it.

And the examples could be multiplied.[1]

---

[1] Some of the Senecan references relating to Trimalchio have been given in another chapter (pp. 129 ff.) and many of the other relevant citations will be found in the works mentioned on p. 195, n. 1, above, although the most complete list of parallels between the *Apocolocyntosis* and the *Satyricon* is in G. Bagnani, *Arbiter of Elegance* (Toronto, 1954), pp. 80 ff. For our present purposes, the following deserve enumeration: of the passages discussed in this section, for *Sat.* 115.8 ff. cf. also *Ep.* 4.7–8; 5.8–9; 49.11; 63.15; 66.42 ff.; 91.4; 102.27; 107.6–7; for *Sat.* 125.4, cf. also *Ep.* 97.14; for *Sat.* 100.1, cf. also the stylistic similarity of *Ep.* 36.11; 44.2–3. There seems a general connection between the *Cena* and *Ep.* 94.70 ff., and 95.23 ff., and between *Ep.* 114 and *Sat.* 1–5 as well as the *Cena*

In the light of the above evidence the conclusion seems hard to resist that the overtly moralizing passages in the *Satyricon*, suspect as they might be anyway in their humorous setting and with their disreputable fictional provenance, are there for literary rather than didactic purposes. It has of course been tempting for modern critics, influenced by the moral strenuousness associated with the tradition of Matthew Arnold, to hope that these reflected, however ironically, Petronius' own inner convictions; that they represented his hidden repugnance to the luxury, affluence, and corruption of the Neronian age. Their oddness in coming from an author who was arbiter of elegance at court and willing to spend a small fortune on a perfumed wine dipper, merely added piquancy to an already intriguing character. But although we cannot say that Petronius did *not* hold these views, we cannot infer that he did from the *Satyricon*. One might add also that the banality of the moral reflections contrasts greatly with the pointed, if debatable, insights of the literary criticism; whereas the whole style of the *Satyricon* is an implicit substantiation of the latter, the moralizing is utterly at odds with the general ambience and intermittent 'obscenity' of the work, which have to be defended, as we have seen, on grounds of realism and the portrayal of everyday behaviour (132.15).[1]

We have already examined in the discussion of the *Cena* (pp. 129 ff. above) how Seneca's *Letters* were put under contribution for individual traits in Trimalchio's character, or even incidents in the dinner. Not all of the use made of Seneca's writing is tendentious in the obvious sense, unless we regard the imaginative handling of Senecan material, or themes common to both authors,

again. For more detailed resemblances compare *Sat.* 11.4 ('*sic dividere cum fratre nolito*') with *Ep.* 88.11 (. . . *sic nescio cum fratre dividere*); *Sat.* 26.9, e.g., with *Ep.* 1.1 ff.; *Sat.* 55.5 with *Ep.* 8.8; *Sat.* 56.7 (*philosophos de negotio deiciebat*) with *Ep.* 88.44 (*omnia negotia de negotio deiecit*); *Sat.* 76.3 with *Ep.* 115.17; *Sat.* 84.4 with *Ep.* 17.5; *Sat.* 116.7–9 with *Ep.* 95.43; *Sat.* 117.12–13 with *Ep.* 91.19; *Sat.* 140.14 with *Ep.* 7.1–2, 6, 10–12; 29.10; *Sat.* 140.15 with *Ep.* 8.3.

[1] Note incidentally the mocking glance in this passage at the Stoic saint, Cato—*constricta . . . fronte Catones*—which contrasts so strongly with Seneca's admiration for his puritanical conscience (*Ep.* 97.8) and his panegyric on his other virtues (*Ep.* 71.8).

for more purely artistic—and therefore Epicurean—purposes as an implicit criticism of their deployment in the service of Stoic morality. But even in the *Cena*, as well as in the set-pieces given Eumolpus and Encolpius, there is recognizable parody of Seneca. For instance, the philosophical banalities emanating from Trimalchio are clearly part of the satiric portrait: his remarks on the variability of human affairs (55.3) and the power of Fortune, put in the form of a trite epigram, both show up his ignorant pretensions and remind the reader of the familiar passage in Horace's *Cena Nasidieni* (*Sat.* 2. 8.61), but the Stoic remarks on the common humanity of slaves, which offer clear allusions to Seneca's *Letter* 47, and the absurdity of what follows (71.1 ff.), prove that a subsidiary aim of mocking Stoic philosophy is not incompatible with the primary artistic intention.

The *Satyricon* then is much more topical in its references and aims than the controversy about its date would have led us to suppose. The period during which Petronius was writing his very literary and offhandedly critical, if comic, serial for recitation to the sophisticated Neronian circle coincides, however closely we date it,[1] with the last period of Seneca's still fertile writing career. On the evidence of the *Satyricon* and other contemporary literary documents, it would appear that Nero's court circle, like most coteries, was not without its literary—and political—undercurrents and conflicts, some of them, as Petronius learnt to his cost, mortal. The early predominance of Seneca as Nero's political and literary mentor had waned by the time the surviving parts of the *Satyricon* were written. No doubt other political and literary stars had risen, and among the latter was presumably Petronius.

The question of Seneca's merits as a writer is by no means a straightforward one. To a rather conservative literary critic such as Quintilian there was much in him to criticize. Petronius may have had similar feelings about the strained and rhetorical prose, if our estimate of his literary principles is correct. But it is doubtful whether there could have been anything but a natural antipathy between the insouciant courtier, whose functions were aesthetic

[1] See K. F. C. Rose, 'The Petronian Inquisition: An Auto-da-fé', *Arion* 5 (1966), 289.

and social, and the earnest counsellor, rapidly losing his influence and doomed to lose even more. Certainly the continuous moral posturings of the *oeuvre*, and the presumably genuine Stoic attitude to life and literature, would be antipathetic to Petronius' Epicureanism, which, from Tacitus' account, was the philosophically cruder if more elegant Roman version of the Master's hedonism.[1] With the decline in Seneca's authority, his works, whether dramatic or philosophical, would offer an obvious target for the parodist. Nor is it irrelevant that Seneca's nephew Lucan, also a Stoic, is even more clearly an object of Petronian criticism. Any more practical motivation for these attacks would not of course affect our estimate of the skill and success with which the parodic and critical elements are woven into the work, and speculation as to the temporal or psychological priority of these motives is sure to be inconclusive. Petronius and his friends may have been interested in gaining or preserving influence with Nero, and Petronius' literary sniping at Seneca may have been part of the campaign. Possibly the Stoic faction at court had been rapidly losing ground for different reasons – Seneca because he was irksome, Lucan because he was too good a poet, or too Republican, in his enthusiasms – and Petronius, in his attacks on each, may have been indulging in the subtle flattery of Nero that Plutarch attributes to him. We cannot know. But despite the machinations of Tigellinus, whose methods were less nice than those one might impute to Petronius, there is little reason to suspect that Petronius belonged to the 'opposition' circles. His Epicurean philosophy would be alien to the ideals of the Pisonian – or indeed of any – conspiracy. On the basis of our ancient testimony one could venture to say that until the very end Petronius flourished in the Neronian ethos. He would have had his philosophical, literary, and perhaps personal antipathies, and like most Roman Epicureans from Lucullus onwards, he seems to have neglected the real spirit of the Master's

---

[1] Seneca's description of this sort of Epicurean, no doubt the type familiar to him in contemporary society, fits Tacitus' account: *Epicureum, laudantem statum quietae civitatis et inter convivia cantusque vitam exigentis* (*Ep.* 88.5). There is a more elaborate and hostile description of this Epicurean wine-women-and-song attitude in *Ep.* 123.10–11.

cautious principles, and his negligence ultimately proved his un-
doing. But although the artist is as mortal as the moralist, the
Epicurean was better fitted for Neronian society than the Stoic.

If there was such a feud as I have described, the fight may not
have been entirely one-sided. Perhaps it is not too fanciful, though
hardly provable, to see in Seneca's later *Letters to Lucilius* a veiled
animus against the attitudes and habits that Petronius is credited
with in the Tacitean portrait.[1] No names or unmistakable references are given, but the *Letters* were, after all, intended for publication, and it seems to have been a convention in Imperial literature,
no doubt for good reasons, that hostile allusions be anonymous.
Petronius does not mention Lucan, and Persius' strictures are as
general as Juvenal's. In fact, considering how free Seneca is with
local colour in some of the letters, one finds him extraordinarily
reticent about the court life, which he must have known so well
and which would have furnished him with a wealth of anecdotes,
examples, and warnings for the edification of Lucilius and his
other readers, had he wished–or dared–to use them. But even
Stoic philosophers are not free, should they decide to publish.
Despite Nero's reported tolerance of the more casual sort of
criticism, Seneca no doubt saw the danger of using the court as
quarry for his moral lessons and of recording for posterity, in
hopefully permanent form, the sort of things that went on around
Nero. He had no wish to publish *and* perish.

---

[1] See especially the attack on the night-owls, the *turba lucifugarum*, in *Ep.* 122,
which is discussed in more detail below (pp. 251 ff.). *Ep.* 123 and 124 also adopt
a hostile tone towards Epicureanism; this is very different from the frequent,
and sympathetic, use of Epicurus' teachings in the first three books of the *Letters*:
cf. e.g. *Ep.* 4.10, 7.11, 11.8–9, 12.10–11, 13.14, 14.17, 15.9, 17.11.

CHAPTER VI

The Humour of Petronius

i. *Some General Considerations*

Nothing is more boring than writing about what is comic, and so one approaches the subject of Petronius' humour with a heavy heart, though it is almost the first characteristic of the *Satyricon* that the reader notices. L. Dugas' sound remarks come to mind:

> Il n'est pas de fait plus étudié que le rire; il n'en est pas qui ait eu le don d'exciter davantage la curiosité du vulgaire et celle des philosophes; il n'en est pas sur lequel on ait recueilli plus d'observations et bâti plus de théories, et avec cela il n'en est pas qui demeure plus inexpliqué. On serait tenté de dire avec les sceptiques qu'il faut être content de rire et de ne pas chercher à savoir pourquoi on rit, d'autant que peut-être la réflexion tue le rire, et qu'il serait alors contradictoire qu'elle en découvrît les causes . . .[1]

Nevertheless it would be cowardly, in a work aiming at some sort of comprehensiveness, to shirk the subject, even though the remarks that follow offer merely one possible pattern of analysis, and do not purport to cover all the possible aspects of Petronius' humour. Some of these have been discussed earlier under different heads, the comic satire, for instance, and the extensive stretches of literary parody. Indeed it is difficult to disentangle the pure humour from the finer play of wit in the style and conception of the work, which offers subtler, but not necessarily inferior, amusement.

[1] *La psychologie du rire* (Paris, 1902), p. 1.

The staple of most humour and comedy is the incongruous, the linking together in unexpected ways of diverse concepts, language, situations, persons, or modes of experience and behaviour. Petronius' humour is no exception. Unfortunately, even this sort of humour tends to be topical and dependent on fashion, and frequently fades within a century. The reason is often linguistic or social change whereby jokes are lost and absurdity diminished. We are not very much amused nowadays by the references to 'horns' in Elizabethan literature. With the *Satyricon*, therefore, a great imaginative effort is often needed to see just what the purely topical incongruities are, although, luckily, some of the humour flows from perennial springs. The basic humour of the *Satyricon* consists in the application of a refined, literary, and stylistically sophisticated narrative medium to the disreputable low-life adventures and sexual escapades of a number of unprincipled and generally worthless characters. The *nostalgie de la boue* that perhaps dictated this choice of subject, which contrasts so strongly with some of the literary digressions, has already been examined, and here we need merely inspect the techniques and mechanisms used. Particularly noticeable is the contrast between the short, polished, and rhythmic sentences, with their constant literary allusions, and the high degree of excitement, despair, astonishment, shame, suffering, laughing, crying, and ecstasy they describe. The narrative is full of references to the narrator's being thunderstruck, frightened to death, delirious with happiness and so on, yet the prose itself, economically and smoothly, records these horrors and raptures without any ornate or effusive reinforcements of the feelings described, except where deliberate parody is intended.[1] The effect is an ironic distancing of the writer's material, which enhances the amusing quality of the work: something of the sort may be seen in the early novels of Evelyn Waugh and Anthony Powell.

Sometimes the incongruity that is fundamental to the humour is between the high moral sentiments, the sensible, sometimes serious, literary criticism, and the persons that voice them, whether

---

[1] For a more complete analysis, see J. K. Schoenberger, *Glotta* 31 (1951), 22 ff., and P. A. George, *Arion* 5 (1966), 336 ff.

the narrator Encolpius, a timorous and suspicious criminal of (to us) strange origins and unknown destination, or the immoral, opportunistic poetaster, Eumolpus. Sometimes the incongruity is between the style of the prose or verse and the lowliness or absurdity of the incidents, or, alternatively, between the high-flown declamatory style of some of the characters, Giton, for instance, or even Chrysis, and the actual station or attainments in life. The tragic style is frequently invoked and parodied, as the references to *tragoedia* (108.11) and tragic subjects (*Thebanum par* 80.3; cf. 132.13) might lead us to expect. The use of epic style and references, especially of Vergilian or Homeric epic, for the most unlikely or obscene subjects is even more noticeable. Not only is the Wrath of Priapus a parody of the Wrath of Poseidon in the *Odyssey*, but Homer is drawn on for such incidents as Lichas' lewd recognition of Encolpius (105.9), which burlesques Eurycleia's identification of Odysseus.

The use of elevated, lyrical, or rhetorical language for unseemly subjects is frequent enough in English literature and may be found in Rochester, Dorset, and in such minor productions as the anonymous *Panegyric on Cundums*, just as the use of elegant and high-flown prose for erotic matters is familiar to us from such novels as John Cleland's *Memoirs of a Lady of Pleasure*. Petronius has a highly differentiated style, or set of styles, but this is certainly one use to which he puts his abilities for comic effect. As Samuel Johnson remarks in his *Life of Cowley*:

> Language is the dress of thought: and as the noblest mien or most graceful action would be degraded and obscured by a garb appropriated to the gross employments of rustics or mechanics, so most heroic sentiments will lose their efficacy, and the most splendid ideas lose their magnificence, if they are conveyed by vulgar mouths and contaminated by inelegant applications.

The best example of this literary erotic humour is the episode with Circe (126 ff.). The narrative contains a number of reminiscences of Ovid's amatory works, particularly in the description of Circe and her powers;[1] the climax of the story (or should one

---

[1] Cf. Collignon, pp. 260 ff.

say anti-climax?), Encolpius' impotence, which is followed by Circe's beratings of him, and his own soliloquy over the offending member, whose failure has deprived him of such joy, draws heavily on Ovid's well-known elegy on *his* impotence (*Am.* 3.7). The theme is a popular one, being found in the roughly contemporary *Priapea* (83, attributed to Tibullus), and it was to enjoy a long history. Maximianus in the fourth century elaborated on the Ovidian description with some originality (*Elegy* V), and the Earl of Rochester's poems, *The Imperfect Enjoyment, On Leaving his Mistress*, and *The Disappointment*, all turn on the topic.

Petronius elaborates on Ovid in a number of ways. He splits up the basic action into several dramatic scenes: Chrysis is brought back as a witness; Giton, rather than another woman, is given the blame; Ovid's simple self-reproaches become in the hero's soliloquy an opportunity for reflections on obscenity (132.15); and the usual Petronian motif of castration is invoked.

Apart from heightening the action in this way, Petronius keeps up the play of literary humour. Ovid is kept continually in mind in this whole section. Even at 135, when Encolpius is seeking a cure for his impotence, we have the parodic allusions to the Baucis and Philemon story, treated by Callimachus in the *Hecale* and rehandled by Ovid in the *Metamorphoses*. Even Encolpius' slaughter of the goose at 136.4 ff. seems to recall the more hospitable slaughter of the goose for Theseus in the Alexandrian epyllion which Ovid inserted into his work (*Met.* 8.620–724). At this point in the *Satyricon*, not content with Ovidian allusions, Petronius adds a parody of Vergil cast in the more suggestive sotadic metre:

> ter corripui terribilem manu bipennem,
> ter languidior coliculi repente thyrso
> ferrum timui, quod trepido male dabat usum.
> nec iam poteram, quod modo conficere libebat;
> namque illa metu frigidior rigente bruma
> confugerat in viscera mille operta rugis.
> ita non potui supplicio caput aperire,
> sed furciferae mortifero timore lusus
> ad verba, magis quam poterant nocere, fugi.
>
> (132.8)

Three times I took the murd'rous axe in hand,
Three times I wavered like a wilting stalk
And curtsied from the blade, poor instrument
In trembling hands–I could not what I would.
From terror colder than the wintry frost,
It took asylum far within my crotch,
A thousand wrinkles deep.
How could I lift its head to punishment?
Cozened by its whoreson, mortal fright,
I fled for aid to words that deeper bite.

Not satisfied with the echoes of Vergil in this poem, Petronius
adds a cento of Vergilian lines to describe the appearance of
Encolpius' penis:

illa solo fixos oculos aversa tenebat,
nec magis incepto vultum sermone movetur
quam lentae salices lassove papavera collo.[1]

(132.11)

She held her eyes averted and down-cast
Nor altered aught her face at this address
Than supple willow or drooping poppyhead.

The piquancy of the wit is irreverently enhanced by the fact that
the first two lines were used by Vergil to describe the pathetic
meeting of Dido and Aeneas in the underworld, and half of the
last line comes from the description of the death of Euryalus.

The parody is not confined to the frankly sexual situations.
Legal language, diplomatic language, and the tones of erotic elegy
also, are employed in more innocent contexts, such as the scene
where Eumolpus negotiates a truce between the adventurers and
their pursuers (109.2), or the episode where he plots against the
legacy hunters (117.5); and Ovid is largely drawn on for Encolpius' initially romantic encounters with Circe. Similar use is made
of philosophical doctrines or commonplaces, Stoic and Epicurean.
As we have seen, Trimalchio's enlightened speech on the common

[1] *Aen.* 6. 469–70; *Ecl.* 5.16; *Aen.* 9.436.

218

humanity of slave and free: '*et servi homines sunt et aeque unum lactem biberunt, etiam si illos malus fatus oppresserit*' (71.1–'Slaves are human too and they drank one and the same milk as us, even if an unlucky fate has put them down'), is meant as the keynote of what, to Petronius, would be his absurd and tasteless treatment of his household, in which undue familiarity and harsh treatment (cf. 28.7, 52.5, 53.3 etc) irrationally alternate. The purpose is, in a way, satiric, and the savagely ironic glance at such sentiments in Seneca's *Epistulae Morales* adds the literary element to the humour.[1]

The attraction of the humour of incongruity and surprise for Petronius may be seen further in the two stories which Eumolpus retells at different points in the narrative, the stories of the Boy of Pergamum and the Widow of Ephesus (85 ff., 111 ff.). In each case, the point of the story lies in the reversal of roles: the young boy becomes the would-be seducer, and Eumolpus is reduced to stern measures to avoid what he formerly desired so eagerly; the Widow, that paragon of chastity, is willing to sacrifice anything, even the husband she doted on enough to die for, to save the new lover she has acquired.[2] The pellucid style of the narrative contrasts vividly with the unseemliness of the themes, and here, as elsewhere, Petronius avoids any vulgar or obscene language of the sort we find in Catullus or Martial. Eumolpus, for all his wicked ways, is as chaste in his prose as in his poetry.

ii. *Mime and Comedy Situations*

A priori, it is perhaps a surprise that the great sophistication of style and literary allusion is at the service not simply of picaresque adventures and sexual descriptions, but also of individual scenes which seem to be drawn from mime and comedy. The picaresque and sexual elements are explicable by Petronius' artistic assumptions, even where we might criticize them, and something of the sort must be invoked to explain his free use of mime, for its

[1] See above, pp. 193 ff.
[2] The story was a very popular one, see E. Grisebach, *Die Wanderung der Novelle von der treulosen Witwe durch die Weltliteratur* (Berlin, 1886) and P. Ure, 'The Widow of Ephesus: Some Reflections on an International Comic Theme', *Durham Univ. Journal* 18 (1956), 1 ff.

influence is unmistakable.[1] The question is, what was the particular attraction of mime and comedy for Petronius, and to what
use does he put this inspiration in the *Satyricon*?

Despite the literary tradition of Sophron, Herodas, and Theocritus, and the perhaps better than average efforts of such Roman
writers as Laberius and Publilius Syrus, who, besides being a
favourite writer of Trimalchio's (55.5), is quoted by Seneca about
nine times in the *Epistulae Morales*, the mime in Rome in our
period was hardly a respectable literary or artistic form. With the
pantomime, it seemed to provide what the twentieth century
gets from soap opera, farce, melodrama, strip-tease, ballet, interpretative dancing in the style of Isadora Duncan, or the miming
of Marcel Marceau. But however trite, obscene, or even cruel it
may have been, its general popularity is well-documented for the
first century.[2] Martial writes with complete unconcern about a
realistic performance of the Pasiphae story in the amphitheatre
and the actual crucifixion of a criminal in a production of the
famous *Laureolus* mime;[3] the notoriety that made such actors as
Latinus and Bathyllus stock butts for the satirists is as indicative
of their standing as are the fierce, if prejudiced, protests of Christian
writers such as Tertullian.[4] An analogous addiction to gladiatorial
games was present in quite well-educated people, the emperor
Claudius being an obvious example (Suet. *Claud.* 21), and Seneca
would at least drop in on them, if only to be shocked (*Ep.* 7.3).
On the other hand we are familiar with professors of philosophy
who like detective fiction or soccer; eminent papyrologists and
literary critics share a fondness for P. G. Wodehouse or thrillers.
Petronius' perhaps condescending interest in mime may have been

---

[1] See M. Rosenblüth, *Beiträge zur Quellenkunde von Petronius' Satiren* (Kiel,
1909); F. Möring, *De Petronio mimorum imitatore* (Münster, 1915), a more
moderate statement; K. Preston, 'Some Sources of the Comic Effect in Petronius', *CP* 10 (1915), 260 ff.; and R. Cahen, *Le Satiricon et ses origines* (Paris,
1925), pp. 38 ff., 70 ff.

[2] For its general characteristics, see H. Reich, *Der Mimus* (Berlin, 1903), vol. I,
pp. 35 ff.

[3] *Lib. Spectac.* 5.7.

[4] Cf. e.g. Juv. 1.36, 6.63; Tert. *Spect.* 17.1–5. For ancient judgments on the
mime and Christian criticisms, see Reich, *op. cit.*, pp. 50 ff., 109 ff.

analogous; and the *nostalgie de la boue*, which has been postulated
as a dominating impulse in him, might find equal satisfaction in
making use of this sort of 'art', particularly if he could fit its
themes, with the resulting incongruity, into his highly literary
framework.

It is perhaps an exaggeration to say that the key to the whole
Satyricon is in the words: *omnia mimico risu exsonuerant*,[1] but words,
incidents, even titles from mime, occur in the narrative. Before
we examine the end to which this art-form is put by Petronius,
it might be well to summarize such relevant characteristics of the
mime in the early principate as might appeal to him.

There is, first of all, the theory of the mime which would com-
mend itself as consonant with Petronius' own literary principles.
Its origin was popularly thought to be *mimetic*, imitative of real
life,[2] hence the naturalism of even such Alexandrian mime writers
as Herodas and Theocritus. By an obvious progression due to the
principles of realism, we have the concentration on the lower
aspects of life, and the careful, if stereotyped, observation of everyday affairs and language, particularly of the lower classes. The
obscenity of the mime, Martial's *mimica licentia*, is not unconnected
with this.[3] To Petronius' mind this art-form would have an aim
similar to his own intentions in the *Satyricon*: to narrate frankly
the behaviour of ordinary, i.e. inferior, people (*quodque facit
populus, candida lingua refert*, 132.15) and the pleasures of sex
(*concubitis, Veneris gaudia*, ibid.).

Other characteristics of the mime, literary and non-literary, that
must have appealed to Petronius would be the colloquial speech,
such stock figures as the procurer or go-between (like Chrysis),

---

[1] E. Thomas, *Pétrone* (Paris, 1912), p. 213.

[2] Diomedes' description (*GLK* I, p. 491), which depends on Theophrastus,
reads: *mimus est sermonis cuius libet ⟨et⟩ motus sine reverentia, vel factorum et turpium
cum lascivia imitatio; a Graecis ita definitus:* μῖμός ἐστιν μίμησις βίου τά τε συγ-
κεχωρημένα καὶ ἀσυγχώρητα περιέχων. Johannes Lydus adds (*De mag.* 1.40):
μιμικὴ τεχνικὸν μὲν ἔχουσα οὐδέν, ἀλόγῳ μόνον πλῆθος ἐπάγουσα γέλωτι
Cf. W. Ridgeway, *The Drama and Dramatic Dances of Non-European Peoples*
(Cambridge, 1915), p. 10: 'Amongst primitive people all dances are mimetic
and pantomimic'.

[3] Mart. 8 *praef.*; cf. Val. Max. 2.10.8.

the *cinaedus*, the excluded lover (cf. Encolpius *inclusus*, 94.7 ff.), and so on. In particular one of the features of mime was imposture and deception, and this alone would relate the whole world of the *Satyricon* to the mime.

Specifically, however, the first direct reference we find is in the Quartilla scene. Quartilla and her maids have arrived; the promises of Encolpius are accepted, and the priestess' threat of possible force has been made. Suddenly the three women burst out laughing, to the surprise and consternation of the trio, and at this point the phrase, if we can trust the variant reading for *nimio, omnia mimico risu exsonuerant* (19.1) occurs. From the context it appears that some sort of deception is being practised on the three; from what follows, it is presumably that the apparently harmless and weak women are backed by forces greater than the trio can hope to match. The laughter is described as *mimicus* because it is the sort of laughter which the stage deception excites, hearty and cruel. Even the mock marriage of Giton and Pannychis (25.1 ff.) has the features of mime, and may have been suggested by Laberius' *Nuptiae*.[1]

The same impression is left by Petronius' use of the word at 117.4, where Eumolpus, having thought of a deception which he can practise on the Crotonian legacy hunters (*mendacium*, 117.2, 5), wishes he had a large stage setting (*scaena*), and better dress and equipment, but asks why they are delaying the production of the mime (*quid ergo cessamus mimum componere?* 117.4), the mime being of course that of the poor old man, who pretends to be rich and ill, and so profitably deceives the legacy hunters.

The motif of the mime is particularly pervasive in the *Cena*.[2] Not only does Trimalchio like real mimes, as the song (35.6) from the *Laserpiciarius mimus* or *The Asafoetida Man*, and the imitation of Publilius Syrus (55.6) indicate, but many of the scenes put on for the entertainment of the guests involve some sort of humorous trick, deception, or joke, and are reminiscent of mimes. There can

[1] Rosenblüth, *op. cit.*, p. 37.

[2] Given the various literary influences that make themselves felt in the *Cena*, Rosenblüth's comparison (*op. cit.*, p. 53) of the whole episode to the mimes of Herodas and Theocritus must not be taken too seriously.

be little doubt that these entertainments, like some of the others put on by Trimalchio, are yet another indication of his low taste. Encolpius' sour remarks make this clear: *pantomimi chorum, non patris familiae triclinium crederes* (31.7). The sneer is directed not so much against mime itself, as against Trimalchio's bad taste in spoiling the dinner and the conversation by his unremitting attempts to impress and amuse his guests. His taste for such things as mime, Atellan farce, and acrobats is genuine (cf. 53.12–13), whereas Petronius' own interest would be self-conscious and critical. As with Herodas and Theocritus, it is the elevation of a popular art form into a higher literary genre or a more sophisticated context.

There are however one or two incidents of a farcical nature in the *Satyricon* which perhaps surprise the non-Anglo-Saxon reader more than anything else, unless of course this type of anal humour appeals to him. Trimalchio's ill-mannered emphasis on excretory functions (41.9, 47.2–6) may be excused as satiric, a fact underlined by the guests' laughter (47.7), but the farting scene with Eumolpus' servant Corax would be more puzzling were it not consistent with the frequently low nature of the incidents in the *Satyricon*. It must also be remembered that this type of humour exercises a certain hearty, or morbid, appeal to some writers. Such Rabelaisian interests may be seen in Ben Jonson, whose *Famous Voyage* also makes use of the mock-heroic style, Jonathan Swift, Mark Twain, at least in his *1601*, and, most importantly for our purposes, Aristophanes, who, in the opening scene of the *Frogs*, has Dionysus' slave Xanthus behave in much the same way as Corax for the same reasons.

In sum, it may be said that mime subjects and situations provide part of the grist for Petronius' sophisticated and literary mill. They provide the melodrama, the movement, and incident, for the picaresque plot and some of its farcical humour. There are swift disappearances, violence, quarrels, concealments, enforced baths, impostures, and dramatic *bouleversements*.[1] Not all should be attributed to the direct influence of mime – satire and comedy have

[1] See Preston (*art. cit.* above) for an exhaustive – and exhausting – survey of the possibilities.

similar features–but the insistence in certain episodes on laughter and applause, ideas so opposed to the upper class Roman notion of *gravitas*,[1] again indicates perhaps that one source of humour that Petronius was drawing upon was, as I have suggested, the fusing of typical incidents from the plots of mime with a highly literary language and treatment–once more the humour of incongruity.

Naturally the modern reader does not always appreciate the references to so unrestorably topical a form. The dead conventions are alien to him, as the conventions of *Gammer Gurton's Needle* and the humour of many Shakespearean comedies are alien also. He will notice of course the contrast between the refined style and literary discussions, and the buffoonery of much of the action, but he will not be able to perceive easily the *deliberateness* of the contrast between the action and the language. One would have to turn to modern analogies to realize the effect that Petronius seems to be aiming at. Several come to mind. A simple analogy may be seen in the novels of P. G. Wodehouse, whose relation to stage comedy with its embarrassing social situations, elaborate plots, and unmaskings, is approximately the same as Petronius' to mime. The analogy is strengthened when one considers Wodehouse's ironic use of English colloquialisms and literary allusions–the inversion of *milieux* corresponds to the difference between a democratic and an aristocratic society's tastes. After all, farcical situations, with some exceptions, are culturally determined. Lovers in chests, or laundry baskets, predicaments so dear to the Romans and the Elizabethans, are out of place in the efficient housing of today. Adulterous lovers who run into family friends at airports fit our different patterns of behaviour, although the situations may be just as comical.

It is important not to claim too much now for the humour of incident in Petronius, although we can realize that his comedy was probably a good deal funnier for his audience than we can properly appreciate, just as his literary allusions, imitations, and parodies must have excited a more immediate response, and thus a greater pleasure, from the instant recognition of incongruity than we can hope to achieve by our laborious restoration of the original con-

[1] Cf. Quint. *Inst.* 6.3.8: *risus res levis et quae a scurris et mimis moveatur.*

texts. Here again, perhaps, the limited analogy of Wodehouse, with Bertie Wooster's mangled Shakespeare, might be borne in mind.

iii. *Verbal Wit*

At the opposite extreme to the farcical incidents employed by Petronius for the action proper, there is the almost equally large element of verbal wit, which more readily satisfies our expectations of such a literate and polished writer. The most obvious form in which this verbal wit shows itself is the pun. Humour of the punning sort was more popular with the Romans than with us, as the extant examples of Cicero's witticisms prove. Even such oddities as a fondness for rebuses, a liking shared by Trimalchio and the Emperor Augustus,[1] exemplify this taste.

Puns may be tendentious, sexual, for example, or simply plays upon words; again they may rely on a simple change of a letter or syllable, or involve the *double entendre* proper. Petronius uses most of these varieties. As an example of the first may be instanced Eumolpus' wry but neat comment on Ascyltos' success in being picked up at the baths: '*tanto magis expedit inguina quam ingenia fricare*' (92.11), which may be translated loosely by 'A polished wick is more profitable than a polished wit'. There are a number of *double-entendres* proper, both in the narrative and the dialogue. Quartilla's little joke on examining Giton's miniature sexual equipment (24.7) provides a convenient example:

'haec' inquit 'belle cras in promulside libidinis nostrae militabit; hodie enim post asellum diaria non sumo.'

Loosely,

'Tomorrow,' she said, 'this will serve nicely as hors d'oeuvre to tempt my appetite. For the present I don't want a common shrimp after such a nice cod-piece.'

The actual joke depends on a double meaning of *asellus*, which can be both a fish and that great Roman symbol of lust and sexual potency, the ass. Similar sexual puns and double meanings may

---

[1] Compare 56.8–10 with Suet. *Aug.* 75.

be found at 11.4 (*dividere cum fratre*); 17.7 ff. (*medicina*); 24.1–4 (*embasicoetas*); 126.10 (*in equestribus sedeo*); 131.7 (the Ovidian *leporem excitavi*); 140.2,7 (*bonitas*); and 140.13 (*deorum beneficia*).

Puns and double meanings, of course, are funnier when they rely on the powerful reinforcement of a sexual reference. And it must be said that most of the puns in Encolpius' narrative and the dialogue outside the *Cena* are of this sort. Trimalchio, however, although he is given his fair share of sexual allusion (e.g. 69.3), is limited in his verbal humour to puns which are either childishly naïve or ponderously artificial; these are not meant in themselves to be funny, but are intended by their very weakness to satirize Trimalchio's deficiencies in wit. Examples of these are: *hoc est ius cenae* (35.7), which plays upon the double meaning of *ius* (*law* and *sauce*); '*Carpe, carpe*' (36.7), which would come over into English as 'Carver, carve 'er!'; and *secundae mensae* (68.1–2), which relies on the literal meaning 'second tables' and the idiomatic meaning of 'dessert'. The joke about *Corinthea vasa* and *Corinthus* (50.2–4) is too weak even to bear explication, as Encolpius' sardonic *ille melius* underlines.

As is clear, these 'jokes' sometimes rely on staging and props to be made at all, and Trimalchio's most elaborate joke is practically a tableau (41.6 ff.). Here a slave named Dionysus plays the different avatars, as it were, of the God of Wine. Trimalchio orders him to play the Italian god of wine, Liber, and the boy interprets this adjectivally as *liber* (free), and puts on a freedman's cap. Trimalchio compounds the joke by adding that the guests cannot deny *me . . . habere liberum patrem*, which plays upon the two possible meanings, *Father Liber* and *a free father*.[1] The fondness for this elaborate situational pun, as we may describe it, may be seen also in the Zodiac dish served by Trimalchio (35.2 ff., 39.4 ff.); here the various foods placed over the signs of the Zodiac generally show some sort of conceptual relationship to their sign, which is explicated at tiresome length by Trimalchio.[2] It would be equally

---

[1] See A. E. Housman, *CR* 32 (1918), 162.

[2] Where the text is nonsensical, I would suggest: *super scorpionem locustam* (following Gaselee), *super sagittarium oculatam*, *super capricornum caprum et cornutam*.

tiresome to examine the rebus-tickets which are distributed among the guests, and which elicit odd presents for them to take home (56.8 ff.). The only bearable example is perhaps 'muraena et littera' (lamprey and a letter), which receives a mouse with a frog attached instead of the expected lamprey (murem cum rana alligata / muraena), and a stick of beet (beta meaning both 'beet' and the Greek letter beta).

All this, of course, in so far as it is funny at all, is purely second-order humour, and is at the service of the satiric portrait. The real humour of the Cena–fortunately–consists in something much more comic and human. Verbal wit is exhibited also in Petronius' choice of names for his characters, although it must be admitted that he lacks the fantasy and richness of a Peacock or a Dickens. Almost all of the names are Greek, a fact that may be explained by Petronius' choice of low characters who, to the Roman mind, would be ex-slaves or Graeculi, and by the fact that Greek names have more expressive possibilities than standard Latin names. Quartilla is one of the few exceptions: her name is a diminutive of the Latin quarta (fourth)–such numerical names being not uncommon for slaves. There might possibly be an allusion in the diminutive to her early sexual proclivities, which she describes at 25.4 ff.: 'Iunonem meam iratam habeam, si umquam me meminerim virginem fuisse' ('Juno's curse on me, if I remember ever being a virgin'). But usually the names are appropriately Greek, with the further exception of Proculus in Trimalchio's circle of freedmen. The importunate poet is ironically named Eumolpus ('the sweet singer'); Ascyltos' name (something like 'Mr. Takeit') fits Eumolpus' envious description of him: 'o iuvenem laboriosum: puto illum pridie incipere, postero die finire' – 'What a man for the job! I think he starts yesterday and finishes tomorrow' (92.9–10). Some of the names are less vividly descriptive. Tryphaena means, roughly, 'luxurious' and so is appropriate for a demi-mondaine who travels around solely in the pursuit of pleasure (101.5). Similarly 'Oenothea' ('Wine-goddess') aptly describes the bibulous priestess of Priapus (134.8 and ff.), as well as being perhaps a humorous allusion to the Homeric Eidothea. Some of the names of the minor characters are simply slave names (e.g. Corax and Psyche). The mythological names on the other hand do usually have point. Circe and 'Polyaenus', Agamemnon and Menelaus, provide mildly joking allusions to Homeric characters, and Lichas, the licentious sea-captain, derives his name from the Hercules myth with a possible overtone of perverse sexual practices (λειχάζειν).[1]

iv. *Characterization*

Petronius' principal genius is for humorous characterization, which is deployed largely through the medium of dialogue, and this perhaps is the side of the *Satyricon* which appeals most to the reader, familiar as he is with the developed techniques of the novel. Encolpius is usually the victim, as the plot requires, and his characterization for various reasons differs from the others (see above, pp. 116 ff.). He is very emotional and suggestible, but his infrequent moments of ecstasy (78.8 and 126.13 ff.), or bravery (82.1 ff.), are more than balanced by his almost immediate return to despair, frustration, or cowardice. He is generally depicted as pessimistic, timorous, and self-pitying. He is rarely allowed to shine, if we except the opening scene and the *apologia* for the work (132.15), where he is presumably voicing the author's own views, and tends more to be the foil, if not a butt, for the other characters. He is the target of Quartilla's practical jokes (24.2 etc); of Ascyltos' sardonic cracks (10.1; 11.4); of Giton's infidelity (80.6; 113.4); of Eumolpus' disdainful unkindness (94.1 ff., 109.8); of Circe's sarcastic irony (128.1; 130.4-6) and brutality (132.2). One has to remember of course that Petronius is not interested in exploring the consistencies or inconsistencies of Encolpius' character as a modern novelist might be, but rather in using him as the excuse for the different episodes or the foil for the other characters.

The characterization of the other figures in the *Satyricon* is predominantly satiric in the conventional sense of the term, even though there is no impression given of moral indignation. With the crew of libidinous women that stalk the pages of the *Satyricon*, the problem for the author is simply one of differentiation, as we have seen (pp. 119 ff.). Not all the techniques employed are humorous, although an exception might be made of the delightfully ironic

---

[1] See further the explanations in the index of names to Ernout's edition.

tone of Circe's letter to Encolpius (129.4-9). The transcendence of Petronius' initial satiric aims by a stronger comic and novelistic impulse in the creation of Trimalchio has been also examined earlier (pp. 151-57 above).

Eumolpus is perhaps the most suitable figure with which to illustrate Petronius' techniques of character depiction in detail. We are first presented with a physical description:

> ecce autem . . . intravit pinacothecam senex canus, exercitati vultus et qui videbatur nescio quid magnum promittere, sed cultu non proinde speciosus, ut facile appareret eum ⟨ex⟩ hac nota litteratorum esse quos odisse divites solent.
>
> (83.7-8)

All of a sudden, however . . . a white-haired old man entered the picture-gallery. His face was lined and seemed to have in it a promise of something impressive. But his appearance was shabby, and this made it clear that he belonged to the class of intellectuals so hated generally by the rich.

As with Quartilla and Circe, his first address is conciliatory and righteous:

> 'ego' inquit 'poeta sum et ut spero non humillimi spiritus, si modo coronis aliquid credendum est, quas etiam ad imperitos deferre gratia solet. 'quare ergo' inquis 'tam male vestitus es?' propter hoc ipsum. amor ingenii neminem umquam divitem fecit . . . non dubie ita est: si quis vitiorum omnium inimicus rectum iter vitae coepit insistere, primum propter morum differentiam odium habet; quis enim potest probare diversa? deinde qui solas extruere divitias curant, nihil volunt inter homines melius credi quam quod ipsi tenent. insectantur itaque, quacumque ratione possunt, litterarum amatores, ut videantur illi quoque infra pecuniam positi.'
>
> (83.8-84.3)

'I am a poet,' he said, 'and a poet of no mean ability, I like to think, at least if bardic crowns are to be trusted when favouritism confers them even on mediocrity. 'Why,' you ask, 'are you so badly dressed then?' For this one reason–concern for the arts never made anyone rich . . . No doubt about it. If a man sets his face against every temptation and starts off on the straight and narrow, he's immediately hated because of his different ways. No one can approve of conduct different from his own. And secondly, those who are interested in piling up money don't want anything else in life regarded as better than what they have themselves. So they persecute lovers of literature in any way possible to show that they too are inferior to wealth.'

As we have observed, Petronius is particularly fond of the humour of contrast and incongruity, and this lofty tone of dedication and disdain for lower pleasures is quickly deflated for the reader by the anecdote of Eumolpus' adventure in Pergamum where he manages by a clever deception to seduce his host's young son. The tale is clearly a familiar *conte*, but at the same time its narration by Eumolpus shows him to be a lecherous and hypo-critical old fraud: Circe's initial demureness and the brutality and libidinousness of her true nature provide an analogous contrast. Eumolpus in fact completely inverts the poetic *topos* that we find in Catullus, Ovid, Martial, and others.[1] Whatever we think of his poetry, it is rarely playful (as at 109.9–10), and never obscene (whereas his life is anything but chaste). Eumolpus becomes then a suitable new rival for Giton's affections, and a natural leader in the imposture practised on the legacy hunters at Croton. The highly sexual episode involving Philomela's little daughter (140) is a perfect example of the combination in him of lechery and deceit. His relations with Encolpius and Giton are a similar blend, and his trickery is evident also in his attempts to deceive Lichas and Tryphaena on board ship (104.3 ff.).

It may be noted, however, that Eumolpus has many virtues; he is resourceful and courageous, as well as lecherous and cunning (cf. 95, 108, 117). Analogously, we do not have to take the literary criticism of the *Satyricon* and the moral criticism as vitiated simply by the speaker. The moralizing speeches (88, 140.14 etc), apart from their parodic intentions, provide a deliberate counterpoint

---

[1] See p. 104, n. 2.

to the immoral actions of Eumolpus and the others. What validity they might have is undercut by their dramatic function, and provide no evidence, positive or negative, by consistency or contrast, of the author's own views. It is unlikely, for instance, that his Epicureanism would be offended by Eumolpus' philosophy of *carpe diem* (cf. 99.1, 132.15, particularly lines 5–8), but its presentation is above all governed by Petronius' sceptical and opportunistic humour. The literary criticism, on the other hand, contrasts with nothing. It is not undercut by issuing from Eumolpus; it is merely appropriate, even when valid, for Eumolpus' important trait is that he is mad about poetry. Inopportune reciters and poets are of course frequent subjects of satire in Latin literature,[1] and the satiric intent here is made quite obvious by the crowd's hostile reception of Eumolpus' poem on the Fall of Troy (90.1), and by Encolpius' own chidings (90.1, 90.3, 93.3). But there is no need to be sceptical about Eumolpus' function as a vehicle of the author's literary criticism (are we to assume that Petronius did *not* think that Horace displayed *curiosa felicitas*?) or to feel that its insights are necessarily out of character when coming from Eumolpus.

I have not tried here to do more than outline the broader strokes used in the delineation of character in the *Satyricon*. Much of the differentiation of character, as was noted earlier, is achieved by a careful attention to the style of each speaker's dialogue, and, where relevant, monologue.[2] This aspect of Petronius' character drawing, however, concerns his parodic intentions, and not, strictly speaking, his comic characterization.

[1] Cf. e.g. Juv. 1.2 ff., 3.9; Mart. 3.44, 45.
[2] See pp. 119 ff., and P. A. George, *Arion* 5 (1966), 336 ff.

CHAPTER VII

The Sexual Themes of the *Satyricon*

i. *The Pornographic Tradition*

So far we have managed to discuss the *Satyricon* without more than glancing at an aspect of the work which has been perhaps responsible more than anything else for Petronius' notoriety with the Common Reader, and his peculiar handling by critics of Latin literature. Not to face this issue squarely would be to produce *Hamlet* without the Prince of Denmark, or to write on D. H. Lawrence without discussing *Lady Chatterley's Lover*. Why there is 'obscenity' in the work at all should be clear from earlier chapters, but it should not be forgotten that what we would call obscene literature had a long and prominent history in the ancient world. The frank acceptance of the physical side of life by the Greeks and the Romans, their glorification of the sexual instinct rather than the sexual object, was only infrequently checked by certain sporadic religious, and social, taboos and philosophies; there was not the systematic fear and suspicion of sex *per se* such as we find in most forms of Christianity, and which have made its literary representation in our culture almost as disreputable (until recently) as the reality. What puritanism we may discern in social attitudes in the classical periods derives from a social, not a religious, morality, the sort of morality represented by the elder Cato, whose advocacy of resorting to prostitutes in order to channel the sexual appetites of the young away from adultery into more socially acceptable modes of expression might have raised modern eyebrows.[1] Similarly, restrictions on the writing and

[1] See Hor. *Sat.* 1.2 and p. 99, n. 1, above.

reading of obscene literature were social, and not religious. We can deduce from the attitude of such worthies as the younger Pliny that the main objection to such literature was the damage it might do to one's public dignity, or one's reputation for *severitas*.[1] The objections were much the same as those against drunkenness. If then my explanation of the genesis of the work is more or less correct, the sexual themes of the *Satyricon* should occasion us no surprise. Obscenity was a treasured part of the literary tradition and a sophisticated coterie would be as amused by pornography as by parody, although of course the usual *apologia* was in order. Petronius' obscenity is not, as it might be with us, *avant garde*, but traditional.

If we look again at 132 we see, in time-honoured terms, the objections put and the defence given. Encolpius has been abusing his impotent penis, but then recollects himself:

> nec minus ego tam foeda obiurgatione finita paenitentiam agere sermonis mei coepi secretoque rubore perfundi, quod oblitus verecundiae meae cum ea parte corporis verba contulerim, quam ne ad cognitionem quidem admittere severioris notae homines solerent.

> Once this vile abuse was finished, I began to regret talking like this, and I blushed inwardly for forgetting my sense of shame, and bandying words with a part of the body that more austere people do not even think about.

The objection clearly is due to Encolpius' sense of shame. His defence is that, if any parts of the body, even such equally un-dignified parts as the belly, may be addressed, then the genitals should have parity of esteem. The poem, which has already been discussed (pp. 98–102), then presents a more general defence of the obscenity of the work. The key lines are:

> quid me spectatis constricta fronte Catones
>   damnatisque novae simplicitatis opus?

and

> quodque facit populus, candida lingua refert.

[1] *Ep.* 3.21 (on Martial), 4.14.4, and 5.3 (where Pliny's list of 'indecent' authors is almost as long as Ovid's in the second book of the *Tristia*).

The defence, as was pointed out, is essentially the argument of candour and honesty. If sex is universal, and unobjectionable, both by popular consensus and by Epicurean arguments, then its literary depiction is equally justifiable on grounds of realism, and Petronius' *nova simplicitas* was as much a matter of treatment and style as a reaction against *prisca simplicitas*.

ii. The Choice of Themes

The main question for our present purposes concerns the *choice* of sexual themes by Petronius. Some of these are easily explained. Eumolpus' story of the Widow of Ephesus is a typically 'Milesian' tale, whose interest for us lies partly in the artistic handling, and partly in its crystallization of a view of women that is present throughout the work for satiric purposes. It is maliciously introduced by Eumolpus to twit Tryphaena and pique Lichas, who remembers his wife's seduction by Encolpius (113.1–2). The idea has had a long, and no doubt wistful, history, and is an obvious satiric postulate. As Alexander Pope put it (*Epistle to a Lady*, 215–16):

> Men, some to Bus'ness, some to Pleasure take;
> But ev'ry Woman is at heart a Rake.

Eumolpus' remark at 112.1 that his audience must know what usually follows a satisfying meal (*ceterum scitis quid plerumque soleat temptare humanam satietatem*) epitomizes the very physical nature of women's sexual appetites, at least as represented in the *Satyricon*. Encolpius' relationship with Giton, although physical, has its romantic elements: Encolpius can talk of 'true love' (*si vere dilexisti*, 114.9). The women in the story are interested simply in the physical act. Even Circe, despite her protestations about fate, is not jealous about Encolpius' relationship with Giton (127.2), but is positively brutal towards him when he proves impotent. Quartilla is just as frank in the earlier episodes.

The other tale told by Eumolpus deals with homosexual seduction. Together they reflect the sexual impartiality of the work. Petronius uses, and no doubt shared, the common assumption of Roman literature that men are potentially, if not actually, bisexual in their inclinations and actions – a belief which in an altered form has entered our modern consciousness only through the work of Freud.[1] The assumption is of course enshrined in ancient mythology, Jupiter and Hercules being obvious examples. In Greek and Roman literature a romantic relationship might equally well be homosexual or heterosexual. Ovid and Propertius may seem to us the elegiac norm in these matters, although Ovid's objections to homosexuality are personal rather than moral, and it may well be that, to ancient eyes, Catullus and Tibullus presented a more realistic picture. In the *Satyricon* the characters turn to love objects of both sexes with almost equal impartiality. Eumolpus seems initially oriented towards males (85 ff., 92.9–10, 94.1–2), but chooses Philomela's daughter rather than her son as his sexual partner (140.4 ff.). Encolpius surrenders his beloved Giton for Circe (127.4), just as Giton shows no reluctance when put into bed with Pannychis (26.3). Even Trimalchio, who has a catamite named Croesus and an eye for pretty slaves (28.4, 74.8), shared his favours between his former master and mistress (75.11).

Given these assumptions of bisexuality and promiscuity, the attitude to sex in the work is what we must consider a fairly standard ancient view, shared by most classical authors outside the philosophers, the moralists, and the few who believed in an age of innocence under the reign of Saturn, or thought sexual licence incompatible with Roman *gravitas* or social order. It might be summed up in Donne's words:

> Whoever loves, if he doth not propose
> The right true end of love, he's one that goes
> To sea for nothing but to make him sick.

Consequently the notion of Platonic love (*Socratica fides*, 128.7) is invoked only as a savage jest, and the humour of the impotence scenes (128 ff.) revolves around the unnatural inability to do what

---

[1] Cf. e.g. Lucr. 4.1053–4; Cat. 32,61.129 ff., 66; Hor. *C.* 4.1.29 ff.; Sen. *QN* 1.16.2; Juv. 1.28 ff.; 6.34 ff; Mart. 7.57, 11.45, 11.78, 11.87, 12.87, 12.97; Suet. *Caes.* 49–52, *Ner.* 29, etc. For the more modern view, see e.g. S. Freud, *An Autobiographical Study*, trans. J. Strachey (London, 1946), p. 69, and *Three Essays on the Theory of Sexuality*, trans. J. Strachey (London, 1949), pp. 14 ff.

is natural, rather than any psychological interest. Of course the literary humour is an important aspect of the episode, as Encolpius' impotence with Circe is at least partially inspired by the classic treatment of the subject in Ovid's *Amores*. Some of the motifs are identical. The attribution of the condition to witchcraft, or to sexual indulgence elsewhere, may be cited, as well as the boasting of former prowess and the classical examples offered of sexual abstinence.[1]

Another literary theme is to be found in the portrait of Circe, who was described by her maid as one of those women who 'get heated up over the absolute dregs and can't feel any passion unless they see slaves or bare-legged messengers' . . . who 'look for something to love among the lowest of the low'. This satirical portrait of Circe has already been discussed, as well as its literary history. But it may be added here that this psychological tendency to prefer a degraded sexual object is, in modern times, found more usually, according to Freud, in men, because of two factors operative in our civilization: the very strong incestuous fixation of childhood, and the frustration by reality suffered during adolescence, which allow such men to enjoy complete sexual fulfilment only by degrading the love-object, and so differentiating it from the earliest incestuous object of their sexual drives. Freud further adds that 'women show little need to degrade the sexual object'.[2] It is interesting to speculate whether the psychological conditions of Roman childhood, the importance of the *pater familias*, and the general restraints on quite young women, including the arranged marriage, were such as to produce in women rather than (or as much as) in men this sexual tendency. (On the other hand, the evidence we have for this female orientation among Roman ladies comes after

---

[1] Cf. *Am.* 3.7.27–36, 79–80 with *Sat.* 128.2, 129.10–11, 131.4–5; *Am.* 3.7.80 with *Sat.* 129.8–9; *Am.* 3.7.23–6 with *Sat.* 129.1; and *Am.* 3.7.21–2 with *Sat.* 128.7. See also *AP* 12.232, which suggests, incidentally, that it may be a traditional theme.

[2] See 'A Special Type of Choice of Object Made by Men' and 'The Most Prevalent Form of Degradation in Erotic Life', *Collected Papers*, Vol. IV (London, 1925), pp. 192 ff., 203 ff. For their possible relevance to other parts of Latin literature, see my 'Castas Odisse Puellas: A Reconsideration of Propertius I, 1', *WS* 74 (1961), 96 ff.

all from male writers, and a sedulously propagated myth serves as well as anything to degrade–or indeed to elevate–women.)

But the literary origin of these sexual themes does not get us to the heart of the matter, even when the Priapus theme is regarded as the author's further justification of the material used. To understand why the non-literary obscenity of the *Satyricon* is what it is needs deeper investigation. The expectations of the court circle, the literary traditions of satire and parody, even of obscene epigram, will carry us only so far in our explanations.

Some may perhaps feel that we should be content with this and press no further in a search for explanations of so seamy an area of the work. Others may feel that the connections I shall try to make are fanciful or, if true, that they diminish the literary value of Petronius' work by focusing our attention on what is essentially biographical or non-literary: the critic should concentrate not on the *what* but on the *why* and the *how*. It is true that the particular choice of sexual themes should not affect our evaluation of Petronius, even though *that* he has chosen them at all will be of relevance. But for those who feel that the dissection of such material limits, or lowers, our estimation of a writer's powers, I can only quote the words of Freud:

When psycho-analytic investigation, which usually contents itself with frail human material, approaches the great personages of humanity, it is not impelled to it by motives that are often imputed to it by laymen. It does not strive 'to blacken the radiant and to drag the sublime into the mire'; it finds no satisfaction in diminishing the distance between the perfection of the great and the inadequacy of the ordinary objects. But it cannot help finding that everything is worthy of understanding that can be perceived through those prototypes, and it also believes that none is so big as to be ashamed of being subject to the laws which control the normal and morbid actions with the same strictness.[1]

[1] S. Freud, *Leonardo da Vinci: A Study in Psychosexuality*, trans. A. A. Brill (New York, 1961), pp. 3 f.

iii. *Scopophilia and Exhibitionism*

Psycho-analytical studies like those of Freud on Dostoevsky, and Jones on *Hamlet*, have thrown considerable light on modern works of literature, but except for such mythological investigations as those of Otto Rank and Theodor Reik there has been little equivalent work undertaken for classical literature. Even the interest in the *Oedipus* cycle is predominantly a mythological interest. Yet ancient authors, just as much as modern, were governed in their art by their individual aims, wishes, stresses, and unconscious preoccupations, and are therefore amenable to similar investigation. The autonomy of art compared with the directed nature of other activities offers the widest scope for the psychology of the individual to show itself, for its manifestations are directed by internal as well as by literary and cultural forces. Psycho-analytical methods applied even to ancient literary works may provide a key for understanding the works themselves and the societies which produced them. It is not impossible that some literary problems may be similarly elucidated with the aid of psychoanalytical methods. The *Satyricon*, as we have said, is partly *realistic* in its intentions; it is a highly self-conscious work of art based upon certain critical theories, which may be established from literary discussions in the work itself. Petronius, in brief, was reacting in language, themes, and treatment, against much of Silver Age literature and following certain tendencies in his society. It was suggested earlier that he also adopted the literary realist's heresy that only the sordid side of life is really life as it is lived. But what is of interest for our present purpose is the *type* of sexual situation chosen for realistic treatment. The first episode which calls for attention is 16–26, where Encolpius and his two friends fall into the hands of Quartilla. The main event of this first episode is the defloration of the seven-year-old Pannychis by Giton, and the conditions under which this takes place:

> itaque cum inclusi iacerent, consedimus ante limen thalami, et in primis Quartilla per rimam improbe diductam adplicuerat oculum curiosum lusumque puerilem libidinosa speculabatur diligentia. me quoque ad idem spectaculum lenta manu traxit,

et quia considerantium haeserant vultus, quidquid a spectaculo vacabat, commovebat obiter labra et me tamquam furtivis subinde osculis verberabat . . . (26.4–5)

And so, when they were shut in and lying down, we sat around the chamber doorway. Quartilla was the first to put an inquisitive eye to a crack which she had naughtily opened, and spy on their childish play with excited eagerness. Her insistent hand dragged me down to have a look too. Our faces were pressed together as we watched, and whenever she could spare a moment from the spectacle, she'd move her lips close to mine in passing and bruise me with sly kisses.

This is the first patent example of scopophilia in the work. Although Quartilla is sexually aroused, Encolpius indicates that he does not enjoy her attentions, possibly because of his exhaustion.

There is a similar incident in the last section of the story where Encolpius is with Eumolpus in Croton. Eumolpus, posing as a rich, childless, and ailing old man, is entrusted with the care of her two children by the unscrupulous Philomela, who hopes for a legacy:

Eumolpus, qui tam frugi erat ut illi etiam ego puer viderer, non distulit puellam invitare ad †pigiciaca† sacra. sed et podagricum se esse lumborumque solutorum omnibus dixerat, et si non servasset integram simulationem periclitabatur totam pene tragoediam evertere. itaque ut constaret mendacio fides, puellam quidem exoravit ut sederet supra commendatam bonitatem, Coraci autem imperavit ut lectum in quo ipse iacebat subiret positisque in pavimento manibus dominum lumbis suis commoveret. ille lente parebat imperio puellaque artificium pari motu remunerabat. cum ergo res ad effectum spectaret, clara Eumolpus voce exhortabatur Coraca ut spissaret officium. sic inter mercennarium amicamque positus senex veluti oscillatione ludebat. hoc semel iterumque ingenti risu, etiam suo, Eumolpus fecerat. itaque ego quoque, ne desidia consuetudinem perderem, dum frater sororis suae automata per clostellum miratur, accessi

temptaturus an pateretur iniuriam. nec se reiciebat a blanditiis
doctissimus puer, sed me numen inimicum ibi quoque invenit.

(140.–151)

Eumolpus, who was such a sexual miser that even I seemed a
boy to him, did not hesitate a moment to invite the girl to some
ritual buttock-thumping (?). But he had told everyone that he
had gout and an infirmity in his loins, and if he did not keep
up his pretence, he would be in danger of ruining the whole
plot–a prickly situation.

So to ensure that the lie was not discredited, he actually per-
suaded the girl to sit on top of the upright nature to which she
had been entrusted, and ordered Corax to get under the bed
he was lying on, and, with his hands on the floor, to move his
master up and down with his bottom. Corax carried out his
orders gently, and the girl responded to his skill with similar
movements. Then when things had the desired result in sight,
Eumolpus loudly urged Corax to hurry up with his job. Placed
like this between his servant and his girl, the old man looked as
if he were playing on a swing. Eumolpus repeated this performance amid roars of laughter, including his own. Not un-
naturally, I for my part, not to get out of the habit through lack
of practice, approached the brother, who was admiring his
sister's tricks through the keyhole, and tried to see if he would
object to being assaulted. The shrewd lad did not object to my
overtures, but the unfriendly god dogged me in this situation
too.

Here then are two cases of *scopomixia*, and in each the scenes witnessed seem to be of a perverse nature. But this is not all. Voyeurism and exhibitionism are psycho-analytical polarities, and the
latter is also exemplified in Petronius. Immediately before the
child marriage occurs the following incident:

stabat inter haec Giton et risu dissolvebat ilia sua. itaque con-
spicata eum Quartilla, cuius esset puer, diligentissima sciscita-
tione quaesivit. cum ego fratrem meum esse dixissem, 'quare
ergo' inquit 'me non basiavit?' vocatumque ad se in osculum

adplicuit. mox manum etiam demisit in sinum et pertractato vasculo tam rudi 'haec' inquit 'belle cras in promulside libidinis nostrae militabit; hodie enim post asellum diaria non sumo'.

(24.5–7)

Giton was standing there while all this went on, and was splitting his sides laughing. Catching sight of him, Quartilla with great interest asked whose the boy was. I replied he was my brother. 'Indeed!' said Quartilla, 'Why hasn't he given me a kiss?' And calling him to her, she pressed her lips to his. Then she slipped her hand into his clothes, and felt his immature little tool.

'This,' she said, 'will serve nicely tomorrow as an hors d'oeuvre to our love feast. For the moment, I don't want ordinary stuffing after a nice piece of meat.'

Despite differences–handling rather than looking at a forbidden object–this is surely a sort of exhibitionism. Not that Giton is depicted as an exhibitionist, but rather that the author here is subjecting Giton to these experiences. After the second instance of voyeurism there is an even more patent example of exhibitionism. Although in his attempt on the boy, who was watching his sister through the key-hole, Encolpius was frustrated by his impotence, yet after a hiatus in the manuscripts we find him talking to Eumolpus:

'dii maiores sunt, qui me restituerunt in integrum . . .' haec locutus sustuli tunicam Eumolpoque me totum approbavi. at ille primo exhorruit, deinde ut plurimum crederet, utraque manu deorum beneficia tractat.

(140.12–13)

'There are mightier gods who have restored me to full health...'
With this I lifted my tunic and showed off all I had to Eumolpus. At first he was stunned, then to convince himself to the full, he ran both hands over the gifts of the gods.

In this exhibitionism there is also the motif of *handling* the genitals, which seems to argue conclusively that the scene between Quartilla and Giton was exhibitionist too in its significance, just as voyeurism is psychologically compatible with the desire to touch what is seen. And another example might be cited from 105, where the narrator is recognized despite his disguise by his enemy Lichas, who 'ran up and looked at neither my hands nor my face, but straightway dropped his eyes, and ran his business-like hand to my genitals'.

Apart from these uncomplicated examples, there is also a less obvious case. Early in the work Encolpius quarrels with his friend Ascyltos over the affections of Giton. Ascyltos leaves in a rage.

> . . . osculisque tandem bona fide exactis alligo artissimis com-
> plexibus puerum fruorque votis usque ad invidiam felicibus.
> nec adhuc quidem omnia erant facta, cum Ascyltos furtim se
> foribus admovit discussisque fortissime claustris invenit me cum
> fratre ludentem. risu itaque plausuque cellulam implevit, oper-
> tum me amiculo evolvit et 'quid agebas' inquit 'frater sanc-
> tissime?'
>
> (11.1–3)

At last our kisses were without restraint. I hugged the boy close to me. I had what I wanted and anyone would have envied my luck. But we were still in the middle of this when Ascyltos came quietly to the door, violently shattered the bolts, and found me having a gay time with Giton. He filled the little room with laughter and applause. He rolled me out of the cloak I was lying in and said, 'What were you up to, you most reverend brother?'

In the light of earlier instances the scopophilic aspects of this are patent. From the narrator's view-point it is exhibitionism. (In the case of fiction, it is the author's psychology that we are concerned with, and the question of the voluntary or involuntary nature of the incident from the character's point of view may be dis-regarded.) On Ascyltos' side it is voyeurism. If the latter is stressed, the usual parallel is not far to seek. Later in the work Encolpius and Ascyltos part, and Giton elects to go with Ascyltos. He is recovered by Encolpius through a chance meeting at the public baths, and they give Ascyltos the slip. It turns out that Giton was in charge of Ascyltos' clothes, which were stolen when he left. Eumolpus describes the subsequent scene:

'. . . circumire omnes angulos coepi et clara voce Encolpion clamitare. ex altera parte iuvenis nudus, qui vestimenta perdiderat, non minore clamoris indignatione Gitona flagitabat. et me quidem pueri tamquam insanum imitatione petulantissima deriserunt, illum autem frequentia ingens circumvenit, cum plausu et admiratione timidissima. habebat enim inguinum pondus tam grande ut ipsum hominem laciniam fascini crederes. o iuvenem laboriosum: puto illum pridie incipere postero die finire.'

(92.6–10)

'I began going around every nook and cranny, and calling out *Encolpius!* in a loud voice. In the opposite direction, a naked young man, who had lost his clothes, was yelling for someone called Giton with equally indignant shouts. And while the boys just ridiculed me as a lunatic with the most impudent imitations, a huge crowd surrounded him with applause and the most awe-struck admiration. You see, he had such enormous sexual organs that you'd think the man was just an attachment to his penis. What a man for the job! I think he starts yesterday and finishes tomorrow.'

From the author's standpoint, the exhibitionism here is not one or two enjoying the sight, but an admiring crowd. A crowd standing around someone in the Roman public baths, where almost everyone was naked, is rather unexpected in a Latin author, and seems to spring from fantasy rather than any probable incident in real life.

We find then in this short fragmentary work two, possibly three, cases of *scopomixia*, and three (if the extension from sight to touch is admitted) of exhibitionism. It would be rash for a modern to pronounce on the prevalence of such perversion in Roman life, but it can be stated with reasonable certainty that it is not a traditional literary topic in extant classical literature in the way the incest motif is.

There is, of course, the retelling in classical authors of certain myths involving scopophilia and exhibitionism. The story of Actaeon, who was torn to pieces by dogs for having witnessed Diana bathing, and Baubo's piece of exhibitionism to amuse Demeter, come to mind. But in general, examples of such things are few in classical literature. The story of Candaules, who hid Gyges behind his bedroom door to enable him to see his wife naked (Hdt. 1.8–12) is not really relevant, as neither Candaules' wife, nor Gyges, was a willing participant, and both were non-Greek. Outside Petronius the only non-mythic examples of scopophilia in literature are covered by a handful of references, generally in the Greek Anthology and Martial.[1] Not that the traits were unknown in the ancient world: the use of mirrors for sexual purposes is evidenced by Suetonius, who attributes the practice to Horace (*vit. Horat. ad fin.*), and Seneca, whose Hostius Quadra appears to have had most of the known vices (*Q.N.* 1.16.2–9). There are certain works of art which depict similar things, generally a man watching a sexual act (*scopomixia*).[2] There is a little evidence to indicate the presence of peepholes in some Roman brothels, similar to those which could be found in some Chicago and San Francisco whore-houses in the nineteenth century. On the exhibitionist side, the gross man, according to Theophrastus (*Charact.* 11), lifts up his tunic in the presence of ladies, and the *cordax*, which Trimalchio in the *Satyricon* is anxious for his wife to perform (52.8), was a popular, and frankly exhibitionistic, dance. But the point is that, although we cannot say for certain what we would find in the literature no longer extant, the evidence we do have points to the *rarity* of these motifs and suggests that Petronius is not following any obvious literary tradition, or borrowing the themes from earlier authors.[3] His large use of them

[1] Prop. 1.10; *AP* 5.225, 12.40, 12.207; Mart. 1.34.6, 11.45.5–6, 11.70, 11.104.5–8, 13–14.

[2] A silver cup in the Museum of Fine Arts in Boston depicts a slave peeping through a door at a pair of lovers; a red-figure *schale* in the Berlin collection (3251) shows a masturbating youth watching a sexual act with masochistic elements.

[3] For peepholes, cf. Mart. 11.45.5–6; female exhibitionism is the subject of Mart. 1.35.

is therefore the more striking, and they must therefore be a genuine reflection of his own psycho-sexual interests, whether these were grounded in his sexual behaviour or in his fantasy life. Petronius is the only ancient author who makes such extensive use of these themes, although the subjects are much more common in modern literature, witness Marcel Proust.

iv. *Disguised Aspects of the Theme*

To understand how pervasive a theme scopophilia is in the *Satyricon*, it is necessary to examine disguised aspects of this instinct by reference to Freud's scheme for it.[1]

α	Subject's looking at his own *sexual organ*	=	Subject's own sexual organ being looked at *by himself*
β	Subject's looking at an *extraneous object* (active scopophilia)	γ	Subject's own sexual organ being looked at by *another* person (exhibitionism)

It is irrelevant whether the characters expose themselves of their own accord, or through force of circumstances, for the author is autonomous here; but, so far, incidents in the *Satyricon* of active scopophilia have been paralleled by overt and covert exhibitionism (Freud's type β and γ). There are, however, instances also of Freud's α category. In the passage quoted earlier (140) Encolpius found himself impotent, a disability he blamed on Priapus. He is first aware of this when he disappoints Circe. After his unsuccessful attempt with her, Encolpius goes to bed alone. The scene then occurs in which Encolpius describes in mock-tragic diction his attempt at self-castration (see above, pp. 70 f.). Encolpius, despite certain feelings of shame, goes on to abuse his genitals for failing him. This incident plainly falls into Freud's α category: even the dual nature of that category is realized, as Encolpius and his penis are treated as separate subjects, occupying our attention in turn. The very ambivalence of Encolpius in this castration attempt (is his penis part of himself or not?) suggests the auto-erotism underlying scopophilia. Petronius thus illustrates all the Freudian classifications, not aetiologically or in their psycho-analytical priority,

[1] 'Instincts and their Vicissitudes', *Collected Papers*, Vol. IV, p. 73.

as Freud expounds them, but as unconnected aspects of the same preoccupation.

In the light of the above, certain elements in the work arguably relate to the less obvious transformations of scopophilia. Some of them are significant only when viewed in connection with the more obvious scopophilic themes, but some also display their scopophilic nature to the most cursory examination.

In *Der Witz und seine Beziehung zum Unbewusstsein*, Freud said: 'it cannot be doubted that the desire to see what is sexual exposed is the original motive of smut.'[1] The *Satyricon* is not pornographic in the full sense, but it does make use of conventionally obscene subjects; their treatment is humorous, and there are frequent examples of obscene wit in the conversations (e.g. 92: '*Tanto magis expedit* inguina *quam* ingenia *fricare*'). The two 'Milesian' tales, *The Widow of Ephesus* and *The Boy of Pergamum*, may now be adduced as similar evidence.

Scopophilia particularly shows itself in the desire to see what is forbidden, whether by law, social custom or, ultimately, incest taboos. Abraham says of a neurotic patient:

> In this as in other cases the prohibition of looking at his mother originated in the more particular prohibition of seeing her naked, and in especial of seeing her genitals.[2]

Along with the mixoscopy of the *Satyricon* there is a concentration on more general *secrets*: the word *secretum* (as well as synonyms like *obscurus* etc) occurs frequently. At times it describes out of the way places, and these instances may well be dictated by the exigencies of the picaresque plot. The same may be argued of the impersonations and disguises of the last two episodes, and the fact that more than half the scenes take place at dusk, or at night, or in an atmosphere of darkness and failing light, guttering lamps, and burning torches. But the use of secrets in the plot itself may be susceptible of deeper interpretation.

[1] *Jokes and their Relation to the Unconscious*, trans. J. Strachey (London, 1960), p. 97.
[2] 'Restriction and Transformations of Scopophilia in Psycho-neurotics', *Selected Papers of Karl Abraham M.D.* (English Edition, London, 1927), p. 177.

Encolpius' offence which made him fall foul of Quartilla (16–26) was the witnessing, and consequent profanation, of some rites of Priapus, an unforgivable sacrilege (*inexpiabile scelus*). Quartilla stresses the secret nature of these rites (*tot annorum secreta*) and the danger of their becoming common knowledge. There were various secret cults in the Roman world but the ceremonies in honour of Priapus are self-avowedly sexual. Expiation for the offence requires a licentious all night vigil in the god's honour, and it is during this that the first scopophilic incident occurs. Throughout this episode there are allusions to secrets (e.g. 'Both of us swore in the most solemn terms that so horrible a secret would perish between us,' 21.3). Again, when Encolpius is apparently the victim of a sexual assault (the text is fragmentary here), Ascyltos 'had covered his head with his cloak; he had been warned it was dangerous to be involved in other people's secrets' (20.3). It may be added that among the verse fragments attributed to Petronius there is a retelling of the story of Midas and his asses' ears, and how the secret leaked out–the moral being that men cannot keep secrets (*Nam citius flammas mortales ore tenebunt/quam secreta tegant*, Fgt. XXVIII). The significance of these features of the work is brought out by Abraham's remark on a neurotic patient:

> . . . the early forcing away of his scopophilic instinct from its real objects and aims led not only to a typical brooding but also to a morbid propensity towards secret and mystical things . . . I need hardly refer to the countless similar phenomena that are to be found in folk-psychology–on the one hand, secret cults, mysteries, occultist movements etc, and on the other, religious prohibitions against inquiring into the most secret things.
>
> (*op. cit.*, p. 219)

Even the two supernatural stories (61–3), and the magical themes in Petronius, may fit in with Abraham's further remarks on the same patient:

> Concerning the significance of ghosts . . . when later the prohibition against looking and knowing had obtained a hold over him, his repressed wish for a repetition of the pleasurable

impressions of childhood was displaced on to 'ghosts'. He longed all the time to see ghosts.

(ibid., p. 220)

Abraham also explains the significance of the Cyclops story in relation to scopophilia and castration anxiety. Allusions to the Cyclops theme in the *Satyricon* are found in 48, 97, 98 and 101—patently it attracted Petronius. The motif of blinding is not specifically used, the story being generally offered as a comparison with some situation in which the characters find themselves. One admittedly dubious instance comes near this, however, and would be psycho-analytically important. In 48, Trimalchio, displaying his inaccurate knowledge of mythology, asks Agamemnon if he knows 'the story of Ulysses, how the Cyclops tore his thumb out with pincers'. Admittedly the text is corrupt, but it looks as though here the underlying notion of castrating the father has been replaced by the more basic anxiety that the father will castrate oneself. Trimalchio's mistake, if our present text is at all to be trusted, is of considerable interest for the author's psychology.

The whole motif of castration in the *Satyricon* must be brought into relation with the scopophilic elements. The castration anxiety evinced may be taken as the fear of punishment for forbidden looking. The reversal by Trimalchio of the traditional Cyclops story is paralleled by the lack of active castration (directed as it was against the father) in the work. The two castration scenes are both concerned with self-castration. The first is Giton's move to castrate himself with a blunted razor, because his sexual attractions have caused so much trouble and jealousy among his friends. He had earlier attempted to cut his throat with the same razor (94). These attempts at self-mutilation or suicide, although not serious on Giton's part, always lead to Encolpius' trying to cut his throat too. These incidents are to be compared with Encolpius' frustrated self-castration in 132 (cited earlier in another connection). This last takes place after his sexual failure with Circe, and thus is connected with the theme of sexual inadequacy and sexual envy.

248

Abraham mentions a patient who had once seen his father naked when he was nine years old and

> . . . had inspected his genitals with great interest. His phantasies
> . . . often reverted to that scene. And yet the thoughts associated
> with it were by no means purely pleasurable; on the contrary,
> he was continually worried by the question whether his genitals
> would attain the size of his father's . . . he fell prey to the tor-
> menting belief . . . that his penis was too small.
>
> (*ibid.*, p. 186)

These are two situations in the *Satyricon* that might be compared to this: the jealous reference to the size of Ascyltos' genitals in 92 (Ascyltos, it will be remembered, being a rival for Giton's affections), and the final return to normal of Encolpius' own genitals in 139, when he exhibits them to his other rival, Eumolpus, a fatherly figure with strong sexual inclinations. Feelings of sexual inferiority are often a motive for certain types of scopophilia, particularly for male interest in male genitals, just as any natural physical disability often prompts curiosity about the hidden part of normal people's lives. All of these sexual incidents fit a scopophilic pattern, and it is to be noticed that Encolpius, the narrator and the hero (or anti-hero) of the work, is the one who generally exemplifies the syndrome.[1] It is he who displays the sexual inadequacy, the sexual envy, the castration anxiety, the scopophilic and exhibitionist traits to the full, and seems therefore the main vehicle of the author's fantasy in these respects, just as Eumolpus is the main vehicle of the author's views on poetry. Encolpius is

---

[1] Not of course invariably. Scopophilic behaviour is found in many of the other characters. Moreover certain characteristics of the famous vulgarian Trimalchio serve also as a vehicle for the less obvious transformations of the instinct that dominates the work. Urolagnia and coprolagnia are part of the complex of voyeurism: Trimalchio (like the Emperor Claudius, cf. Suet. *Claud.* 32) is greatly interested in the excretory functions, and gives a long and vulgar description of his own internal economy (47); references to chamber-pots and similar subjects are frequent in this part of the work (cf. 27, 41 *et al.*). One might add here Freud's remarks: 'Excremental things are all too intimately and inseparably bound up with sexual things; the position of the genital organs—inter urinam et faeces [*sic*]—remains the decisive and unchangeable factor': *Collected Papers*, Vol. IV, p. 215.

not made out a sympathetic character, he is more of an unfortunate scapegoat.

v. *Sadism in the Satyricon*

We may even fit into this pattern the frequent incidents of an apparently sadistic nature, which occur with almost equal regularity in the work. There is, for example, the sexual (and general) maltreatment of Encolpius and Ascyltos by Quartilla and her entourage (20 ff.); the beating of Encolpius by Ascyltos (11.4); the scourging of Encolpius and Giton by Lichas' crew (105.4); the extreme punishments inflicted on Encolpius by Circe's household (132.2–4); his further beating by Proselenus (134.3–4); and the painful attempts to cure his own impotence by urtication and worse (138.1–3). Other scenes might be included, such as the mauling of Eumolpus by the lodging-house slaves, but the scenes of violence and beating involving Encolpius bulk curiously large in the short extant narrative we possess. It has to be admitted that there is no loving lingering over these incidents: the treatment is brief and witty, and has nothing in common with the modern 'hard-core' pornography on this subject, which aims to excite, or pander to, such an interest in the reader. Nevertheless the regular choice of such incidents for insertion into the narrative may reflect an unconscious pattern of attention, and the following considerations may just be worth offering.

The following passage from Otto Fenichel summarizes adequately the possible connection between these incidents and the basic sexual theme:

> Very often sadistic impulses are tied up with scopophilia: the individual wants to see something in order to destroy it (or to gain reassurance that the object is not yet destroyed). Often looking itself is unconsciously thought of as a substitute for destroying ('I did not destroy it; I merely looked at it').
>
> The typical obsessive idea in women that they must compulsively look at men's genitals often represents a distorted expression of the sadistic wish to destroy men's genitals.[1]

---

[1] *The Psychoanalytic Theory of Neurosis* (London, 1946), p. 71.

The implications of this passage for the behaviour typical of many of the women in the *Satyricon* needs, of course, little stress, and the reader may be left to work out the details for himself.

Although, like Proust's narrator, Encolpius does not seem aware of the perverseness of some of these scopophilic and sadistic situations, Petronius takes care to *place* Encolpius in a way Proust does not in comparable situations. This is as indicative of Petronius' artistic sensibility as the incidents chosen are of his psychological preoccupations, just as his narrative style, however erotic the subject, never makes use of the obscene words that figure in Catullus, Martial, and even Horace.

vi. *Some Psycho-analytical Deductions*

Petronius, then, has chosen as the main element of his realism various sexual motifs and has concentrated on such perversions of the sexual instinct as are related to scopophilia, and its polarity, exhibitionism. In this I suggest that he was directed by his own fantasies and sexual interest; the frank nature of the work allowed his preoccupations much greater rein, as they were here less fettered by literary models, conventions, or stock themes. Even the pre-eminently sensible Collignon says: '*Le choix même du sujet est un indice de son caractère. Une certain conception de la vie se manifeste par la manière dont il imagine, conduit, dénoue les aventures de ses héros*' (p. 52). Consequently more might be deducible about his psychology than is usual with many ancient or modern authors, and if the evidence presented above does reveal a preoccupation with scopophilic themes, the rarity of these in ancient literatures may allow psycho-analytical deductions to be made.

Certainly there may be one practical application. The material presented above could perhaps offer another possible argument for the attribution of the *Satyricon* to the Petronius of Tacitus. The most interesting features of Tacitus' account in *Ann.* 16.17–20, which may be related to the feature of the *Satyricon* I have been discussing, are Petronius' nocturnal habits and the great interest he showed in the Emperor's sexual life. To examine them in order: Petronius did not simply use the nights for pleasure; this might be dependent upon general conventions, which were not so different, at least in the early empire, from what they are now. He used them also for work – this may point to a deliberate avoidance of daytime as a time for any activity at all. It is important however that Tacitus specially refers to this habit, and so implies it was at least a significant characteristic deserving the historian's comment.[1] In the work itself perhaps half of the episodes take place in darkness; the characters are frequently lost in the dark; lamps and lighting are often mentioned. In all cases, as obviously in some, this might be demanded by the situation, and it would be unwise to deduce much from it. But one of the characteristics of scopophilia is the fear of light and the avoidance of it. Abraham is again the most convenient text (*op. cit.*, pp. 201–6), where he says that darkness has both a positive and a negative significance for the scopophilic. Obviously Abraham is drawing on case-histories of neurotic patients, and it is unlikely that Petronius had any really neurotic intolerance of daylight. This would be hardly feasible in view of his record as a capable administrator. But he did have a preference for night, which Tacitus took pains to point out, and this may well indicate a scopophilic disposition. The most important relevant feature for us of the courtier's portrait is surely the great interest he took in the details of the sexual life of the Emperor. This was a dangerous interest, and Silia suffered on suspicion of pandering to it. It was a strong interest, which must have involved close questioning of Silia (if it really was she who was his source) about Nero's associates, and the practices in which she took part. This interest must strike us as morbid to some degree, and reflects the scopophilic instinct in its vicarious aspect. The connection of graphic and verbal obscenity with scopophilia is well known.

---

[1] Of course it was not (and is not) too unusual. Seneca refers scathingly to the *turba lucifugarum* (*Ep.* 122.15), which included such people as Acilius Buta and Sextus Papinius. The whole letter is worth consulting, as it is a lengthy attack on the sort of Epicurean and aesthete that Petronius clearly was: compare *Quomodo cultu se a ceteris distinguunt, quomodo elegantia cenarum, munditiis vehiculorum, sic volunt separari etiam temporum dispositione* (122.18) with Tac. *Ann.* 16.18 and *Sat.* 72.4. I suggested above (pp. 211 ff.), as a partial explanation of Petronius' parody of Senecan moralizing, that the two would be mutually antipathetic, and that this letter might well be a disguised criticism of the courtier; see P. Faider, *Études sur Sénèque*, pp. 15 ff.

Prompted by revenge, Petronius chose to write down a careful account of all he knew about the Emperor's sexual proclivities, based on careful study, it would seem, for the blow struck home to Nero, and produced a violent reaction. This connects the courtier with our author, and it is on this fact in particular that a psycho-analytical argument for the attribution of the *Satyricon* to the Petronius described by Tacitus may be based. It has at least slightly more definition than the traditional psychological arguments which have held the field for so long.[1]

[1] See e.g. J. Wight Duff, quoted above, p. 31, n. 1.

CHAPTER VIII

Conclusion

An evaluation of Petronius that will convince everyone is perhaps impossible: the *Satyricon*, as we have it, even after the most searching attempts at reconstruction, is too fragmentary, the movement, and the dénouement of the plot too obscure. But there is enough of it left to allow some sort of judgment on its merits as a cultural and literary document, and a more or less informed assessment of its probable intentions and success. Were enough not extant, it would be hard to explain, pragmatically or plausibly, the interest aroused by it and the labours expended on it. Several obstacles have stood in the way of any attempt to see what its virtues are, or to relate it to the development of Latin literature in general: besides the mutilated text, the persistent doubts about its date and authorship, although, to my mind, largely unnecessary, made critical comment hazardous, just as the scabrous nature of some of the episodes made a scholarly interest in the work eccentric or suspect. (Arguably, the whole question of the sexual strain that runs through Latin literature – and Greek, for that matter – is overdue for serious scrutiny, with the hope of separating what is, and what is not, of true literary and human interest to the twentieth century. But perhaps, as Fordyce's recent bowdlerization of Catullus suggests, classical scholarship is not quite ready for this.) It was, no doubt, this lack of moral earnestness, real or apparent, and its *recherché*, and therefore incomprehensible, literariness that militated against its survival intact through periods whose growing Christianity went hand in hand with increasing intellectual barbarism. The rather specialized nature of its sexual interests – homosexuality, voyeurism, and castration–and its learnedly allusive and blatantly topical qualities might appeal as a combination to a *jeunesse dorée* of low habits and refined tastes, but hardly to those whose hopes of heaven denied them a number of more earthly interests. A modern reaction to this standard view has been to read into the work the sort of seriousness we associate with the classics of moral satire or the philosophical novel.

In this book I have tried to dispel, as far as possible, the factual uncertainties about the *Satyricon* and its historical setting; I have tried to counter certain critical, perhaps even unconsciously moral, assumptions about the necessary nature and inner spirit of all satiric forms in Latin literature. However we finally evaluate his achievement, Petronius was, in certain clear senses, a literary opportunist. Menippean satire presumably suggested itself as a very suitable form for such opportunism because of the comparative freedom it offered in terms of structure and theme. The *Satyricon* was almost certainly written for the amusement–the *literary* instruction at most–of Nero's court circle. There seems evidence that it was used, incidentally and without too great a fuss, not only to present a classical critique and an Epicurean theory of literature, but also to snipe at various literary and philosophical targets, such as Lucan and Seneca, rhetorical moralizing, and Stoic doctrine in general. What prompted the dislike behind this sniping, whether personal antipathy, literary or philosophical disagreement, the wish to please or influence the emperor, we naturally have no means of deciding. Luckily the purely personal motives of an artist are irrelevant to an assessment of his aesthetic principles and actual success. Such principles must underlie an author's responsible choice of sexual, local, biographical, political, or literary themes, and dictate his handling of them; as such, they are a proper subject of our concern. They may be invoked to explain local inadequacies or limitations, just as the unifying vision behind the work determines our total impression of its larger intentions and its classic status.

The main question, touched upon earlier in these pages, now has to be posed directly. Is Petronius a true satirist? There have been many attempts to make him one, and, as with any classical author, the defence counsels have been learned and ingenious. He has been credited with personal satire against his own ex-slave, against various court ladies such as Agrippina, and even against Nero himself; he has been depicted as dwelling on the turbulence and unhappiness of passion and vice simply to inculcate the lessons of Epicurean *ataraxia* and contented imperturbability; he has been ascribed more traditional castigation of the luxury, materialism, and sensuality of his Roman contemporaries; and, more subtly, he has been praised as seeing the skull beneath the skin of his world, of seeing around him a Waste Land, with fear in a handful of dust. This Waste Land is supposedly represented in the *Satyricon* by such things as Trimalchio's obsession with death and by the sterile childlessness and materialistic preoccupations of his company. The only sane answer amid all this is that given by the Sibyl to the teasing children: 'I want to die' (48.8). Doubtless T. S. Eliot's use of this story as an epigraph for *The Waste Land* helped, if it did not suggest, such a critical interpretation. The world that Petronius presents, then, would be

> A heap of broken images, where the sun beats,
> And the dead tree gives no shelter . . .

I find it difficult, however, to substantiate any of these interpretations. There seems to be an occasional hit at some contemporary fashion at court or at large, but the theory of a consistent satire, directed against a person or persons, will not stand up to an examination of the literary and historical evidence. The advocacy of a morality associated more with Epicurus himself than with his later, less orthodox, Roman followers, such as Lucullus and Petronius, as posited by the more strenuously moral apologists for the work, seems flatly contradicted, not merely by what we know of the author's own life, but also by the views expressed at 132.15, where Epicurean principles about literature and sex are invoked to quite different effect. The passages in the prose and the verse that present some straight moralizing, and which are used to buttress the theory that Petronius, in a conventional but sincere manner, is satirizing the vices of his times, become suspect through the irony of their context, because of the disreputability of the *personae* that utter them, and in the light of their parodic intentions.

Even the subtler, though (to me) anachronistic, interpretation that claims a consciously felt, and expressed, *Angst* or *Weltschmerz* simply does not survive an inspection of the humorous irony that pervades the work, and the interested vitality that comes through all the elaborate literariness. Such evidence for this as may be collected from the repetitive themes and images in the *Cena* may be explained as examples of philosophical parody or satiric characterization: the middle and lower classes of many societies *are* preoccupied with money, and many Romans, including Pacuvius and Seneca, were, like Trimalchio, obsessed with the thought of death, whether their attitude was one of didactic resignation or fearful preparation. But in Petronius, the *Cena* seems to depend, for this aspect of it, on the satirical and amused observation, not the disgusted and symbolic condemnation, of a society.

The words 'satire' and 'satirical' turn up constantly, when one is clarifying Petronius' aims, techniques, and achievements. And it may seem paradoxical to deny him his status as a major satirist in despite of this. But Petronius' use of the satiric mode, however original and inventive in some ways, is not, as it were, classical: he employs themes and techniques, he follows certain models, of the genre, but he is not interested in morality in the larger sense, but only in art. And this means that the centrality of the great satirists, Horace at his best, Persius, Donne, Pope, Johnson, and Byron, for instance, is beyond him–or not his main concern, depending on the criteria we choose to apply.

When I speak of 'great satire', I do not mean satiric elements or even 'negative' satire, although this may be forceful and brilliant. Satire has always presented critical problems, and there is (or used to be) a tendency to dismiss all satirists as somehow impure or inferior artists, or think of them in terms recalling Louis MacNeice's lines:

> He is not creative at all, his mind is dry
> And bears no blossoms even in the season,
> He is an onlooker, a heartless type,
> Whose hobby is giving everyone else the lie.

The best satire, to my mind, has to be conceived as an art form that is self-avowedly concerned in some sense with morality (including under this head aesthetic and intellectual principles) and it expresses, implicitly or explicitly, an ethical or para-ethical standpoint. This constitutes, as it were, the centre from which the description and the treatment of the objects of the satire emerge. The best satire embodies, in proper artistic form, a coherent and positive sensibility. One need hardly point out that just to have a moral or semi-moral position and good intentions is not enough: it is the intimate fusion of art and morality that makes satire *literature*. This also generates the critical problems, particularly as the reader does not have to, and often does not, share the ethical assumptions of the satirist. But the triumphs, the paradigms, of the genre, *The Dunciad*, *The Vanity of Human Wishes*, *Don Juan*, effectively dispel any *a priori* doubts we might feel.

A satirist of this type Petronius is not. He is, so to speak, Alexandrian—in the modern rather than the ancient sense. His unswerving devotion to literature and his more or less coherent aesthetic theory go hand in hand with a deliberately limited 'realism'; it looks like the selective and seamy 'realism' of the genuine satirist, who naturally focuses on the darker side of life, but the impulse behind his restricted choice of low characters, cynical motivation, and the high preponderance of sexual situations (in so far as this is not to be analysed in social or psychological terms), is a *literary* impulse, and devoid of any obvious moral commitment. The satiric subjects are chosen on literary grounds, for their traditional connotations or humorous possibilities, not the other way around, as might be the case with the true satirist.

The result is a curious distancing, a wry irony, which at times makes the author seem almost ambivalent towards his characters, and distracts him from their consistent presentation, although it does, for one thing, drain the more shocking episodes of any pornographic effect; for instance, the rich Latin vocabulary of obscenity is hardly ever called upon, except for an inoffensive joke or a sexual pun. Petronius' self-conscious sophistication may be seen in the careful dissociation of the author from the ostensible narrator, who is constantly made the unconscious butt of the author's ridicule and satire to achieve this very purpose. This in

258

turn blunts the edge of the conventional satire against other targets in the work, by removing any acceptable moral criteria, except for the uninteresting possibilities in the reader's stock responses. The satire seems then the product of a literary, rather than a moral, impulsion, a view that is confirmed by the very traditional satiric themes selected. Even when Encolpius steps out of his dramatic role to deliver the well-known defence of the work, to claim that it is prompted by candour, and that it described life as it is, this partial revelation of the author's principles is nevertheless presented in an ironic and mocking context of literary allusion.

All this surely must throw doubt on any claim that Petronius is a genuine classic, however minor, of satire in the proper sense. If there is a 'quasi-moral' principle at work, it is the principle, invoked sometimes by Horace also, of taste, be it taste in literature or behaviour, but taste itself dictates that even this be not taken too seriously–*surtout pas de zèle*. Petronius tries to strike a balance –and he is sometimes successful–between the traditional demands of his chosen genre, which he cannot altogether resist, and the spirit that animates his work. And perhaps this indicates that he had in mind something different from the true satirist.

An English critic, W. W. Robson, long ago pointed out to me that there are two kinds of judgment that one makes about literature. In one case, and this covers light reading and the literature of escape or time-killing, one judges the thing as a specimen of a class: the mere subsumption in a category predetermines the *range* of critical predicates. And this allocation to genre, as we tend to call it in academic studies, is not as dull, trivial, or futile as might be suggested by the perusal of our drier literary histories–or some of the discussions of the *Satyricon* as an example of satire, parody, or adventure story. It can be a way of indicating what things are relevant to the critical examination. Accordingly, if one condemns an adventure story or a thriller as lacking in suspense, everyone would agree that the comment, whether true or not, was to the point. One may say that thrillers are a shocking waste of time, and that the desire for suspense is unworthy of a mature reader, but no one can question the relevance of the criterion. The judgment operates in terms of a *class* of literature, and thus whether the work in question has or has not certain expected properties. But with the other sort of literary judgment, which is perhaps best exemplified in such verdicts as 'that's a good poem', or 'that's a significant novel', one is not assigning to a category, and the audience has virtually no idea of the range of appropriate predicates.

Of course the criteria for good poems, indeed for any works in which creative originality is an important element, seem far more varied than the criteria for good thrillers. It looks as though whenever we judge a poem good, we are not thereby considering it to have satisfied some pre-existing criteria for a particular class or category of poems. We seem to be valuing the thing as it is in itself as something unique. And we may contrast with this such judgments as 'that's a good set of elegiac verses', or 'that's a skilful use of dochmiacs', judgments that have gone out of fashion in modern literary discussion, because they imply some anterior formula or recipe which the poet has successfully followed, and so seem to degrade the artist into a mere craftsman.

Naturally our usual literary discussions are full of overlappings of these two types of judgment. In classics, there is the further complication of making a preliminary decision, often on the basis of an incomplete set of facts, about what the work was intended to be in its entirety, or even what it said or meant locally. Both of these problems are important and relevant to such fragmentary works as the *Satyricon*. When, however, we compare two works with a view to establishing a preference between them, we may only do this in virtue of some hypothetical end or aim which they are presumed to share; but in so doing, we must give up the claim for either of them of an ideal purity and singularity of intention. On the other hand, when we analyse a work with a view to showing how it attains its characteristic effect, we may, if we wish, retain the implication that its particular realization of its individual aim is unique. Of course in practice the critical and descriptive vocabulary we employ, if it is to be intelligible, has to relate to the audience's experience of other works: comparison is implicit generalization. It is important, however, to be aware when we are doing the one or the other; to know what criteria are relevant and when; and to see where and why we can convincingly invoke, with reasonable safeguards, the privilege of singularity for a given work.

In the light of this, denying Petronius his claim to be a serious satirist doesn't mean denying him all claim to an integrating vision or to artistic seriousness in other ways. And the principle of uniqueness is a tempting one to invoke for a work that is so manifestly different from the rest of Latin literature; certainly the adjective 'unique' occurs frequently in critical comment on the *Satyricon*. We have examined the reason for Petronius' decision to use humorous narrative as the vehicle for his artistic ends–and *ad hoc* purposes: the form was flexible, and so adaptable to his particular aims and even to his Epicurean views on the non-utilitarian value of literature. Behind the basic conception of the *Satyricon*, there was some hard and critical thinking. Certainly some of the literary discussions interspersed in the narrative echo certain important critical debates, common to the Neronian and earlier periods, that affected, to some degree at least, Petronius' aesthetic principles. The controversies that obviously influenced the genesis of the *Satyricon* were, first, that carried on between the Atticists and the Asianists over style in general, as well as some of its remoter ramifications, and, secondly, the more defensive fight waged by the writers of satire, epigram, and the earthier, more 'realistic', genres of Latin literature against both moralistic censors, waving the banner of Cato, and the exponents of the loftier, more prestigious, and ambitious types of poetry and prose-historical and mythological epic, drama, and philosophy. If my estimate of the framework, style, subject-matter, and narrative method of the *Satyricon* is correct, Petronius was on the side of the Atticists and, despite his admiration for Vergil and the other classics, the 'realists'. The other factors governing his choice of sides are not difficult to guess at. As far as we can see, there was a sterile imitativeness about much of Neronian literature, both in poetry and rhetoric. The evidence is there in the harsh criticism of Persius' first satire, in Lucan's radical attempt to get away from the traditional mythological structure of epic, and in the minor literature that has survived from the period. Almost in the spirit of Callimachus, who turned away from the grander forms of poetic composition, not because of their intrinsic inferiority, but because they had reached their peak with such predecessors as Homer, and were now unsuited to the demands and talents of a very different, sophisticated, and academic, age, Petronius chose the Latin tradition that offered him, as it did Persius, Martial, and Juvenal, the greatest freedom for experiment and originality, and the desired tolerance of such things as criticism, parody, literary versatility, and the sophisticated treatment of subjects that were alien to more classical forms. This tradition, whose vitality did at least ensure that the evolution of Latin poetry, a sicklier, if more precocious, child of the Roman and Italian genius than Latin prose, did not come to a halt with the Augustan or Neronian eras, but continued to produce classics, in the standard sense, well into the second century A.D. Petronius' exploration and expansion of the comparatively minor sub-genre, Menippean satire, was prompted by the many opportunities it offered, although, like the novel or *vers libre* in more recent times, it also presented certain temptations to self-indulgence.

Of course the 'freedom' that modern authors like to think they possess was psychologically impossible for any, even the most revolutionary, Roman writer. The power of tradition, of formal conventions and requirements, of literary decorum, even of the audience's expectations, was greater than our romantic and modernist imaginations can readily grasp–yet it was gladly acknowledged. Revolutions in literature took place within established, or at least acceptable, frameworks: they were not violent or anarchical attempts to trample underfoot the achievements of predecessors, or the heritage of Greek and Latin literary theory. The call for *novae tabulae* in Rome was always political, never literary, whatever the faults of contemporary practitioners in the eyes of the reformers. For all his originality, Petronius is no exception to this rule.

The *Satyricon* has still to conform, minimally at any rate, to the rules of *satura*, which was still a more encompassing form than our *satire*, even though by this time it was, one suspects, being gradually pressed into what was to become the Juvenalian mould. It remained of course an appropriate form still for literary, as well as moral, criticism and for humorous parody as well as philosophical censure; it invited also coarseness and sexuality, not always strictly relevant or necessary, which presumably appealed to the Roman readers of Catullus, Horace, Martial, and Juvenal, and which has certainly distressed many of their more modern admirers.

The *nostalgie de la boue* which went with such tastes, and which which must be postulated in the simultaneously refined and gross upper class circles of Petronius' age (and later), the impulse that sent Nero the *artifex* wandering and brawling through the lower quarters of Rome like any *Tityre-tu* in seventeenth-century London, is hard to overlook in the *Satyricon*: it is visible in the lack of admirable characters; in the sympathetically detailed, if ironic, description of Trimalchio and his milieu; and, above all, in the recurrent, bizarre sexual scenes. This had to be a determinant of the choice of form and subject-matter, just as the motive behind the criticism of Lucan's *Pharsalia*, and the parody of Seneca's tragedies and of the later philosophical work produced by that presumably uncongenial Stoic, was another. The form once fixed upon exercised its prerogatives in stricter ways: *some* satire, in our standard sense, had to be introduced to satisfy its demands. Petronius was obliged, as it were, by his literary principles to gratify somehow the expectations of his hearers. Fundamentally his engagement, apart from minor excursions into topical, or even personal, matters, was with literature, which is as much a part of life, of course, as any other, but he had now to set up, with misleading consequences for us, at least some of the standard moral targets of his predecessors in satire, whether this went against his artistic grain or no. Into the accommodating framework of his comic *Reiseroman*, therefore, with its affectionate parody of the Homeric Wrath of Poseidon, he inserts such obviously 'satiric' episodes as the Crotonian imposture (against legacy hunters); the *Cena Trimalchionis* (against wealthy and pretentious freedmen); and, most congenially for his sexual 'realism', the various scenes portraying that favourite subject of satirists through the ages, female lust—in the persons of Tryphaena, Quartilla, the Ephesian matron, Circe, Proselenos, and Oenothea. The number and variety of these characterizations of what is, at bottom, a simple enough literary and satirical type provide a clue to Petronius' real achievement: how he transcended, to a great extent, the limitations and exigencies (for him) of his chosen but, in certain ways, uncongenial form, and, to an admittedly limited extent, unified the disparate intentions of the different parts of the work. As a result, a piece of coterie writing, a loosely-knit assortment of occasional criticism, parody, humorous adventure, and perverse sexual themes, impresses us, by some standards and in certain areas, as artistic writing of a high order.

The Flaubertian objectivity of his style; the complete absence of the author's personality from the main narrative, achieved through the use of a dissociated and carefully 'placed' narrator; even the ironic and detached expression of his principles through the medium of different (and differentiated) *personae*; while these cannot, or at any rate do not, produce great satire in the classical sense, they are Petronius' means to a different sort of end: a creative and humorous presentation of an imaginatively realized world. (Despite her satiric potentialities, Emma Bovary is not satirized either.) It is not a world that corresponds to our world, nor one that stretches as far as the horizons of the very greatest and most humane writers of other ages. But it is the sort of creation that one is hard put to parallel, except occasionally, in comparable Latin writers: the microcosm of Plautus and Terence is schematic and insubstantial by comparison, and the universe of Apuleius is as dreamlike and unlocalized as Cupid's palace in the story of Psyche.

In the most obvious and impressive case, the episodes involving Trimalchio, we see how an initial conception, which might have developed along traditional satiric lines, as does Horace's *Cena Nasidieni*, is transformed into something different in kind rather than degree; so vigorous is the artistic power, and so vivid the delineation, that the subordinate motives of Senecan parody, and the topical criticism of current fashion and earlier folly, are fused into, rather than stand in the way of, the total effect. A sardonic caricature of a volatile, ignorant, superstitious, and boastful freedman, who seems initially arraigned for condemnation on grounds of taste, would be no difficult feat for a writer as good as Petronius, given also the wealth of earlier literary models and the material for observation offered by first-century Rome. But by an impressive variety of structural devices: changes of tone and point of view; ironic reversals of the expected signals and responses; carefully planned rhythm and dynamic symbolism; and plausible detail and dialogue, the episode ends up a convincing and sympathetically *felt* creation of a memorable fictional character, or rather of a whole society. The rounding out of what might have been an essentially flat figure in a comparatively static situation is accomplished by the gradual revelation of Trimalchio's personality, and by a corresponding and increasingly complex development of our attitude towards him: he is presented through his physical surroundings; then through Encolpius' own personal impressions of him; then through the conversation of his guests; we are given, concomitantly, a prejudiced account of his behaviour and hospitality by Encolpius, the effect of which is offset by an unwittingly naïve account of his own poor behaviour; finally, the last strokes are added with Trimalchio's great outburst at Fortunata, followed by his autobiographical reminiscences and his mock funeral. He is dramatically presented from successive points of view, much as Socrates is presented in Plato's *Symposium*, and this is a true novelist's technique. (One remembers that D. H. Lawrence, in *Surgery for the Novel – or a Bomb*, described Plato's dialogues as 'queer little novels'.)

So if satire in the full sense was alien to Petronius' genius and outlook, the more disinterested and tolerant observation of the novelist was not. The satiric realism he limited himself to, in following the tradition, does indeed concentrate on the blacker, meaner, and seamier aspects of life, but this limitation, although serious enough by the highest standards, which are not anyway in question here, is partially surmounted by Petronius' refusal to associate himself (as the omniscient author, say) with Encolpius' narrative, criticism, or self-pity. His humorous and ironic detachment ensures that we do not see the low-life adventures and cynical immorality of the characters through pessimistic eyes, but with amusement, and even, in the cases of Trimalchio and perhaps even Eumolpus, whose devotion to poetry is touching, if a little absurd, with sympathy. Trimalchio is admittedly larger than life, but this in no way excludes the careful and controlled observation that is characteristic of the detached sympathy of the artist, as opposed to the directed and highly selective purview of the satirist. It has been said that the future of realism in literature may lie in the ease with which it can sustain, as it does in certain recent English and American novels in the picaresque vein, the properly timed commentary of humour. When all reservations are made, the *Cena* stands out as an early anticipation of this, a successful and self-contained example of such comic realism. The *Cena* accordingly offers us a standard for the rest of the work, and it is not without reason that this part has received most scholarly attention, although the comparatively intact text and the relatively inoffensive nature of the realism have also helped. And Petronius' claims as an imaginative writer must begin from this. Admittedly none of the other characters in the work can compete with Trimalchio. Encolpius, although sometimes a vehicle for the author's critical views, is too drastically distanced by Petronius' self-conscious irony for us to have more than an idea of his character. He has to step out of his dramatic role at least twice, and his reaction to situations seems partly motivated by an effort on Petronius' part to milk the humour of each episode rather than to present Encolpius as all of a piece. As a consequence, his behaviour is not just melodramatic but psychologically inconsistent also, without any discernible artistic reason. The rest of the characters, the women, for instance, are unfortunately known to us only from very fragmentary episodes. Eumolpus is, in a way, an important exception, but the consistency of his amusing hypocrisy and his satirized *furor poeticus* is rather marred by his selection as an alternative vehicle for some of the author's literary views. His poetic effusions, which have to be taken seriously by him and Encolpius in the context of the narrative, have, after all, parodic or exemplary purposes from the point of view of Petronius and his audience: their rationale and his eminently reasonable critical remarks do not properly jibe with the dramatic presentation. Here Petronius' local opportunism has meant artistic sacrifices. This ironic knowingness, of course, protects the author from too much responsibility for his literary exercises and opinions. But this in turn strikes the reader as an ambivalent attitude to a literary creation, and produces in him a sense of unease.

Indeed, one might say, in general, that this sort of opportunism *is* a crucial weakness in the work as it stands; it is one of the temptations inherent in any sort of *satura*, and perhaps Menippean satire particularly is subject to it. The form, as we can see, leads to other and similar self-indulgences, partly because it is expanded by Petronius beyond its original circumscribed limits. Petronius works hard to impose, and keep obvious to the reader, the mock-epic structure that to some extent unifies the *louche*, unpredictable adventures of Encolpius; true, the *Cena* may be defended as a digression that is a self-contained and successful work of art, but even so, Petronius, perhaps in response to his local and circumstantial incitements which his arguably serial method of composition and publication may have encouraged, is sometimes too ready to display his artistic versatility, and this leads to a blurring of the dramatic focus and an inconsistency of treatment. Almost any opportunity may serve for the introduction of a rhetorical parody or an amusing, or clever, and *ad hoc* poem, which cannot, in the nature of things, rise to any great heights. And this willingness to be irrelevant shows itself in larger ways.

The humorous realism of the *Cena* is almost thrown aside in the Croton episodes; the realism in these is confined to the sexual scenes, and the rest of the story has an air of unreality, which is alien to the tone so far developed in the work. The themes of legacy hunting and cannibalism, although not in themselves incapable of humorous treatment, lack the ironic gravity that a Swift might bring to them. The humour is usually farcical, and is liable to strike the reader as rather heavy-handed even when he allows for the fragmentary state of the text at this point. And this crystallizes the main dissatisfactions that one feels with Petronius, the want of a unified view-point throughout the successive episodes – Encolpius is not enough for this – and the lack of a properly controlled tone, or at least recognizable justification for its inconsistency. And the suggested circumstances of its production, with perhaps the haphazard, and *ad hoc* or *ad hominem*, selection of themes and models once the basic plot and general scale were established, serve only to *explain* these faults.

These criticisms suggest some further reflections. If one had to characterize the vision that dominates the work, as distinguishable from the narrator's pessimistic outlook, it might be described as amused and snobbish, but interested and tolerant, acceptance, in literary terms, of things as they are. In Petronius' world they are not altogether well or admirable, unless the neo-Epicurean defences, ironic humour and the refined humane pleasures of literature, social life, and taste, are kept intact. Much like Lucretius, looking squarely at what is, for ordinary people, a cold, blind, and depressing universe and accepting it in a philosophical spirit, so Petronius looks at a world of men, which he deliberately, and unnecessarily, depicts as uniformly mean, immoral, and ridiculous. And he is saved from pessimism, if my reading is correct, by two things: an interest in the sheer vitality and variety of even this sort of life, particularly when it is the material of art, and, secondly, by his sophisticated irony and humour. For many, it may be that the deliberately limited subject matter that the *Satyricon* presents is scarcely saved by the author's subtle and disengaged style, and by his unemotional observation of his world. Nevertheless, the horrors *are* distanced, even become funny, when observed with his ironic, and yet sympathetic, detachment.

In fine, it must be confessed that Petronius' literary theories and artistic practice finally impress the reader, despite their successes, as not quite fully thought out. His complaints about the unreality of contemporary rhetoric are not consonant with his traditionalist's admiration of Vergilian epic; his defence of the realism of the *Satyricon*, so decisively limited in its scope anyway, conflicts with the differently conceived fantasy of much of the Crotonian episode, as well as with many of the irrelevant insertions, prose and verse, which serve merely to display his stylistic invention and skills. His choice of a satiric genre, his rehandling of various conventional satiric topics, although partly dictated by this very choice of a loose and adaptable form, are admittedly suspicious in the absence of any consistent and positive standards. Here his detached irony and meticulous style may, or may not, have interesting results: it may produce a Trimalchio or the bizarre, if scarcely pornographic, scene with Philomela's children. His conception that the artist, in epic or satire, must be highly literate and well-read is of course almost a commonplace of Roman criticism and literary practice, and it is obvious how seriously he took it himself. Still, there are temptations in a form as loose as Menippean satire to display gratuitously one's familiarity with earlier models, and the range of one's reading. And Petronius is sometimes guilty of this. Yet this might also be seen as breaking in a different way the rule he lays down for epic: that *sententiae* should be subordinated to the narrative. Perhaps some of Petronius' literary setpieces might be similarly criticized in terms of the whole work.

Against these deeper faults, which are not entirely to be laid at his door, but may be partly attributed to the straitjacket of Latin literary theories and the tastes of his milieu, we have to set the cleanness, clarity, and vigour of his style; the pace, humour and invention of his narrative; the independent treatment of his models and his chosen form; and his correct decision as to the strength of the Latin literary tradition. Despite his admiration for Vergil he eschewed the desiccated banalities of mythological or historical epic to which Valerius Flaccus and Silius Italicus were to succumb; he avoided, in general, some of the stylistic Sirens to which Seneca listened in both his prose and his verse. And if his achievement, apart from the *Cena*, seems more art than matter, Silver Latin writers have left us works that are notable for neither. If Petronius has profited too much from the mystery of the *Satyricon*'s genesis, other writers without even the excuse of that mystery have profited from our inertia.

Bibliography

This is not a complete bibliography of Petronius, as there is little here on the text or the manuscript tradition, on the details of the language and style, or on the various philological and historical problems. It does however include the main editions, and some of the general, or critical, works on Petronius, as well as the more important articles and books on the work and its background which are cited in the notes. A reasonably complete bibliography may be compiled with the aid of S. Gaselee, 'The Bibliography of Petronius', *Trans. of the Bibliographical Society* 10 (1909) 141–233; M. Stirling, *Addenda et Corrigenda to 'The Bibliography of Petronius' by Stephen Gaselee*, Pts. I and II, 1931 (MS in the Cambridge University Library); *L'Année Philologique;* E. Lommatzsch, *Bursians Jahresberichte für das klassische Altertum* 175 (1919) 98 ff.; 204 (1925) 215 ff.; 235 (1932) 142 ff.; 260 (1938) 94 ff.; R. Helm, *ibid.* 282 (1945) 5 ff.; R. Muth, *Anzeiger für die Altertumswissenschaft* 9 (1956) 1–22; H. C. Schnur, *CW* 50 (1957) 133–6, 141–3; and A. Rini, *Petronius in Italy* (New York, 1937).

Abbott, F. F., 'The Use of Language as a Means of Characterisation in Petronius', *CP* 2 (1907) 43 ff.
— 'The Origin of the Realistic Romance among the Romans', *CP* 6 (1911) 257 ff.
Altamura, D., 'Quibus ex Graeca lingua translatis verbis in Cena Trimalchionis enarranda Petronius usus sit', *Latinitas* 6 (1958) 194 ff.
Arrowsmith, W., *The Satyricon of Petronius*. Translated and with an Introduction. Ann Arbor 1959.
— 'Luxury and Death in the *Satyricon*', *Arion* 5 (1966) 304 ff.

Auerbach, E., *Mimesis, the Representation of Reality in Western Literature* (trans.) (New York 1957).

Bacon, H. H., 'The Sibyl in the Bottle', *Virginia Quarterly Review* 34 (1958) 262 ff.

Bagnani, G., 'And Passing Rich', *Phoenix Supplt.* 1 (Toronto 1952) 218 ff.

— *Arbiter of Elegance, Phoenix Supplt.* 2 (Toronto 1954)

— 'Encolpius: Gladiator Obscenus', *CP* 51 (1956) 24 ff.

— 'The House of Trimalchio', *AJP* 75 (1954) 16 ff.

— 'Trimalchio', *Phoenix* 8 (1954) 77 ff.

Bailey, C., *Epicurus*, Oxford 1926

Baldwin, F. T., *The Bellum Civile of Petronius*, New York 1911.

Balsdon, J. P. V. D., *Roman Women*, London 1963

Barnes, J. W. B., 'Egypt and the Greek Romance', *Mitteil. aus. d. Papyrussamml. d. Öst.-Nat. Bibl.* n.s. 5 (1956) 29 ff.

Beck, C., *The Age of Petronius*, Cambridge, Mass. 1856

Bendz, G. 'Sprachliche Bemerkungen zu Petron', *Eranos* 39 (1941) 27 ff.

Bickel, E., 'Petrons Simplicitas bei Tacitus', *RhM* 90 (1941) 269 ff.

Birt, T., 'Zu Petron', *PhW* 45 (1925) 95

Bogner, H., 'Petronius bei Tacitus', *H* 76 (1941) 223 f.

Boissier, G., *Étude sur la vie et les ouvrages de M. T. Varron*, Paris 1861

— *L'Opposition sous les Césars*, Paris 1875

Bonner, S. F., *Roman Declamation under the Empire*, Liverpool 1948

Borszák, K., 'Die *Simplicitas* und römische Puritanismus', *EPhK* 70 (1947) 1 ff.

Browning, R., 'The Date of Petronius', *CR* 63 (1949) 12–14

— 'The Date of Petronius', *CR* 63 (1949) 28–9

Bücheler, F. *Petronii Arbitri Satirarum Reliquiae*, Berlin 1862

Bürger, K., 'Der antike Roman vor Petronius', *H* 27 (1892) 345 ff.

Burman, *Titi Petronii Arbitri Satyricôn quae supersunt*. Curante Petro Burmanno. Editio altera. Amsterdam, 1743

Cahen, R., *Le Satiricon et ses origines*, Paris 1925

Carratelli, G. Pugliese, 'Tabulae ceratae Herculanenses', *PP* 3 (1946) 381

Ciaffii, V., *La Struttura del Satyricon*, Turin 1955
— *Petronio e Apuleio*, Turin 1960
Cichorius, C., 'Petronius und Massilia', *Römische Studien*, Leipzig 1922, pp. 438 ff.
Cizek, E., 'Autour de la date du Satyricon de Pétrone', *Stud. Clas.* 7 (1965) 197 ff.
Collignon, A., *Étude sur Pétrone. La Critique littéraire, l'imitation et la parodie dans le Satiricon*, Paris 1892
Cordier, A., *L'allitération latine. Le procédé dans l' 'Enéide' de Virgile*, Paris 1939
Courtney, E., 'Parody and Literary Allusion in Menippean Satire', *Philologus* 106 (1962) 86 ff.
Crum, R. H., 'Petronius and the Emperors', *CW* 45 (1951) 161 ff., 197 ff.
de Guerle, J. N. M., *Recherches Sceptiques sur Pétrone*, Paris 1797
de Vreese, J. G. W. M. *Petron 39 und die Astrologie*, Amsterdam 1927
Desmouliez, A., 'Sur la polémique entre Cicéron et les Atticistes', *REL* 30 (1952) 168 ff.
Downer, J. W., *Metaphors and Wordplays in Petronius*, Waco, Texas 1913
Duff, A. M., *Freedmen in the Early Roman Empire*, Cambridge 1958
Dugas, L., *La psychologie du rire*, Paris 1902
Enia, M., *Il Satiricon e il suo autore Petronio Arbitro*, Palermo 1899
Ernout, A., *Le Satiricon de Pétrone*. Texte et Traduction. 4th edn. Paris 1958
Faider, P., *Études sur Sénèque*, Ghent 1921
Feix, J., *Wortstellung und Satzbau in Petrons Roman*, Breslau 1934
Ficari, Q., *La figura di Trimalchione nel 'Satiricon' di Petronio Arbitro*, Lucera 1910
Freud, S., *Jokes and their Relation to the Unconscious*, London 1960
Friedländer, L., *Petronii Cena Trimalchionis*, 2nd edn. Leipzig 1906
Garrido, I. M., 'A Note on Petronius' Satyricon 135', *CR* 44 (1930) 10 f.
Gaselee, S., *Some Unpublished Materials for an Edition of Petronius*, (1909). Unpubld. Diss. Camb. Univ. Lib.
George, P. A., 'Style and character in the Satyricon', *Arion* 5 (1966) 336 ff.

Gottschlich, J., 'De parodiis Senecae apud Petronium', *Miscellaneorum Philologicorum libellus zu Friderici Haase Jubiläum* (Breslau 1863)

Gresseth, G. K., 'The Quarrel between Lucan and Nero', *CP* 52 (1957) 24 ff.

Griffin, M. T., 'De Brevitate Vitae', *JRS* 52 (1962) 104–13

Grimal, P., 'Sur quelques noms propres de la *Cena Trimalchionis*', *RPh* 16 (1942) 161 ff.

Griesbach, E., *Die Wanderung der Novelle von der treulosen Wittwe durch die Weltliteratur*, Berlin 1886

Grube, G. M. A., *The Greek and Roman Critics*, London 1965

von Guericke, A., *De linguae vulgaris reliquiis apud Petronium et in inscriptionibus parietariis Pompeianis*, Gumbinnen 1875

Haley, H. W., 'Quaestiones Petronianae', *HSCP* 2 (1891) 1 ff.

Haskins, C. E., *M. Annaei Lucani Pharsalia* (ed.). With an Introduction by W. E. Heitland. Cambridge 1887

Hausrath, A., 'Die ionische Novellistik', *NJA* 33 (1914) 441 ff.

Headlam, W., *Herodas*, Cambridge 1922

Heinz, K., *Das Bild Kaiser Neros*, Bern 1948

Heinze, R., 'Petron und der griechische Roman', *H* 34 (1889) 494 ff.

Heitland, W. E., see Haskins

Helm, R., *Der antike Roman*, 2nd. edn. Göttingen 1956

Heraeus, W., *Die Sprache des Petronius und die Glossen*, Leipzig 1899

Herter, H., *De Priapo*, Giessen 1932

Hertling, C., *Quaestiones mimicae*, Strasburg 1899

Highet, G., 'Petronius the Moralist', *TAPA* 72 (1941) 176 ff.

— *Juvenal the Satirist*, Oxford 1956

Hirzel, R., *Der Dialog*, Leipzig 1895

Housman, A. E., 'Jests of Cicero, Plautus and Trimalchio', *CR* 32 (1918) 162

Iannelli, C., 'Dissertatio tertia qua Petronii Arbitri aetas constituitur', *In Perottinum codicem . . . Dissertationes Tres* (Naples 1811) pp. 117–316

Jensen, C., *Philodemus über die Gedichte, fünftes Buch*, Berlin 1923

Kent, R. G., see Sturtevant

Kempe, P., *De clausulis Petronianis*, Greifswald 1922

Kindt, B., 'Petron und Lucan', *Philologus* 51 (1892) 355 ff.

Klebs, E., 'Zur Komposition von Petronius' Satirae', *Philologus* 47 (1889) 623 ff.

— 'Petroniana', *Philologus Suppltbd.* 6 (1893) 659 ff.

Lavagnini, B., *Eroticorum Graecorum fragmenta papyracea*, Leipzig 1922

Le Coultre, J., 'Notes sur Pétrone', *Mélanges Boissier* (Paris 1903) pp. 326 ff.

Levi, M. A., *Nerone e i suoi tempi*, Milan 1949

Lommatzsch, E. (with J. Segebade), *Lexicon Petronianum*, Leipzig 1898

Ludwig, E., *De Petronii sermone plebeio*, Marburg 1869

McCague, E. S., *Clausulae in Petronius* (1930). Unpubl. Thesis. Univ. of Pittsburgh

MacKendrick, P. L., 'The Great Gatsby and Trimalchio', *CJ* 45 (1950) 307 ff.

Maiuri, A., *La Cena di Trimalchione di Petronio Arbitro*, Naples 1945

— 'Petroniana', *PP* 3 (1948) 103 ff.

Marbach, A., *Wortbildung, Wortwahl und Wortbedeutung als Mittel der Characterzeichnung bei Petron*, Giessen 1931

Marchesi, C., *Petronio*, Rome 1921

Marmorale, E. V., 'Cena Trimalchionis' *testo critico e commento*, Florence 1947

— *La questione Petroniana*, Bari 1948

Martin, J., *Symposion, die Geschichte einer literarischen Form*, Paderborn 1931

Martins, F., 'A crise do meravilhoso na epopeia Latina', *Humanitas* 1 (1947) 25 ff.

Mason, H. A., 'Is Juvenal a Classic?': *Critical Essays in Roman Literature: Satire*, London 1963, pp. 93 ff.

Mendell, C. W., 'Petronius and the Greek Romance', *CP* 12 (1917) 158 ff.

Michenaud, G., 'Les sons du vers Virgilien', *LEC* 21 (1953) 343 ff.

Momigliano, A., 'Literary Chronology of the Neronian Age', *CQ* 38 (1944) 96 ff.

Möring, F., *De Petronio mimorum imitatore*, Münster 1915

Mössler, J. G., *Commentatio de Petronii poemate 'De Bello civili'*, Breslau 1842

— *Quaestionum Petroniarum specimen quo poema 'De bello civili' cum 'Pharsalia' Lucani comparatur*, Hirschberg 1857

Müller, K., *Petronii Arbitri Satyricon*, Munich 1961

— (with W. Ehlers), *Petronius Satyrica: Schelmengeschichte*, Munich 1965

Münscher, K., *Senecas Werke, Untersuchungen zur Abfassungszeit und Echtheit, Philologus Suppltbd.* 16 (Leipzig 1922)

Nelson, H. L. W., *Ein Unterrichtsprogramm aus neronischer Zeit, dargestellt auf Grund von Petrons Satiricon, c. 5*, Amsterdam 1956

Norden, E., *Die antike Kunstprosa*, Leipzig 1909

Pack, R., 'The Criminal Dossier of Encolpius', *CP* 55 (1960) 31 ff.

Paratore, E., *Il Satyricon di Petronio I–Introduzione, II–Commento*, Florence 1933

Pepe, L., *Studi Petroniani*, Naples 1957

— 'Sul monumento sepolcrale di Trimalchione', *GIF* 10 (1957) 293 ff.

Perrochat, P., *Commentaire exégétique et critique du Festin de Trimalchion*, 2nd edn. Paris 1952

Perry, B. E., 'Petronius and the Comic Romance', *CP* 20 (1925) 31 ff.

Pétrequin, J. E., *Nouvelles recherches historiques et critiques sur Pétrone*, Paris, 1869

Preston, K., 'Some sources of the comic effect in Petronius', *CP* 10 (1915) 260 ff.

Raith, O., *Petronius ein Epikureer*, Nuremberg 1963

Rattenbury, R. M., 'Romance: The Greek Novel', *New Chapters in Greek Literature. Third Series*, Oxford 1933, pp. 211 ff.

Reich, H., *Der Mimus*, Berlin 1903

Révay, J., 'Horaz und Petron', *CP* 17 (1922) 202 ff.

Ribezzo, F., 'I frammenti di libro XIV di Petronio', *RIGI* 15 (1931) 41 ff.

Rohde, E., *Der griechische Roman und seine Vorläufer*, 3rd edn. Leipzig 1914

Rose, K. F. C., *The Date and Author of the Satyricon* (1962). Unpubld. Thesis. Bodleian Library, Oxford

— 'The Author of the *Satyricon*', *Latomus* 20 (1961) 821 ff.

— 'The Date of the *Satyricon*', *CQ* 12 (1962) 166 ff.

— 'Time and Place in the *Satyricon*', *TAPA* 93 (1962) 402 ff.

— 'The Petronian Inquisition: An Auto-da-Fé', *Arion* 5 (1966) 275 ff.

Rosenblüth, M., *Beiträge zur Quellenkunde von Petronius' Satiren*, Berlin 1909

Rostagni, A., 'Filodemo contro l'estetica classica', *Scritti Minori* I (Turin 1955) pp. 349 ff.

Rowell, H. T., 'The Gladiator Petraites and the Date of the *Satyricon*' *TAPA* 89 (1958) 12 ff.

Rudd, W. J. N., *The Satires of Horace*, Cambridge 1966

Sage, E. T., 'Atticism in Petronius', *TAPA* 46 (1915) 47 ff.

Salonius, A. H., *Die Griechen und das Griechische in Petrons Cena Trimalchions*, Helsingförs–Leipzig 1927

Schissel von Fleschenberg, O., 'Die künstlerische Absicht in Petrons "Saturae" ', *WS* 33 (1911) 264 ff.

Schmid, D., *Der Erbschleicher in der antiken Satire*, Tübingen 1951

Schnur, H. C., *The Age of Petronius Arbiter* (1957). Unpubld. Diss. New York Univ.

— 'The Economic Background of the *Satyricon*', *Latomus* 18 (1959) 790 ff.

Schoenberger, J. K., 'Zum Stil des Petronius', *Glotta* 31 (1951) 22 ff.

Schraidt, N. E., 'Literary and Philosophical Remains in the *Satyricon* of Petronius Arbiter', *CJ* 35 (1939) 154 ff.

Segebade, J., see Lommatzsch

Sgobbo, I., 'Frammenti dello libro XIV delle "Saturae" di Petronio', *RAL* 6.6. (1930) 355 ff.

Shero, L. R., 'The *Cena* in Roman Satire', *CP* 18 (1923) 126 ff.

Sinko, T., 'De famis et libidinis in fabula Petroniana momento', *Eos* 36 (1935) 385 ff.

— 'De reconstructione fabulae Menippeae Petronii', *Meander* 12 (1957) 79 ff.

Sochatoff, A. F., 'The Purpose of Petronius' *Bellum civile*: A Re-examination', *TAPA* 93 (1962) 449 ff.

Sparrow, J., *Half-Lines and Repetitions in Virgil*, Oxford 1931

Steele, R. B., 'Literary Adaptations and References in Petronius', *CJ* 15 (1920) 283 ff.

Strilciw, N., 'De arte rhetorica in Petronii saturis conspicua', *Eos* 30 (1927) 367 ff.

Stubbe, H., *Die Verseinlagen im Petron, Philologus Suppltbd.* 25 (Leipzig 1933)

Studer, G., 'Über das Zeitalter des Petronius Arbiter', *RhM* 2 (1843) 50 ff., 202 ff.

Sturtevant, E. H. (with R. G. Kent), 'Elision and Hiatus in Latin Prose and Verse', *TAPA* 46 (1915) 148 ff.

Sullivan, J. P., 'Realism and Satire in Petronius': *Critical Essays on Latin Literature: Satire*, (London 1963) pp. 73 ff.

— *Petronius: The Satyricon and the Fragments. Translated and with an Introduction.* (Penguin Classics) Harmondsworth 1965.

Süss, W., *De eo quem dicunt inesse Trimalchionis cenae sermoni vulgari*, Dorpat 1926

— *Petronii imitatio sermonis plebei qua necessitate coniungatur cum grammatica illius aetatis doctrina, Acta et Comm. Univ. Tartuensis* 13 (1927) 103 ff., Dorpat 1926

— 'Zu Lucilius' (§ II) *H* 62 (1927) 349 ff.

Thomas, E., *Pétrone*, 3rd edn. Paris 1912

— 'Pétrone et le roman grec', *RIPB* 45 (1900) 157 ff.

Thomas, P., *L'âge et l'auteur du Satyricon*, Ghent 1905

Trampe, E., *De Lucani arte metrica*, Berlin 1884

Tremoli, P., *Le iscrizioni di Trimalchione*, Trieste 1960

Trenkner, S., *The Greek Novella in the Classical Period*, Cambridge 1958

Ure, P., 'The Widow of Ephesus. Some Reflections on an International Comic Theme', *Durham Univ. Journ.* 18 (1956) 1 ff.

Usener, H., *Epicurea*, Leipzig 1887

Veyne, P., 'Vie de Trimalchion', *Annales Économies Sociétés Civilisations* 16 (1961) 213 ff.

— 'Trimalchio Maecenatianus', *Hommages à Albert Grenier* (Brussels 1962) pp. 1617 ff.

Veyne, P., '*Arbiter Elegantiae*', *RPh* 37 (1963) 258 f.
— 'Le "je" dans le *Satiricon*', *REL* 42 (1964) 301 ff.
Westerburg, M., 'Petron und Lucan', *RhM* 38 (1883) 92 ff.
Wilamowitz-Moellendorf, U. von, 'Asianismus und Atticismus', *H* 35 (1900) 1 ff.
Wilcken, U. 'Ein neuer griechischer Roman', *H* 28 (1893) 92 ff.
— 'Eine neue Roman-Handschrift', *Archiv f. Papyrusforschung* 1 (1901) 255 ff.
Wilkinson, L. P., 'Philodemus and Poetry', *G & R* 2 (1933) 144 ff.

Index of Petronian Passages

Figures in bold type indicate the more substantial discussions

Index of Ancient Authors

Achilles Tatius, 93
Aelian, 121 n.
Albinovanus Pedo, 185
Apollonius Rhodius, 176, 183
Apuleius (*Metamorphoses*), 36, 39, 77 n.,
   96, 112, 121 n., 123 n., 264
Aristophanes, 49 n., 66, 121 n., 223
Aristotle (*Poetics*), 102, 102 n.
Athenaeus, 126
Ausonius (*Epig.*), 65 n.

Boethius, 91

Callimachus, 262; (*Hecale*), 217;
   (*Aetia*), 86, 87, 184
Calpurnius Siculus, 187
Capitolinus (*Verus*), 101 n.
Catullus, 193, 219, 230, 235, 235 n.,
   251, 254, 263
Chariton, 93
Cicero, 85, 91, 103 n., 164, 164 n., 165,
   192, 225; (*Ad Att.*), 99 n.; (*Brut.*),
   58 n.; (*De opt. gen. orat.*), 164;
   (*Tusc.*), 70 n.
Claudian, 185
Clement of Alexandria (*Paed.*), 123 n.
Cornelius Severus, 185
Cresconius Corippus, 185

Demosthenes, 91, 163, 165
Dio, 24 n., 84 n., 89 n., 101, 101 n.
Diomedes (defining mime), 221
Dioscorides (*Materia Medica*), 49 n.

Ennius (*Annales*), 85, 87, 165
Epicurus, 181, 193
Euripides, 103, 163

Fulgentius, 77 n.; (*Mythologiae*), 35

Heliodorus, 93, 95
Herodas, 121, 123 n., 139, 220, 221,
   222 n.
Herodotus, 121 n., 244
Hesiod, 130
Hipponax, 42
Homer, 41, 42, 67, 75 n., 88, 91, 92,
   92 n., 93, 96, 125, 130, 163, 165, 167,
   168, 176, 181, 183, 184, 185, 216,
   227, 228, 262, 263
Horace, 23, 27, 58, 67, 85–6, 87, 89, 90,
   91, 108, 116, 118, 167, 171, 190, 191,
   192, 193, 193 n., 211, 231, 235 n.,
   244, 251, 259, 263; (*Ars Poetica*), 89;
   (*Cena Nasidieni, Serm.* 2.8), 82, 92,
   126–8, 167 n., 264; (*Ep.*), 104 n.;
   (*Sat.*), 54 n., 89, 100, 104 n., 118,
   118 n., 170, 193, 193 n., 232 n.
Hyperides, 163

Iamblichus, 93
Isidorus (*Origines*), 168 n.

Johannes Lydus, 114, 221 n.
Julian, 112, 113
Juvenal, 27, 76 n., 84, 86, 90, 99 n., 100,
   101 n., 104, 104 n., 105, 108, 109 n.,

General Index

(*The Satyricon* is throughout referred to incidentally as 'S')

ship, 65–6; moves on to Croton, 66–67; Circe and 'Polyaenus' incidents, 70; again impotent, 69, 70; rough handling by Proselenus and Oenothea, 71–2; attempts self-castration after indignities from Circe's servants, 70; his poem on this occasion, 70, 98–102; questions Giton on Ascyltos' sexual prowess, 71; incurs wrath of Priapus, 71–3; various attempts to restore his virility, 72–3; fails to seduce son of Philomela, 75; Mercury comes to aid of, 73 n., 75; is increasingly worried by Eumolpus' success (legacy-hunter incidents), 75–6; possible endings to adventures, 76–8

(b) some interpretations: the Encolpius-Giton story as possible parody of Greek romantic situations, 94; characterization of, essential ambiguity of (role of narrator), 116–119, 152–3, 159; as 'anti-hero', 39; the point of his character inconsistencies, 228; as vehicle of Petronius' views, 116–19, 160, 194; seen as anti-plague scapegoat, 40–2; seen as victim of Priapus' wrath, 40–2; sexual ambivalence of, 39, 234; Freudian interpretations of castration attempts, sadistic assaults on, etc., 245, 250–1 (see Freud); as vehicle of scopophilic preoccupations, 249; as speaker of *sermo urbanus*, 25; cf. the 'Encolpos' of Aelius Lampridius and Martial, 117; for expansion of Encolpius themes, see Giton

Ephesus, the Widow of (and Boy of Pergamum) as recurring 'Milesian' stories, 79, 97, 124, 164, 219, 234, 246; 'Boy of Pergamum', 61, 64, 97, 219, 246

Epic: attitudes to, 88; debt of Greek romance to, 96; criticism of contemporary historic in S, 165–70; as likelier target of satire in S than Greek novel, 93–8; 'divine machinery' usual to, Petronius' use of, 172–7, 181–5; Lucan's avoidance of 'divine machinery', 183, 185–6; Silius' use of it, 186; secondary epic as difficult genre, 184

Epicureanism: attitudes of Petronius to, 33, 88, 108, 110, 212; ousting Lucan's Stoic tenets, 181; Epicurean attitudes to: art, literary *decorum*, 87, 103, 109; dreams, 63, 63 n.; sex as vital element, 70, 98, 99, 99 n.; Senecan approach to, 212 n.; Epicurean morality of S, 103, 107, 108, 133

Epistle as literary genre, 89

Ernout, A., 42 n., 53 n., 272

Erotic situations in various literary genres, 97, 97 n.; realism of as literary principle, 104

Eumolpus: first meeting with Encolpius, 60–1; as rival for Giton's affections, 61–2; joins Encolpius and Giton in robbery, plunder, etc., 61–66; exploits legacy-hunting in Croton, 66–76; reveals himself as traditionalist in poetic style, 66–7; seduces daughter of legacy-hunter Philomela, 75; frightens Encolpius by repeated successes, 74–5; feigns death and has will read, 76; probable death of, 76, 80; one literary purpose of effusions of, 98; as bisexual and promiscuous, 235; characterization of, 229–31; chaste language of, in all circumstances, 219; as critic, for Petronius, of decadence of age, 204–208; Epicurus invoked by, 110; function of, as vehicle of Petronius' literary criticism, 26, 158 seqq., 180,